A TWENTY-FIRST CENTURY APPROACH
TO TEACHING SOCIAL JUSTICE

Studies in the
Postmodern Theory of Education

Joe L. Kincheloe and Shirley R. Steinberg
General Editors

Vol. 358

PETER LANG
New York • Washington, D.C./Baltimore • Bern
Frankfurt am Main • Berlin • Brussels • Vienna • Oxford

A TWENTY-FIRST CENTURY APPROACH TO TEACHING SOCIAL JUSTICE

Educating for Both Advocacy and Action

EDITED BY

Richard Greggory Johnson III

PETER LANG
New York • Washington, D.C./Baltimore • Bern
Frankfurt am Main • Berlin • Brussels • Vienna • Oxford

Library of Congress Cataloging-in-Publication Data

A twenty-first century approach to teaching social justice:
educating for both advocacy and action / ed. By Richard Greggory Johnson III.
p. cm. — (Counterpoints: studies in the postmodern theory of education; v. 358)
Includes bibliographical references and index.
1. Social justice. 2. Social justice—Study and teaching. I. Title.
HM671.J64   303.3′72—dc22   2008043972
ISBN 978-1-4331-0514-2 (hardcover)
ISBN 978-1-4331-0513-5 (paperback)
ISSN 1058-1634

Bibliographic information published by **Die Deutsche Bibliothek**.
Die Deutsche Bibliothek lists this publication in the "Deutsche
Nationalbibliografie"; detailed bibliographic data is available
on the Internet at http://dnb.ddb.de/.

Cover design by Clear Point Designs

The paper in this book meets the guidelines for permanence and durability
of the Committee on Production Guidelines for Book Longevity
of the Council of Library Resources.

Printed in the United States of America

To the memory of my mother, Mrs. Jeannette Johnson,
who will live in my heart forever.

TABLE OF CONTENTS

III. SOCIAL CLASS AND SEXUAL ORIENTATION

IV. GLOBAL PERSPECTIVES ON SOCIAL JUSTICE

ACKNOWLEDGMENTS

First of all, to the folks at Peter Lang Publishing, thank you all. I am particularly grateful to Chris Myers for being such a gem to work with and for standing behind the importance of this book. I am also grateful to Shirley R. Steinberg and Sophie Appel for their positive and enthusiastic feedback and assistance with this project.

To my University of Vermont (UVM) colleagues and friends: Fayneese Miller, Wanda Heading-Grant, Judith Aiken, Susan Dinitz, Wolfgang Mieder, Susan Comeford, Robyn Warhol-Down and Robert James Nash. Thanks for walking with me along this journey.

Finally, to the contributors of this amazing volume...thank you all for your wonderful sense of commitment and dedication to improving our global society. Cheers to you all.

A TWENTY-FIRST CENTURY APPROACH to TEACHING SOCIAL JUSTICE

Educating for Both Advocacy and Action

Richard Greggory Johnson III

Introduction

I suspect that this collection of narratives came out of my life's experiences as an African American, gay man focused on social justice advocacy and action. This is who I am and my hope is that anyone reading this volume will understand the complexities of at least some of the social justice issues addressed here and move beyond a stage of awareness to a stage of advocacy and action.

In the Beginning

Growing up in the Bronx, New York during the 1970s and early 1980s, I was acutely aware of injustices within the American and global society, though I did not have the language to name them. My parents were hard working but were not politically inclined, nor were they active in civic organizations. At sixteen or seventeen I would ask my parents why there was such suffering in the world on a macro level and such poverty in our community on a micro level. My parents simply replied that this was all part of God's master plan. They never did tell me what God's master plan was, nor could I somehow buy into a God who would allow racial, gender and social class injustices to occur time and time again.

During my childhood I watched my mother, a beautiful, heavy-set, dark-skinned woman with a high school education, clean White women's (the Kahn sisters) apartments on 34th Street and Lexington Avenue in New York City until I was in middle school. Later she obtained a job as a cook in an elementary school in the Bronx. I wondered why my mother would love a God who kept the institution of power and privilege alive and well for most of her life. My father tall at 6' 5", was a star basketball player in high school and won a full basketball scholarship to play for DePaul University during the mid-1960s. Instead, he joined the Marines, married my mother, and starting having kids (my brother and I are ten months apart). For thirty years, he worked as a correctional officer for a prison in NYC and never had time to think about the racial and social issues that plagued him on a daily basis.

Social justice was not something I thought of majoring in during college, graduate school, or doctoral studies during the mid-1980s to the early 1990s. My parents wanted me to pursue a field that would offer me job opportunities such as political science or law. I wanted to major in performing arts, specifically dance or voice, which of course did not happen. Instead, I majored in Urban Planning, a field that twenty years later I know nothing about and regret having majored in to appease my parents.

Obtaining a Framework for Social Justice Advocacy and Action

After completing my doctorate from Golden Gate University in 1995 (in public policy), I was twenty-eight and felt hopeless about my future as an African American gay man, albeit with an advanced graduate degree. This was a time of great despair for me as I witnessed countless friends, gay and straight, friends of color and European Americans, die from AIDS. Again, I wondered where was the justice in the pain, suffering, and ultimately death of good and talented people. I could not make sense of this horrible disaster, nor could I make sense of a God who would sanction such a disease. I shut down, emotionally, physically, and intellectually. In order to make sense of my life and the injustices around me, I turned to the stacks in the library at Georgetown University for answers. I was not sure if pursing another graduate degree would answer my questions, but I was willing to try a new path dedicated to my own personal growth and development. Prior to entering the social and public policy/liberal studies masters program at Georgetown in 1996, I knew nothing about this academic field or concentration called social justice. However, I learned and I read, and I talked to Georgetown scholars and professors who were sincerely interested in researching and teaching about matters of human rights and human uplift. For the first time in my life and my academic career, I learned about issues of oppression, race and racism, homophobia, white privilege, and gender inequities. I was beginning to develop a language for the inequities that I could not articulate during my youth. I also learned more about myself as a feminist. Prior to attending Georgetown, I did not know that men could actually be feminist, though some feminists still continue to argue that men cannot be feminist. I also attended programs hosted by Georgetown's Berkley Center for Religion, Peace, & World Affairs as well as the Center for Social Justice, Research, Teaching, and Service. I graduated from Georgetown in spring 2000 with a M.A. in Social and Public Policy/liberal studies. I was now armed with a tool that would help create my life's work as an academic and as a human living in the global society.

In 2003 I became an assistant professor in the Educational Leadership and Policy Studies Program at the University of Vermont, after having been employed at the University since 1999 as Director of TRIO Programs. The Educational Leadership program includes an undergraduate, masters and doctoral program and has a strong social justice commitment reflected in its curriculum. The social justice foci of the program is not unlike the social mission of the University, which, among other things, admitted the first African American student to the Phi Beta Kappa Honor Society in 1877. The University also defied custom and admitted two women as full-fledged students in 1871 (http://www.uvm.edu/about_uvm/).

In spring 2005 I taught Race and Racism in the United States and Leadership for Social Justice, Democracy, and Diversity. Both classes were geared toward advancing a student's understanding of marginalized and underrepresented populations in the United States and abroad. I had been using such texts as *Funds of Knowledge* (Gonzalez, Moll and Amanti, *2005), Reframing Education Politics for Social Justice* (Marshall and Gerstl-Pepin, 2006), and *Readings for Diversity and Social Justice* (Adams et al 2000). While all of these books continue to be worthwhile and add value to the social justice literature, none of them discussed "cutting edge" topics for the 21st century, nor did any of them speak to my students in terms of a call to action. In recent years, I have also used *Leadership for Social Justice: Making Revolutions in Education* (Marshall and Oliva, 2006), whose book addresses the issue of educational leadership action. The criticism of their text is that not all students want to become school leaders, such as principals or superintendents. As the instructor, I tried to fill in the gaps as my students (education and non- education majors) posed the question "so what?" This is what prompted me to edit a book addressing social justice topics with a specific emphasis on action for all students and faculty regardless of discipline. This is why Section II: Social Justice across the Academic Disciplines is central to the core of this volume as the authors give their perspectives on social justice from their field.

Social justice as an academic field may still be considered fledgling with very few United States of America universities offering graduate degrees solely in the area. This is not unusual, as Oldfield, Candler and Johnson argue in their 2006 article that criticizes the academic field of public administration and policy for being behind the curve on embracing many cutting-edge issues such as social class and sexual orientation (pp.,156). Other disciplines in other nations may also be as reluctant to teach or publish on cutting edge social justice topics as well. Indeed, the "elephant" in the room continues to loom large in many respects.

Framework and Organization of Book

The purpose of this book is to provide the reader with a fresh perspective on social justice topics. The book seeks not just to introduce the reader to a different set of social justice frameworks; equally important is how the reader may get involved with action to address the chapter's issue. The definition of social justice remains nebulous at the best. However, social justice in the context of this book is defined as issues pertaining to the marginalization of communities based on gender, race, social class, sexual orientation, religion, and disability. The book addresses these topics from the lenses of thirteen college professors and doctoral students from around the United States and Australia, which take the reader from awareness to advocacy and action. All of the contributors are committed to social justice both in their careers and personal lives.

The book is divided into four distinct parts: I Gender Inequities; II, Social Justice Action across the Disciplines; III, Social Class and Sexual Orientation and IV, Global Perspectives on Social Justice. Each of the chapters is written using a narrative, qualitative or quantitative approach. I have found from my years of teaching social justice that individual students respond better to certain types of scholarship and certain writing styles. Therefore, this book is designed to address the different learning styles of a diverse group of college/graduate students and even readers not associated with higher education.

The chapter written by Dr. William Leap and his doctoral students from American University, *Beyond the Knowledge/Action Divide: Studying Race, Gender, and Social Justice in American University's Department of Anthropology*, uses a narrative approach and provides a refreshing look at the process by which an academic program or department decides on certain foci and why certain students are interested in partaking of such foci. This message is particularly important as it demonstrates the power and determination of "voice" which stem from the students and Dr. Leap who serve as coauthors of the chapter.

Dr. Ciaran O'Faircheallaigh's chapter, *Social Justice, Aboriginal Leadership, and Mineral Development in Australia*, uses a theoretical approach to provide the reader with an "insider's" look at some of the turmoil happening within the Aboriginal community in Australia. Such a chapter is critical to conclude the volume with as it alerts the reader to think globally about marginalization outside of the United States. It is less complicated to think about discrimination and suffering through a national lens. But the power of global awareness and advocacy is life altering.

Thank you for taking the time to read this volume. I hope it provides each reader with a new or renewed sense of passion and enthusiasm about what can be done when we all act justly.

Bibliography

Marshall, C. & Oliva, M. (2006). *Leadership for social justice: Making revolution in education*. Boston, MA: Pearson.

Oldfield, K., Candler, G. & Johnson III, R.G. (2006). Social class, sexual orientation, and shaping a new agenda for social equity policy. *American Review of Public Administration*, 36(2), 156-172.

I. GENDER INEQUITIES

CHAPTER 1

UNEQUAL JUSTICE
Losing Ground in Higher Education

G.L.A. Harris

Despite the overall progress that women faculty have made in the academy in terms of the number of tenured and tenure track positions secured, much of the gains have been lost and continue to recede (American Association of University Professors (AAUP), 2006). This is an issue of social justice and equity because "The barriers …raise questions of basic fairness, but place serious limitations on the success of educational institutions themselves" (p.4). The AAUP selected four performance indicators as gauges of gender equity in higher education; namely, employment status, tenure status, full professor rank, and average salary, and found each to be wanting. More importantly, the findings revealed that when such issues fall short of representing women faculty, not only does the academy suffer, but the absence of women's voices in helping to determine the agenda that are important to women faculty and to higher education as a whole, are not addressed. Using the AAUP's four performance indicators, the succeeding chapter delves into the challenges that women faculty face in the academy, the strategies they employ to reconcile the tensions they experience, and what students can learn and thereby do constructively to help facilitate the increase in female faculty at all levels of academia (AAUP, 2006).

The Struggle for Legitimacy

Since Title IX of the Civil Rights Act of 1964, amended in 1972, banned gender discrimination in education (20 U.S.C. Section 1681), women have consistently witnessed a retrenchment in faculty positions and at a time when institutions are graduating women with doctoral degrees at unprecedented levels (AAUP, 2006). In 1972, women earned 16 percent of doctoral degrees and represented 27 percent of higher education faculty (U.S. Department of Education, 2005). Yet today, although at least women earn 48 percent of doctoral degrees with 43 percent as faculty in higher education, only 24 percent have attained the rank of full professor.

The largest of women faculty are found in nontenure part-time and full-time employment and are less likely to be in tenured and tenure track positions. Women also earn less than their male peers at each faculty rank. McElrath (1992) sees this disparity as hypocritical in tolerating such differentials among colleagues. Clearly, while women have made significant strides in higher education, their present status calls into question why they continue to encounter obstacles and fail to sustain advances by translating them into a legacy of achievements. Multiple reasons have been cited for this lack of progress.

Intent to Enter the Academy

Perhaps part of the problem is that men and women perceive similar issues differently thus impacting the extent to which each gender desires to enter the academy. Van Anders (2004) found that although men and women in graduate programs considered the same factors surrounding the pursuit of academic careers, they did so at different rates. For instance, men and women ranked teaching, research, and research competence as highly yet markedly differed when such factors as parental leave, childcare, and mobility were measured. Women ranked these issues highly but negatively as a perceived lifestyle that was incompatible with their own. The paucity of women's rise in the academy may at least be attributed in part to some self selecting out of academia or from situations that women perceive as conflicting with parenting and mobility. Both men and women viewed academia as not an ideal occupation for individuals contemplating these concerns. Yet, it is overwhelmingly women who suggested that they would be more adversely impacted by these decisions. It is then no surprise that more women than men perceive barriers to advancement in academia at higher rates than men.

The Problem of Gender

There is an inherent asymmetry that renders women to assume subordinate roles (i.e., wife and mother) to men (Ostriker, 1998; Gunter & Stambach, 2003) even when such roles are important to society (Ridgeway & Correll, 2004). When the female is as committed to her vocation as her husband, the demands of family and career force her to choose between them. These status characteristics (Ridgeway & Correll, 2004) mark extensions of gender that bind women to role expectations and punish them when they are wayward. In effect, a woman's role is to either be that of a mother or a professional, but not both. For as Ostriker (1998) asserts, "...a truth universally acknowledged, that a woman might produce books or babies, but not both, just as she might organize her life around marriage or a career, but not both" (p.3). It is through these lenses of perceived weaknesses and the endowed roles of wife and mother which women faculty struggle against old mores, cultural biases, and the traditional normative values of society dictate.

The disproportionate burden that women bear for family, many argue, creates an unfair disadvantage that reinforces the asymmetry between men and women and constrains women's success outside of the home. The family and the academy are thus greedy institutions that make unreasonable demands on women (Currie, Harris and Thiele, 2000). Female faculty are caught between satisfying themselves and other forces that compete for their attention. And the academy uses the biological trajectory for childbearing against women that predisposes them to choose between career and family (Armenti, 2004). Some go further by applying critical feminist theory to help explain this inequity and the biological trajectory argument by referring to the problem as one of domesticity; the need for men to keep women and their perceived private matters out of the public venue (Acker & Armenti, 2004; Armenti, 2004). For example, childbearing has largely been invisible and only becomes an issue to those who experience it. And, there have always been pressure to suppress childbearing as it is still believed to be the sole domain of women (Finkel & Olswang, 1996).

Male faculty are also consistently invoked as the standard against which women faculty are judged. Bensimon and Marshall (2003) posit that doing so demeans female faculty when the issues are so framed. In the case of publications where it is often implied that female faculty lag behind the productivity of male peers, these issues should be reframed to focus on how all faculty can enhance their publications as such comparisons only pit one group against the other.

The Need for More Research

Acker and Armenti (2004), expanding the work of Bensimon and Marshall (2003), have expressed regret that research on women faculty has fallen off precipitously. They point to the effective application on the inequities in pay, rank and representation, publication, and promotion and tenure and the success in presenting these issues as systematic discrimination against women faculty. By providing large but divergent samples of women faculty with similar experiences, advocates have increased the utility of this rationale (Aisenberg and Harrington, 1988). Acker and Armenti (2004) caution that these gains are no reason for complacency. They point to the enduring tensions between work and family that women faculty struggle to balance. While there were clear generational differences, baby boomers and Generation Xers faced common challenges. Both groups of women complained about the stress that is often manifested as health-related complications. Many felt that while they were as committed and worked harder than male faculty, their work often went unrecognized. Further, these women believed that workloads were apportioned according to gender. Much of the women's experiences have been echoed by multiple studies on the subject (Currie, Harris & Thiele; 2000; Armenti, 2004; McElrath, 1992; Acker & Feuverger, 1996; Finkel & Olswang, 1996; Gunter & Stambach, 2003; Hensel, 1991; Jorgensen, 2000; Ostriker, 1998; Park, 1996). It is then evident that the issues of the past continue to plague today's women faculty and provide warning signs for yet unfinished work.

Demographic Inertia

Hargens and Long (2002) refute the sentiments of Acker and Armenti (2004) and other like-minded researchers. While Hargens and Long submit to discrimination against women faculty and in turn their representation in academia, they scold colleagues for not recognizing other factors that may be germane to the issue and should be part of the equation. Demographical variables like the age and gender of the initial composition of entering faculty along with changes that may occur over time within the existing faculty can help to explain the sluggishness in the growth of female faculty.

Assuming that the available number of male and female Ph.D.s. for employment have similar qualifications, individual modeling was employed to anticipate changes within faculty composition every five years (Hargens & Long, 2002). Researchers factored the age and gender at the entry of employment, the composition of the existing faculty in which faculty are entering, that no retirement and/or attrition occurred within the existing faculty, that existing faculty will retire at age 65, and that the number of entering faculty is equal to the rate of those who are leaving. Given these five year increments, little, if any changes will occur as there will not be much movement in the faculty. For any change to occur, some of the male faculty must begin to retire every five years. But even after 25 years or when the last male faculty was expected to retire, researchers argued that the existing faculty will be comprised of 46 percent female and only within another 5 years or by 30 years or 35 years will women faculty achieve parity with men. In essence, it will take between 30 years and 35 years for changes that are significant enough for female faculty to achieve complete parity. Hargens and Long admit that this research design would not be feasible nor can the findings be generalized to future Ph.Ds. and gauging the growth of female faculty over time should be in accordance with each discipline and department.

Competition for Resources

Kanter's (1977) seminal work on women in predominantly male organizations provided the impetus for subsequent research on gender specific roles. Kanter referred to this imbalance in the ratio of men to women as tokenism. This highlights the many similar experiences that women faculty today, particularly those in the still non-traditional fields of engineering and the sciences, continue to experience. The need to demonstrate competence by outperforming male peers, the feelings of isolation and the pressure to assume gender appropriate roles, according to Kanter, are to be attributed to the skewed ratios of men to women that result in women being perceived as tokens. Kanter believed that as the number of men and women approached some balance, it would become less critical for men to call attention to the differences in women. The pressure to place women in gender specific roles would then decrease. However, to strike a discernible dent in representation for resonance, the minority group, in this case women, must reach a minimum of 15 percent of the workforce in each occupation.

Although Yoder (1991) credits Kanter with enlightening our understanding about women's experiences in organizations, specifically in gender-stereotyped roles, she disputes the significance of tokenism. Yoder sees tokenism as a factor in the biases experienced by minority groups within majority organizations but she contends that bias is more than about tokenism. Accordingly, Kanter (1977) did not fully capture the nuances of her research, as it was more about the gender inappropriateness of her sample at the time. The majority perceived the minority to be of a lower status and therefore their presence as intrusive. Blalock (1967) validates Yoder's (1991) logic as a competition for resources that becomes the primary threat to the majority more so than the mere presence of the minority. Any increase in the minority group would constitute a corresponding increase in discrimination by the majority group.

Following a Male Trajectory

Another contributing factor that is purported to stagnate and even reduce the number of prospective female faculty is their absence as role models in the academy. This is critical at especially large research universities and in engineering and the sciences. A comprehensive study of tenured and tenure track faculty in the nation's top 50 science and engineering departments illustrated that although women Ph.Ds. in these fields have substantially increased, faculty represented are still overwhelmingly white and male (Nelson & Rogers, 2004). Even more disappointing is that the fields in which women traditionally pursue and outnumber men in the Ph.Ds. conferred, white males still surpass them in faculty positions held.

DiPlama's (2005) analysis of women's progress in academia confirmed that even in fields like social work, the greater gains for women have only occurred at the assistant professor rank. To compound this conundrum, when women in any discipline enter the academy, few if any female faculty are available as role models. Thus female faculty are forced to follow a male academic career path. This, some believe, is what contributes to the prevalence of the problem (Finkel & Olswang, 1996). According to Nelson and Rogers (2004), "There is a drastically disproportionate number of male professors as role models for male students" (p.130). And, following a male trajectory does nothing to advance the issues that are important to female faculty. As Finkel and Olswang (1996) allege, by maintaining the status quo, women become complicit in the problem.

Promotion and Tenure

Many of the above factors have separately and collectively contributed to women faculty's lack of ascent in academia. But perhaps the most frequently invoked and egregious reason cited is the promotion and tenure system. Much research have borne out that many regard the promotion and tenure system as insensitive to the needs of women faculty (Currie, Harris & Thiele, 2000; Moore & Sagaria, 1993; Lie & Malik, 1994; Acker & Feuverger, 1996; Park, 1996; McElrath, 1992; Finkel & Olswang, 1996; Gunter & Stambach, 2003; Armenti, 2004; Acker & Armenti, 2004). Some go as far as describing the system as intractable (Lawler, 1999). Most complaints surround the structure of the promotion and tenure system that appears to advantage male faculty and is punitive to female faculty that range from failing to recognize women faculty for commitment to their work as much as male faculty (Currie, Harris & Thiele, 2000; Acker & Armenti,2004; Armenti,2004; Gunter & Stambach, 2003; Park, 1996; Acker & Feuverger, 1996), and gendered roles that include greater teaching loads for women faculty (Park, 1996; Acker & Feuverger, 1996; Acker & Armenti, 2004; Currie, Harris & Thiele, 2000) to not taking women's inordinate responsibility for childbearing and family seriously (Acker & Armenti, 2004; Armenti, 2004; Ward & Wold-Wendel, 2005; Finkel & Olswang, 1996). Female faculty, especially at the pre tenure phase, frequently do not take the appropriate leave time, even when entitled to, fearing reprisals that could adversely impact the tenure outcome (Finkel, Olswang & She, 1994).

It is for these reasons, and perhaps more, that many researchers believe that women faculty are still being besieged by problems within the academy. And, it is for these reasons that some like Acker and Armenti (2004) and McElrath (1992) point to as the force behind which women faculty must galvanize toward the struggle for legitimacy.

Gauges of Gender Inequity

The AAUP's (2006) bleak assessment of where women faculty stand in the academy serves as indicators of an unfinished agenda. The challenges faced by women are disproportionate, especially when compared to those of women in the private sector. Women with doctorates are produced at record rates yet fail to secure comparable employment in the academy as their male peers. They are overly concentrated in part-time

positions which almost never lead to tenure, and when in full-time positions, women faculty are more likely to be found on nontenure track
status. The AAUP believes that this trend creates a vicious cycle, which if
left unchecked, will lead to an uneven playing field for women. Female
graduate students will be less likely to pursue academic careers, thus
diminishing the already small pool of prospects. Ironically, in academic
medicine, while women are more likely than men to pursue academic
careers, they seldom receive academic rank or higher academic rank appointments as their male peers (Nonnemaker, 2000).

The outlook for underrepresented minority women is far less san-
guine. Institutions with greater underrepresented minority faculty are
more likely to have more underrepresented minority students (Cregler,
Clark & Jackson, 1994). Hence, underrepresented minority students not
only have enhanced opportunities for role models, but more importantly,
those role models look like them (Lewis-Stevenson et al., 2001). The survey of 113 medical schools revealed that while women were half as likely
to occupy full-time and part-time faculty positions in family medicine,
they were 25 percent less likely than men to hold academic appointments
as assistant professors and 50 percent less likely to hold positions at the
associate professor rank. What is alarming is that 75 percent of the
schools' departments of family medicine had no female faculty at the associate professor rank. And with the exception of one predominantly
black medical college, the few underrepresented minority faculty who
were not identified as minority female faculty, were assistant professors.

Women faculty of color also experience the dual marginalization of
gender and race (Viernes-Turner, 2002) and Asian American women
were not the most represented (Hune & Chan, 1997). Viernes-Turner
(2002) described the complex interplay between race and gender. In addition to the challenges already experienced by women faculty, women
faculty of color faced additional impediments of being undermined plus
a host of other obstacles.

Coping Strategies

Given the prevailing challenges that women faculty experience within
the academy, women have devised strategies to survive the onslaught.
While all women faculty are vulnerable, those in either dual-career families or families with children, are especially vulnerable. Much of the re-

search on the difficulties for women faculty is dedicated to navigating the system in light of these obstacles. Women at the pre-tenure phase of their academic careers may neither have the benefit of experience nor similarly situated female faculty to guide them. Many have start up families by the time of their assistant professor appointments or are contemplating these decisions. This is a critical period as by the time of tenure consideration, female faculty are on average in the age range of their mid to late thirties (Armenti, 2004). Should female faculty also desire additional time to prepare for the tenure and promotion process, they may opt to stop the clock, if their institutions offer it. However, many believe that doing so may be perceived as either not being as committed to their careers or not possessing the brawn to endure and survive the tenure process. Many pre-tenure female faculty, therefore, forgo applying for this much needed time off.

Female faculty have thus concocted various mechanisms to help cope with the stress of academic life. To avoid taking time off for maternity leave, for example, some women faculty have employed what Armenti (2004) calls "the hidden pregnancy phenomenon" (p.212). The strategy involves getting pregnant during May of the previous year in order to give birth around June of the following year. This prevents the female faculty from taking additional time off during the academic year by using the summer months to become adjusted to life as a mother. This area alone has perhaps been a key source of contention for women faculty and one that causes them to experience the most angst. This area has also generated the most research on women in academia.

For faculty who are more geographically mobile, and should they be denied tenure, particularly from an elite institution, they can parlay this association with the first institution to increase the likelihood of securing tenure at the second institution (Whicker, Kronefeld & Strickland, 1993). Some women have interrupted their academic careers for various reasons but with the intent of continuing at the same or another institution (McElrath, 1992). However, it has been shown that those who take this option, upon returning to academia, may or may not be perceived as committed enough to their careers, and as a result, are more likely to experience a negative tenure outcome. Some women faculty, although they remain in academia, secure mostly part time positions for the purpose of flexibility. However, these part time positions generally never lead to tenure (Finkel & Olswang, 1996). Finally, there are those women faculty who have made the deliberate decision not to have children. This option allows the incumbent to enjoy family life while not having children allows them more time to dedicate to career aspirations. However, by engaging in the above strategies, Finkel and Olswang (1996) contend that women have simply become part of the problem and by accommodating the existing system, especially with regard to promotion and tenure, women do not force the system to change.

Facilitating Change: Lessons from the Classroom

The AAUP (2006) has made a cogent case that the rates at which women faculty are represented and lack of advancement within the academy is disturbing. While women have come a long way as reflected in the record numbers of doctorates or equivalent conferred annually at the nation's universities, they have not been equally represented within the ranks of faculty. And, their meager gains have not only receded over time, but the very issues that were thought to have provided the impetus for change leading to increasing acceptance toward gender equity are consistently being revisited.

Some like Acker and Armenti (2004) and McElrath (1992) argue that women have not been strident enough in advancing their interests, and in many ways, have become part of the problem. Others like Hargens and Long (2002) counsel that only with patience over time will change in faculty composition come about. Kanter (1977) found that for any minority group to make discernible change and bring about a lasting effect, the representation of the minority group must be sustained at a minimum or change will dissipate. The battle then for achieving gender equity in academia may lie in a multifaceted approach that includes working at every level of the higher education system. Therefore, the impetus for increasing female faculty must begin in the classroom.

Male students have boundless opportunities for male faculty as role models at much greater rates than female students (Nelson & Roger, 2004). When female role models are absent from the classroom, women are less likely to pursue academic careers in those fields from which role models are absent. The presence of female role models then becomes a reliable predictor for even success of female students at the undergraduate level, for instance. Institutions like Princeton University and Duke

University and the National Science Foundation have been deliberate in helping to bring about change in the ranks of female faculty (Bettinger & Long, 2005). They have each earmarked funding for increasing female faculty in science and engineering. Female students who took courses in the sciences, for example, and from a female instructor, were twice as likely as other students to take more courses related to the initial course taken and took 5.2 times more credits in related courses than other female students.

Studies on the reasons why doctoral students remain or left their degree programs demonstrated common themes that can be used as lessons learned in such programs to better prepare and/or orient female students for success (Golde, 2005; Maher, Ford & Thompson, 2004; Gibson, 2004). The attrition for students who prematurely leave doctoral programs stands at 40 percent (Golde, 2005). It then goes without saying that if most entering students are better prepared, attrition rates can be significantly reduced. Data on former doctoral students from four academic disciplines at a research 1 university cited six themes as most responsible for premature departure from doctoral programs. Subjects soon came to realize that their goal expectations were incompatible with those of their disciplines and departments; there was misalignment between their expectations and those of their departments; they were ill prepared for graduate academic life; their experiences were mismatched with those of their advisors; graduate life was not as expected; and at the time of entry and throughout their doctoral programs' pursuit, the employment picture was unfavorable. Finally, the nature of each discipline was such that they felt isolated from each other as well as from the faculty (Golde, 2005).

A second study of another research 1 university reflected dissimilar themes (Maher, Ford & Thompson, 2004). The study focused on those who successfully completed their doctoral studies; early finishers (< 4.25 years) vs. late finishers (> 6.75 years) (p. 390). What appeared to separate the two groups beyond the length of time that it took for successful completion was the level of commitment; stability of financial support; focus and selection of one's dissertation topic; and the working relationship with faculty. Early finishers experienced fewer constraints than late finishers who were further burdened by family-related responsibilities. Finally, Gibson's (2004) study of mentored faculty revealed that women faculty benefited most from either formal or informal mentoring as reported by a feeling of connection with their mentors, a supportive environment, affirmation of one's work, not feeling isolated, and understanding the politics of their experiences.

What can then be gleaned from the current body of research is that when students do not receive the essential information and/or guidance for increasing success in graduate school, the likelihood of their failure increases. Students' experiences can be enhanced through role modeling and/or mentoring relationships. The experiences of recently appointed junior faculty at six research institutions showed how institutional environment plays an important role in faculty retention (Trower & Bleak, 2004). Overall, female faculty were far more likely than male faculty to be less satisfied. And when the data was disaggregated, female faculty were less satisfied with their institutions and departments as well as were less likely to recommend their institutions to colleagues for employment opportunities.

In light of the increasing number of doctorates conferred to women each year and despite their low recruitment and retention rates, the academy should take note of key differences between male and female faculty and what it will take to attract and retain them. An increase in faculty can in turn create opportunities for prospective students who may or may not be considering academic careers. By beginning in the classroom, students can use their experiences to help build the future pipeline of available female scholars. Over time, a new generation of women scholars can begin to make a difference as role models for incoming students in all academic fields of study.

Conclusion

Despite the notable achievements that women have made in the academy over the past 35 years since the passing of Title IX (1972) of the Civil Rights Act of 1964, the journey for gender equity remains illusive. Recent data have shown that although women are fast gaining parity in the number of doctorates earned, they still significantly lag in representation among the faculty ranks. A gnawing pattern has been consistently observed; the higher the degree offered and the more prestigious the institution, the less likely that women faculty will be present. This trend has had diminishing returns that adversely impacts all phases of academic life, from the number of female students in the classroom to the decreasing presence of females within faculty ranks. Women have, in essence, lost ground in academia over time and struggle to maintain current faculty levels. The AAUP's (2006) four measures of performance for gender equity, employment status, tenure status, full professor rank, and average salary, is testament to the persistent inequities in the academy.

The literature points to prominent and recurring themes for these disparities which include but are not limited to women's differing perception of issues that may result in self-selecting out of academia; the perceived problem of gender and the associated cultural and societal biases for role expectations; the call for more research on issues that are important to women; competition for resources between majority (white male faculty) and minority (female faculty) groups; the presence of few female faculty to serve as role models; the need for female faculty to follow a male faculty career path; and problems with the promotion and tenure system. Consequently, women faculty have resorted to devising novel mechanisms as a way to cope with the complexities of their academic lives, many while balancing the inordinate responsibilities of career and family.

While it has been correctly suggested that facilitating change can only be realized by attacking all stages of the educational system beginning in the classroom, some complain that perhaps women faculty may not be asking the right questions to influence change. Gordon and Lee Keyfitz (2004) remark on Nelson and Rogers' (2004) study of female faculty representation in the nation's top science and engineering institutions but identify areas that were worthy of exploration that were not included as part of the analysis. Worthy of mention in the study should have been that some newly minted Ph.Ds. assume post-doctoral positions as a conduit to building their research agenda. And, because most of the scientific disciplines are employing more at the international level, the female faculty representation reported in the study might have only been a reflection of those who were based within the United States.

Winkler (2000) offers some sage advice for women entering the academy. First, become well versed about the field and institution that one is about to enter. Know what the female to male ratio is, especially in your discipline. Second, seek out female faculty from similar and/or divergent disciplines, if necessary, and solicit information about their challenges within the institution. Third, as a novice in the field, women may not readily be aware of the female to male faculty ratio. A female faculty may be more comfortable in a department with a more balanced female to male ratio or where at least the new female faculty will not feel isolated. Winkler cautions against being the first and/or only female faculty in a department as one may encounter resentment or a culture of resistance. Fourth, find out how well female faculty members have fared in the department. It is therefore prudent to pose questions during the interviewing process about how well female faculty have integrated in the department and whether or not male faculty have collaborated with female colleagues and the relationships between them. Fifth, upon securing an academic position, be aware of the criteria for a successful career within the department. If you believe that you are being short-changed in terms of the resources to which you are entitled as a faculty member, discuss the concern with your department chair. Winkler notes, however, that new female faculty should choose their battles by pursuing only those that directly affect them.

Given misperceptions by students about female faculty behavior, it will be important to know how students will behave around a new female faculty and what strategies to develop for effective classroom communication (Winkler, 2000). Knowing what difficulties that female faculty are inclined to experience will help new faculty to better handle challenging situations and avoid self-blame. Tenure is precarious and women faculty much more than men faculty tend to have negative experiences with the process. Winkler recommends that new female faculty know what the criteria are for publishing, for instance, as well as actively seek out others for collaboration on projects. She advises not to depend upon male colleagues to extend the offer to collaborate. More importantly, female faculty should enter the academia with the intent to "hit the ground running" (Winkler, 2000, p.746). When, if ever, female faculty believe that they have not been given due process for reappointment or promotion and tenure, Winkler counsels the aggrieved to use the institution's appeal process to state ones case. Finally, it is incumbent upon female faculty not to remain silent. While being on a tenure track position is uncertain, "we cannot justify our silence" (p.746).

Winkler (2000) also has recommendations on how institutions can facilitate the increase in female faculty. She believes that institutional support is needed to help facilitate change. Leaders should focus on both the recruitment and retention of female faculty and be cognizant that the institution's policies and practices may be fostering a negative environment. Most important, institutional leaders and male students must tap their own feelings and perceptions in order to eliminate gender discrimination within higher education.

Bibliography

Acker, S., & Feuerverger, G. (1996). Doing good and feeling bad: The work of women university teachers. *Cambridge Journal of Education*, 26, 401-422.

Acker, S., & Armenti, C. (2004). Sleepless in academia. *Gender and Education*, 16 (1), 3-24.

Aisenberg, N., & Harrington, M. (1988). *Women of academe: Outsiders in the sacred grove*. University of Massachusetts Press.

American Association of University Professors (AAUP). (2006). Faculty gender equity indicators 2006. Martha S. West and John W. Curtis.

Armenti, C. (2004). Gender as a barrier for women with children in academe. *The Canadian Journal of Higher Education*, XXXIV (1), 1-26.

Armenti, C. (2004). May babies and post tenure babies: Maternal decisions of women professors. *The Review of Higher Education*, 27 (2), 211-231.

Barnett, R.C., Carr, P., Boisnier, A.D., Ash, A., Friedman, R.H., Moskowitz, M.A., & Szalacha, L. (1998). Relationships of gender and career motivation to medical faculty members' production of academic publications. *Academic Medicine*, 73, 180-186.

Bell, L.A., (2000). More good news, so why the blues? *Academe*, 12-95. March-April.

Bellas, M.L., Ritchey, P. Neal., & Parmer, P. (2001). Gender differences in the salaries and salary growth rates of university faculty: An exploratory study. *Sociological Perspectives*, 44, (2), 163-187.

Bensimon, E. M., & Marshall, C. (2003). Like it or not. feminist critical policy analysis matters. *The Journal of Higher Education*, 74, (3), 3337-349.

Bettinger, E.P., & Long, B. T. (2005). Do faculty serve as role models? The impact of instructor gender on female students. *American Economic Review*.

Blalock, H.M. (1967). *Toward a theory of minority group relations*. John Wiley Press.

Coser, L. (1974). *Greedy institutions. Patterns of undivided commitment* The Free Press. McMillan Publishing.

Cregler, L.L., Clark, L.T., & Jackson, E.B. (1994). Careers in academic medicine and clinical practice for minorities: Opportunities and barriers. *Journal of the Association of Academic Minority Physicians*, 5, 68-73.

Currie, J., Harris, P., & Thiele, B. (2000). Sacrifices in greedy universities: Are they gendered? *Gender and Education*, 12, (3), 269-291.

DiPalma, S. (2005). Progress for women faculty in social work academia. *Afflia*, 20, 71-86. Spring.

Finkel, S. K., & Olswang, S.G. (1996). Child rearing as a career impediment to women assistant professors. *The Review of Higher Education*, 19, (2), 123-139.

Finkle, S.K., Olswang, S.G., & She, N. (1994). The implications of childbirth on tenure and promotion for women faculty. *The Review of Higher Education*, 17, (3), 259-270.

Gibson, S.K. (2004). Being mentored: The experience of women faculty. *Journal of Career Development*, 30, (3), 173-188. Spring.

Golde, C.M. (2005). The role of department and discipline in doctoral student attrition: 1essons from four departments. *The Journal of Higher Education*, 76, (6), 669-700. November/December.

Gordon, C., & Lee Keyfitz, B. (2004). Women in academia: Are we asking the right questions? *Notices of the American Mathematical Society (AMS)*, 51, (7) 784-786.

Gunter, R., & Stambach, A. (2003). Balancing act and as game: How women and men science faculty experience the promotion process. *Gender Issues*, 24-42. Winter.

Hargens, L.L., & Long, J. S. (2002). Demographic inertia and women's representation among faculty in higher education. *The Journal of Higher Education*, 73, (4), 494-517. July/August.

Harper, E.P., Baldwin, R.G., Gansneder, B.G., & Chronister, J.L. (2001). Full-time women faculty off the tenure track: Profile and practice. *The Review of Higher Education*, 24, (3), 237-257.

Hensel, N. (1991). Realizing gender equality in higher education: The need to integrate work family issues. ASHE-Eric Higher Education Report, No. 1. School of Education and Human Development. George Washington University.

Hune, S., & Chan, K.S. (1997). Special focus: Asian american demographic and educational trends. In D.J. Carter and R. Wilson (Eds.) *Minorities in Higher Education: Fifteenth Annual Status Report* (p.39-67). Washington, D.C.: American Council on Education.

Jorgenson, J. (2000). Interpreting the intersections of work and family: Frame conflicts in women's work. *The Electronic Journal of Communication*, 10, 3-4.

Kanter, R.M. (1977). *Men and women of the corporation.* Basic Books, Inc. Publishers.

Lawler, A. (1999). Tenured women battle to make it less lonely at the top. *Science*, 286, (5443), 1272-1278.

Lewis-Stevenson, S., Hueston, W.J., Mainous III, A.G., Bazell, C., & Ye, Xiaobu. (2001). *Family Medicine*, 33, (6), 459-465.

Lie, S.S., & Malik, L. (Eds.). (1994). *The gender gap in higher education*. World Yearbook of education. London, Kogan Page.

Long, S.J. (1992). Measures of sex differences in scientific productivity. *Social Forces*, 71, 159-178.

Maher, M.A., Ford, M.E., & Thompson, C.M. (2004). Degree progress of women doctoral students: Factors that constrain, facilitate, and differentiate. *The Review of Higher Education*, 27, (3), 385-408.

McElrath, K. (1992). Gender, career disruption and academic rewards. *Journal of Higher Education*, 63, (3), 269-281.

Moore, K.M., and Sagaria, M.A.D. (1993). The situation of women in research universities in the United States: Within the inner circles of academic power. In B.K. Townsend (Ed.), *Women in Higher Education: A Feminist Perspective* (1st Ed.). Needham Heights, MA: Ginn Press.

Nelson, D.J. and Rogers, D.C. (2004). A national analysis of diversity in science and engineering faculties at research universities.

Nonnemaker, L. (2000). Women physicians in academic medicine: New insights from cohort studies. *New England Journal of Medicine*, 342, 399-405.

Neumann, A., & LaPointe Terosky, A. (2007). To give and to receive: Recently tenured professors' experiences of service in major research universities. *The Journal of Higher Education*, 78, (3), 282-310. May/June.

Olsen, D., Maple, S.A., & Stage, F.K. (1995). Women and minority faculty job satisfaction. *The Journal of Higher Education*, 66, 267-293.

Ostriker, A. (1998). The maternal mind (in) *The family track. Keeping your faculties while You Mentor, Nurture, Teach, and Serve.* Constance Coiner and Diane Hume George (Eds.). University of Illinois Press.

Park, S.M. (1996). Research, teaching and service: Why shouldn't women's work count? *The Journal of Higher Education*, 67, (1), 46-83.

Perna, L.W. (2001). Sex and race differences in faculty tenure and promotion. *Research in Education*, 42, (5), 541-567.

Ridgeway, C.L.., & Correll, S.J. (2004). Motherhood as a status characteristic. *Journal of Social Issues*, 60, (4), 483-700.

Schuster, J.H., and Finkelstein, M.J. (2006). *The american faculty: The restructuring of Academic Work and Careers.* Baltimore: The Johns Hopkins University Press.

Sonnert, G. (1995b). What makes a good scientist?: Determinants of peer evaluation among biologists. *Social Studies of Science*, 25, 35-55.

Trower, C.A., and Bleak, J.L. (2004). The study of new scholars. Tenure-track faculty job satisfaction survey. Gender: Statistical Report. www.gse.harvard.edu/news/features/trower0412204.pdf.

U.S. Department of Education. (2005). *Digest of education statistics* http://nces.ed.gov/programs/digest/d05_tf.asp.

Van Anders, S.M. (2004). Why the academic pipeline leaks: Fewer men than women perceive barriers to becoming professors. *Sex Roles*, 51, 9/10, 511-521.

Viernes Turner, C.S. (2002). Women of color in academe. *The Journal of Higher Education*, 73, (1), 74-93.

Ward, K., & Wolf-Wendel, L.E. (2005). Work and family perspectives from research university faculty. *New Directions for Higher Education*, 130, 67-80. Summer.

Wennerds, C., & Wold, A. (1997). Nepotism and sexism in peer review. *Nature*, 387, 341-343.

Wenzel, S.A., & Hollenshead, C. (1998). Former women faculty: Reasons for leaving one research university. Center for the Education of Women, University of Michigan.

Whicker, M.L., Kronefeld, J.J., & Strickland, R.A. (1993). *Getting tenure.* Sage Publications.

Winkler, J.A. (2000). Faculty reappointment, tenure, and promotion: Barriers for women. *Professional Geographer*, 52, (4), 737-750.

Yoder, J.D. (1991). Rethinking tokenism. Looking beyond the numbers. *Gender and Society*, 5, (2), 178-192.

CHAPTER 2

TEACHING TRANSGENDER ISSUES
Global Social Movements Based on Gender Identity

Jillian Todd Weiss

Transgender Identity

The term "transgender" is unsettled, but the term is generally used to refer to individuals whose gender identity or expression does not conform to the social expectations for their sex assigned at birth (Currah, Juang & Minter, 2006). "Transgender" is often called an "umbrella term," in the sense that it refers to all gender-variant people and includes many different identities. For example, it would include a person who has undergone surgical intervention to live full-time as a member of the opposite sex (sometimes referred to as a "transsexual"), a person who occasionally cross-dresses in private (sometimes referred to as a "crossdresser"), and someone who identifies as both male and female, or neither (Weiss, 2001).

This definition is a useful starting place, but it obscures many complexities of transgender identity. It makes it seem as if each transgender person has a gender that is fluid and constantly shifting, a notion which is incorrect. Many transgender people transition from one sex to another at one point in their lives, but their gender remains stable and fixed. As an example, a person who is called female at birth may find, as they mature, that their gender is masculine, and their gender identity is male. This can occur because sex has both biological and gendered attributes. The biological attributes, such as genitalia, chromosomes, and hormones, do not tell the whole story. Gendered attributes, including psychological, behavioral, and social traits, may bear no relation to the person's biological attributes. The person born with female genitalia and assigned to the female sex may have a deep-seated and unshakeable belief that they are male (referred to as "gender identity"), may behave in ways stereotypically considered male (referred to as "gender expression") and may be seen by society as a male (referred to as "passing"). They may also have medical and surgical intervention to help them reassign their biological characteristics from one sex to another. To say that such a person has an ambiguous gender is more denying their gender than describing it. In fact, it would usually be inaccurate to say that their "gender" has changed, for these gendered psychological, behavioral and social traits are usually felt from a very young age, and memories of gender identity may go back to age three. The definition is particularly troubling to such persons because it suggests that they should not be accepted fully in the new sex because of the historical ambiguity between birth sex and present sex, events which may be separated by decades, and which may bear no relation to their currently unambiguous presentation (Namaste, 2000; Prosser, 1998).

The term "transgender" is relatively new, dating from the late 1980s, and it was not until the mid-1990s that it was used in its current popular sense as an umbrella term that refers to all gender-variant people (Boswell, 1991) Because this term groups together identities that have different personal and political aims, its use is disputed within the transgender community. For example, some transsexuals who transition from one gender to another through sex reassignment surgery, seeking to be recognized as unambiguous members of their new sex, are not sympathetic to the cause of advocates who seek governmental recognition of gender identity without medical intervention. Their concern is that such claims are ignore the social significance of sexual anatomy and the experience of transsexuals who, from a young age, feel trapped in the "wrong body" (i.e., in a body of the wrong sex). They feel an imperative to obtain sex reassignment surgery based on severe and persistent cross-gender feelings, discomfort in the gender role of their birth sex, and distress that causes impairment in functioning in society. Those who do not seek to obtain sex reassignment surgery are perceived as having different issues from true transsexuals (Namaste, 2000). Since many people have accepted the idea that sex reassignment surgery is the line of demarcation between one sex and another, the claim that one can change sex without sex reassignment surgery is considered suspect by many transsexuals. Another political rift in the community involves the inclusion of intersex people in the transgender community. Intersex refers to those born with non-standard sexual biology, such as Androgen Insensitivity Syndrome, in which infants have female genitalia but male chromosomes. Unlike transgender conditions, which most (but not all) authorities consider a purely psychological phenomenon not appearing until the age of 3 or older, intersex conditions are present at birth (although many remain undiagnosed). Some feel that intersex conditions are physical medical conditions constituting disorders of sexual differentiation (DSD), and are medically and socially unlike transgender conditions. They strenuously object to lumping people with intersex conditions into the transgender community (ISNA, 2008). These and other political differences within the transgender community raise the question whether there is, in fact, a "transgender" community, and whether the imposition of the term "transgender" on everyone who could be classified as gender variant is appropriate and ethical. Despite these concerns, the term transgender is in wide usage in many places, particularly the United States, and gay advocates consider "transgender" people to be a part of the gay community, as indicated by the acronym "GLBT" (gay, lesbian, bisexual and transgender), which is widely used to describe sexual minorities.

It is important to distinguish between "gender identity," one's self-identification as male or female (or both or neither), and "sexual orientation," one's orientation towards romantic partners of a particular sex. "Male" and "female" are gender identities, whereas sexual orientation refers to "heterosexual" (orientation towards opposite sex partners, sometimes called "straight"), "homosexual" (orientation towards same sex partners, sometimes called "gay" or "lesbian") and "bisexual" (orientation towards partners of more than one sex). A person who is transgender can be of any sexual orientation (Weiss, 2001). For example, a person who transitions from male to female may be gay, i.e., they prefer females as romantic partners. Such a relationship is a same-sex relationship because giving respect to a transgender person's gender identity means that their new sex is the one that is used for purposes of determining sexual orientation.

The question of when one "changes sex" is a troubling one because different authorities have different opinions on the matter, leading to difficulties for transgender people. Some legal and medical authorities will not recognize a person's gender identity if it differs from their assigned sex at birth, even when there has been sex reassignment surgery and the person is living unambiguously as the opposite sex for years. This can cause problems for transgender persons in circumstances where legal sex is important, such as bathrooms, prisons, and marriage rights (and attendant issues such as spousal inheritance and step-parent adoption). Some authorities will recognize a reassigned sex where there has been sex reassignment surgery, but even here there are difficulties. There are a number of surgeries used to aid in sex reassignment, and genital surgery may be unavailable due to medical or financial reasons. This problem is particularly acute for female-to-male transsexuals because the state of the art in phalloplasty (creation of a penis) is still relatively primitive compared to the vaginoplasty available for male-to-female transsexuals, and three to five times as expensive. Thus, many female-to-male transsexuals obtain hormone treatments which lower their voices dramatically and give them a full beard, and have some surgical procedures to aid their sex reassignment, such as hysterectomy, but do not have a phalloplasty. Because society regards the presence of anatomically correct genitalia to be the determining factor, such a person may be living and passing as a man, but some governments regard him as female. Other governments will consider the person's gender identity to have changed when that person declares a change, and takes certain steps facilitating the change, such as consulting a psychotherapist specializing in gender change and/or taking cross-gender hormones. This approach permits greater flexibility in permitting transsexuals to function in society with fewer barriers.

Different societies have different names referring to transgender people, as well as different social locations for transgenders. In many countries (and in many languages), the term "transgender" does not exist, or is largely unrecognized, and the older terms "transsexual" or "transvestite" are used in the vernacular, or entirely different terms, such as "hijra" or "kathoey," with varying degrees of acceptance and pejorativeness, are used (Nanda, 1999). In such places, these terms are used to describe a wide variety of transgender identities, and do not have the narrowed meanings found in the United States (where "transsexual" describes only those who have or plan to have genital surgery, and "transvestite" describes only those heterosexuals who crossdress in private). For example, there is a term "transgenero" in Spanish, but most Spanish speakers do not recognize the term, responding instead to "transsexualismo" or "travesti," neither of which are completely synonymous with their English cognates, "transsexuality" and "transvestite," and are often defined by inclusion of elements of what is considered "sexual orientation" in the US. In some cultures, transsexuals consider themselves "gay" or "homosexual," whereas other cultures have a sharply defined distinction between transgender and gay identities. These differing language elements reflect more than simple linguistic differences, but rather show significant social and political differences in the understanding and inclusion of gender variant citizens.

One of the most difficult questions to address is the size of the transgender population because the estimate depends greatly on one's definition. If one looks only at those who have undergone sex reassignment surgery, the population is probably in the range of 1 per 50,000 people where such services are obtainable. In a world with a population of 6 billion, this means 600,000 people (a population density of approximately 1 per 80 square miles). If, however, one seeks to include all people with gender variance, then the number is probably closer to 1% of the population, which would include 60 million people (a population density of approximately 1 per square mile) (Conway, 2002).

Transgender Social Justice Issues Generally

There are a number of social justice issues that are common to transgender people everywhere in the world. Social justice organizations working on transgender issues address the following types of problems:

1. private, domestic and state-sponsored violence, particularly among youth
2. governmental and private discrimination in basic human needs
3. governmental refusal to recognize gender identity in identity documents
4. inability to use appropriate gender-segregated facilities
5. governmental refusal to recognize gender identity in regard to marriage
6. inequality in adjudication of refugee asylum petitions

(SRLP, 2007)

The most serious issue facing transgender people is private, domestic and state-sponsored violence, particularly among youth. (Amnesty International, 2005) In many places, family violence greets young people who exhibit transgender characteristics. This violence may involve parental coercion, through physical or emotional abuse, to hide gender variance, and ejection from the family home if such coercion is unsuccessful. On the street, homophobic individuals may feel justified in expressing their disgust through verbal or physical harassment, and a tradition of police impunity contributes to the perpetuation of such conduct. Privately, homophobic people who unwittingly become acquainted with transgender people, and later learn of their transgender status, have committed assault and murder, often claiming panic in defense of their actions. Many police officers that live in societies where transgender people are considered socially unacceptable will ignore or downplay complaints by or on behalf of transgender victims, and will themselves harass or assault transgender people, whom they consider to belong largely to a criminal class of prostitutes and petty thieves. A transgender person who has been subjected to such repeated violence from government officials, and who seeks refugee status and asylum in another county on that basis, may find asylum officials unsympathetic because transgender status is not officially recognized as a protected identity in the asylum law of that country.

In many societies, there is much governmental and private discrimination against transgender people in basic human needs, such as education, employment, public accommodations, housing, public benefits and transgender-specific medical care (Weiss 2001). Education, which holds the key to social and economic success, is often very difficult for young people who exhibit gender variant behaviors. Homophobia and severe harassment coming from teachers, administrators and other students is common, and this makes school an unsafe environment for many transgender young people. The difficulty of educational attainment contributes to severe employment discrimination, making it very difficult or impossible for transgender people to obtain employment consistent with their level of education or ability. This contributes greatly to marginalizing transgender people, pushing many male-to-female transgender people, particularly the young, into the shadow economy of prostitution. Transgender status, if revealed, can make it very difficult to obtain housing, as apartment owners and managers often refuse to rent housing to transgender people. Public benefits, such as welfare or medical care, may be denied when unsympathetic officials are aware of an applicant's transgender status, particularly if transgender behavior is viewed as frivolous or anti-social. Transgender-specific medical care, such as gynecological or urological examinations, endocrinological care for hormone therapy, surgical treatment, and general health examinations are often unavailable because physicians are untrained in treating transgender patients, or denied because transgender medical care is excluded from the health care system. There are many areas in which discrimination plays a role that is impossible to discuss here all of the issues caused by discrimination. For example, another area where transgender discrimination occurs is in divorce cases. Where one parent has transitioned or is transitioning to another sex, courts in the United States have found that the transgender parent should not be allowed to have custody or even to visit their natural children because of the risk of psychological harm to the children by virtue of being exposed to a transgender parent.

Governmental refusal to recognize gender identity in identity documents means that transgender people are living as one sex, but carry documents that carry a different gender marker. This means that transgender status will be revealed every time government officials and private institutions view identification. This creates a chilling effect on the use of a wide range of government and private resources requiring identity documents, which can be as important as obtaining medical care or as simple as using a public library (Weiss 2001). The governmental refusal to recognize gender identity is also related a number of other social justice issues, including inability to use appropriate facilities that are gender-specific, such as bathrooms, and denial of marriage and related rights, such as spousal inheritance and step-parent adoption laws. When government identification fails to match a person's gender presentation, this makes usage of a public bathroom difficult, particularly in employment situations, where employers are more likely to be aware of their employee's transgender status. It also means that transgender persons who are incarcerated may be placed in dangerous situations because of their gender identity, and transgender people whom being placed in the wrong ward or other embarrassing situations. Failure of government recognition also means that a transsexual who marries a person of the opposite sex (opposite to their new sex) may find that their marriage is invalidated when they attempt to access government assistance, such as obtaining a divorce, suing a medical provider for the negligent death of a spouse, or obtaining a spousal inheritance right. A transgender person who marries someone from another country, and seeks to move to their spouse's homeland, may find that the immigration rules do not consider them a "spouse" entitled to immigration rights. In the United States, where some states have enacted a secondary form of marriage called "civil union" reserved for same sex couples, transgender people who wish to marry are in legal limbo as government officials try to decide whether the couple is entitled to civil union or to marriage.

The "Transgender Community" as a Social Movement

While it is useful in some respects to theorize the existence of a "transgender social movement" emanating from a "transgender community," with a homogenous core of social justice issues, it is important not to obscure the divisions within the transgender community. There are at least a dozen gender-variant identities that fit within the transgender "umbrella," and understanding these differences is important to community cohesion and political representation. When these differences are obscured, the need to proclaim identity boundaries within the community makes community cohesion and political representation difficult. Indeed, it may even be a misnomer to speak of a "transgender community" where these differences are obscured, because such communities tend to constitute only a small sample of the entire transgender population, but claim to represent all transgenders despite the lack of representation of all other transgender identities. For example, some transgender organizations claim to be "national" and open to all transgenders, but have largely White and upper-middle class transsexual members.

Measuring the Global Social Movement

Although, as set forth above, there are certain issues common to the transgender movement in various countries, the conditions of the movement in each country and world region are dramatically different. This can be easily grasped by an overview of the formal legal frameworks of international and national law. The United Nations Universal Declaration of Human Rights (1948) states that "Everyone is entitled to all the rights and freedoms set forth in this Declaration, without distinction of any kind, such as race, color, sex, language, religion, political or other opinion, national or social origin, property, birth or other status." The language of "other status" is tracked in the International Covenant on Civil and Political Rights (1976), which specifically includes the right to equal protection of the law and freedom from discrimination. In 1994, the United Nations Human Rights Committee affirmed in its decision in *Toonen v Australia* (1994) that "other status" is to be understood broadly and includes sexual orientation as a protected status. While there has been no specific decision on whether gender identity or expression is also included in the term "other status," it is difficult to imagine an argument that sexual orientation is included but gender identity or expression is not included. This does not, however, require legal recognition of a transgender person's gender identity. It should be noted that, while sexual orientation and gender identity are usually understood as separate identities in the contemporary context, this was not true in the past. Therefore, while some countries have laws prohibiting discrimination based on sexual orientation, few countries have laws prohibiting discrimination based on gender identity or expression. Laws prohibiting discrimination based on sexual orientation, particularly those enacted in the twentieth century, are often understood to also include gender identity and expression. As a result of this ambiguous legal status, one cannot determine the legal landscape of transgender social movements simply by counting countries that include "gender identity" in their legal codes, because countries that protect "sexual orientation" may include transgender persons within its scope. Further complicating the understanding of the international situation is the fact that there is no publicly available current listing of countries that specifically recognize transgender identity or prohibit discrimination based on sexual orientation or gender identity. Countries that are notable for their leadership in formal legal protections for transgender status include Canada, the United Kingdom, Germany, and South Africa.

Looking at the formal legal protections against discrimination for transgender persons is, however, not an adequate measure of the social situation. In some countries, street violence is the most serious problem for transgender people, while in others it is economic marginalization, unemployment, education, or government recognition. Some countries have relatively low levels of street violence and unemployment, but transgender voices are suppressed from public view through legal prohibitions on organizing or social sanctions for calling public attention to disfavored identities. In addition, measuring the level of legal protection does not give an adequate picture of conditions because there is often a disconnect between the laws on the books and the law in action on the streets. Some areas have much formal legal protection, but it is coupled with a low level of social acceptance, leading to non-enforcement of the formal law by police and courts. Other places may have relatively high levels of tolerance for transgender identity in general, but turn a blind eye on those occasions when transgender identity is targeted for street violence, extrajudicial killings by police or economic discrimination.

As an example of the difficulty of generalizing about the movement, it is sometimes assumed that the most successful transgender movement may be found in the United States, where, as compared to many other countries, there are higher levels of tolerance for sexual minorities, a very permissive attitude both legally and socially towards public organizing and freedom of speech, and much emphasis on formal legal protections. As compared to Canada, England and Germany, however, the transgender movement in the United States has been hampered by a number of problems. From a social point of view, there is a high degree of variability of acceptance of transgender identity in different regions. There is a high (though uneven) degree of acceptance in the Northeast, particularly in large cities like New York City and Boston, a lower level of acceptance in the Midwest, and little in the South and West, except in certain large cities like San Francisco, Austin and Atlanta. The fragmentation of most government authority in the United States into fifty different jurisdictions without supervision from the federal government (except on certain national issues, such as immigration and interstate commerce) means that there is no national policy on transgender issues at the time of this writing, although there are currently efforts to create to ban employment discrimination. Unlike Canada, England and Germany, transgender persons cannot receive recognition of their gender change from any central authority, and have to deal with a patchwork of regulations from state and local authorities that often do not accord any credence to their identity. Their gender identity may be recognized by, for example, the driver's license bureau, but not by a federal agency, such as the Immigration and Naturalization Service, a city Registrar who has the power to amend birth certificates, a jail warden or homeless shelter social worker who places inmates into male and female institutions, or a judge hearing a case involving the right change one's name to a name typically associated with the opposite sex. A number of courts have ruled that a heterosexual marriage (such as that between an MTF and a natal male, or an FTM and a natal female) is invalid, despite the fact that the transgender partner had received recognition of their new sex on their birth certificate. This has resulted in invalidation of inheritances, inability to sue for wrongful death of a spouse, and loss of child custody. There is no national health care system, and transgender health care is routinely excluded from private insurance schemes. The United States also has no nationwide protection against employment discrimination based on transgender identity. While some U.S. states and cities have included "gender identity" in their anti-discrimination laws, government enforcement is quite uneven and civil lawsuits are difficult to win because of legal loopholes. Furthermore, a detailed report from Amnesty International indicates that transgender people are targeted by police in the United States for violence, and that impunity is routinely granted to police officers who inflict such violence (Amnesty International). A website which tracks murders of transgender people has a list of approximately 250 U.S. transgender murder victims from 1970 through the time of this writing, more than any other country listed (Smith, 2008).

By contrast, in the United Kingdom, national law makes discrimination based on transgender identity is a crime and subject to civil liability. In addition, the Gender Recognition Act (2004) allows transgender employees to obtain a "Gender Recognition Certificate" from authorities, requiring government and employers to recognize a change in gender. The certificate can be obtained upon a showing that they have been diagnosed with "gender dysphoria" by a psychiatrist and have lived in their new role for at least two years, or have had sex reassignment surgery. The law also makes it a crime, with a fine of up to £5,000, to disclose that a person has a Gender Recognition Certificate. It is a strict liability offense, so "reasonable necessity" or "mistake" is not a defense. In addition, a transgender person is not obliged to disclose whether they have obtained a certificate. Another law, the Data Protection Act (1998), requires that information should only be retained while it is relevant. Keeping a copy of the Gender Recognition Certificate in the agency's or employer's files may violate the law if the file is accessed by unauthorized personnel. While this relatively recent law has not eliminated discrimination in the U.K., the creation of an environment in which the rights of a transgender person are entitled to enforcement by a court makes for a much more positive socio-legal climate than in the United States.

Much research needs to be done in order to begin to properly assess the accomplishments and the needs of transgender social movements around the globe. A comparative listing of formal legal protections on the international level is needed, as well as documenting of statistics on the size of transgender populations, education levels, unemployment and underemployment rates, and hate crimes based on gender identity. This work is hampered by the fact that transgender advocacy remains woefully under funded, and there are only a small number of scholars and advocates who work on documenting transgender social movements in the international context. There are hopeful signs of progress in this regard, but it will probably take decades for transgender social movements to reach the level of effectiveness associated with other, more mainstream social movements.

Bibliography

Amnesty International (2005). *Stonewalled: police abuse and misconduct against lesbian, gay, bisexual and transgender people in the united states.* http://www. amnestyusa.org/outfront/stonewalled/report.pdf accessed April 24. 2008

Boswell, H. (1991). The Transgender Alternative. *TV/TS Tapestry Journal 59*, 31-33.

Conway, L. (2002). *How frequently does transsexualism occur?* http://ai.eecs.umich.edu/people/conway/TS/TSprevalence.html accessed April 24, 2008

Currah, P., Juang, R., & Minter, S. (2006). *Transgender Rights.* Minneapolis: University of Minnesota Press.

Data Protection Act, 1998 (Eng.) www.opsi.gov.uk/Acts/Acts1998/ukpga_19980029_en_1 accessed April 25, 2008

Gender Recognition Act, 2004 (Eng.) www.opsi.gov.uk/acts/acts2004/ukpga_20040007_en_1 accessed April 25, 2008

ISNA (2008). Intersex Society of North America. http://isna.org accessed April 24, 2008

Namaste, V.K. (2000). *Invisible lives: the erasure of transsexual and transgendered people.* Chicago: The University of Chicago Press.

Nanda, S. (1999). *Gender diversity: crosscultural variations.* Chicago: Waveland Press

Prosser, J. (1998). *Second skins: the body narratives of transsexuality.* New York: Columbia University Press.

Smith, G.A. (2008). *Remembering our dead.* http://rememberingourdead.org accessed April 25, 2008

SRLP (2008). *Transgender Issues.* http://srlp.org/index.php?sec=03A&page=issues accessed April 24, 2008

United Nations (1948). *Universal Declaration of Human Rights.*

United Nations Human Rights Committee (1994). *Toonen v Australia.* Case No. 488/1992.

Weiss, J.T. (2001). The Gender Caste System: Identity, Privacy and Heteronormativity. *The Journal of Law and Sexuality. 10*, 123-186.

CHAPTER 3

THE DOWN LOW PHENOMENON
A Case for Reinventing African American
Male Hyper Masculinity

Richard Greggory Johnson III and George Stuart Leibowitz

Introduction

Anti-oppressive and anti-racist paradigms have become increasingly utilized in social justice-minded academic curricular in the social sciences, education, social work, and related professions (Dominelli, 1988; Healy, 2005), and these approaches provide a framework to address the Down Low phenomenon. Influenced by Marxism, and radical ideologies such as feminism, anti-oppressive paradigms urge the development of a critical consciousness and self-reflection in addressing and responding to social problems (Healy, 2005). Anti-racist pedagogy and practice requires an awareness of the ways our membership in certain class and social divisions shapes experiences and access to opportunity, as well as offers a critique of the institutional structures, and their associated language, that promotes oppression. Additionally, anti-oppressive theory applies a multidimensional model of oppression that, in additional to analyzing structural inequalities, includes psychological and cultural dimensions (Dalrymple & Burke, 1995).

Critical and anti-oppressive social work addresses power differentials and stigmatizing exclusion, and offers an analysis of the causes of problem behavior in individuals as bound to the macro social structures that construct the behavior (Millar, 2008). Further, the understanding of oppression may be deepened by an analysis of power as distinguished, on one hand, as the coercive sexual behavior of individuals (the psychological dimension) manifest in the case of the Down Low, and on the other hand, behavior that is not only psychological, but embedded in socio-political contexts and in the way societies function (the cultural and structural dimensions).

Critical social scientists have offered a view of social phenomena, such as sexual relationships, as constructed by the power discrepancies between the dominant discourse and marginalized groups (Healy, 2005).

These groups are divided between those who are members of privileged, dominant groups, e.g., heterosexuals, males, Whites, etc. and those who are members of oppressed groups, e.g., queer communities, African Americans, etc. Freire's (1970) empowerment model for education, which is consistent with the multidimensional model of anti-oppressive practice discussed in this chapter, illuminates the power differentials emanating from the construction of privilege, i.e., between the white educator and the black student. Moreover, Freire emphasizes the importance of criti-cally challenging the multiple forms of inequality and oppression. His utilization of authentic pedagogical dialogue with oppressed people in Brazil is a difficult theoretical approach to imagine in practice, since it requires a form of unconstrained communication of the oppressed. In this chapter, following a detailed discussion of the definitions, and the consequences of the Down Low, an action plan is adapted from an anti-oppressive framework.

Johnson and Rivera (2007) found that African American men were stereotyped as thriving, unintelligent, athletic, and criminals. Most of the stereotypes pointed to the physical prowess of African American men and their bodies. Conversely, white men were stereotyped as successful, intelligent, and CEOs. The significance of Johnson and Rivera's study is that its findings speak to the fact that the United States has a rich history of viewing Black men through hetero-normative and macho lenses. These lenses can in part be the reason for the Down Low phenomenon, and can provide additional insight into our analysis of Down Low as contextualized expressions of power, rooted in inequality, and a impor-tant feature of social relationships based on the construction of race and masculinity.

This chapter attempts to define the Down Low as a social justice is-sue and identify some of the causes for the phenomenon. Critical social justice theory and anti-oppressive practice (Healy, 2005; Millar, 2006) is utilized to analyze these causal factors and construct an action plan. The social work literature has been particularly active in developing antirac-ist paradigms, and although its integration into practice is largely an un-finished project, the robust discussion contained in these paradigms about the way racial identities have been constructed has applicability to understanding African-American men on the Down Low. The chapter also draws a correlation between the phenomenon and the rising

HIV/AIDS infections in the African American community. One of the main challenges associated with the analysis of the Down Low phenomenon is conceptualizing a place in society where African American men can feel acknowledged and accepted, regardless of their sexual orientation. This chapter concludes with an action plan based on anti-oppressive pedagogy and practice, and a case study, for understanding and addressing the issue of the Down Low phenomenon.

Background and Definition of the Down Low

The term "Down Low" originated in the African American community during the late 1990s and refers to African American men who have sex with other men on an on going basis, shrouded in secrecy and denial, while continuing to have sexual relationships with their wives or girlfriends. Moreover, these men often reject an openly gay lifestyle, and discount societal constructions about sexuality and masculine identity. Yet, they seem invested in presenting themselves as hyper-masculine. Indeed, perceptions about dominant masculinities are fluid, and the highly contextual nature of sexuality will be highlighted as we consider the definitions and causes of the Down Low phenomenon.

To begin with, homophobia within the African American community and the absence of black gay sporting and media celebrities may be responsible for the appearance of the Down Low phenomenon. Additionally, Christianity may also be responsible for the phenomenon as well (McBride, 2005), in that religious organizations have made it challenging for individuals in general to have open discourse about homosexuality, and for the African American community, in particular. Down Low may have emerged as a result of various forms of social exclusion and racial bias. The production and reproduction of racial disparities that is partially responsible for the emergence of the Down Low phenomenon, is further complicated by the intersection of two marginalized groups- African Americans and gays. Consequently, there are structural and institutional explanations for the Down Low subculture (discussed further in this chapter).

Clearly, attention has been paid to this phenomenon in the media; talk show host Oprah Winfrey has aired the issue on one of her past shows, Denizet-Lewis (2003) in the *New York Times* wrote about the "double lives" and the "hyper masculinity" of black men on the Down

Low, and some attention has been given to the betrayal, risks, and emotional abuse experienced by woman involved with men on the Down Low. However, to date, the Down Low (or DL) issue has not received much attention within academic journals or other scholarly pursuits. Indeed academics writing on issues of social class, race and sexuality have been remiss in studying the Down Low population.

On the surface, one might label this group of men as bisexual since they continue to have sex with both men and women. However, the Down Low experience is not merely a matter of having sex with both male and female partners, but is a hidden lifestyle. In 1991 Harris brought the issue of black male sexuality and bisexuality to light with his novel *Invisible Life*, in which he suggests that African American men have been engaging in sex with both genders since the beginning of time. But what is significant about Harris's work is that it connects the complexity of black male sexuality with black male identity with black male economics. Murray and Roscoe (1998) argued that Black homosexuality has been around for centuries. The authors debunk the myth that Africans started to engage in same-sex relationships due to colonization by Europeans. This theory is incorrect, according to Murray and Roscoe, because sexual orientation is not created from racial constructs. Even though Murray and Roscoe's research was conducted using fifty African societies, these data and other evidence on the "realness" of black sexuality have had little to no impact on the African-American community, in terms of acceptance.

As a result of the work done by Harris and Murray and Roscoe, the issue of African American men who sleep with other men has received some attention from fraternal organizations (Villarosa, 2001). Such attention is coming from the four historically African American sororities, namely, Alpha Kappa Alpha, Delta Sigma Theta, Zeta Phi Beta and Sigma Gamma Rho, who all hold workshops to talk about the Down Low issues with members of the organization, campus and community women and, high school women.

As mentioned earlier, when analyzing the concepts of bisexuality and the Down Low, one might conclude that both are the same. However there is a clear distinction between the Down Low and bisexuality. Bisexuality is a term that can be applied to any race, class, or gender. But the term on the Down Low refers exclusively to working class or poor

African American men who secretly have sex with men, while maintaining a heterosexual appearance in public. African American men who label themselves as being on the Down Low only do so around other African American men also on the Down Low. However these same men may talk openly about their sexual relationships with women in public, at work or other public events (Lichtenstein ,2000).

Denizet-Lewis (2003) suggests that African American men on the Down Low do not consider themselves bisexual, but rather heterosexual men who sleep with other men, despite the fact that these men may frequent bars or other places where other Down Low men congregate. This is a particularly important point because trying to conduct research on this "invisible" population becomes challenging—even for those academics generally trying to find solutions for challenges associated with being on the Down Low. Researchers must note that typical avenues for ascertaining information on sexuality must be abandoned when studying the Down Low population. Keith Boykin points out that not all gay men can be found in the Castro District of San Francisco, the Dupont Circle district in Washington D.C., Santa Monica Boulevard in Los Angeles or Christopher Street in New York City (Millennium March, 2000). But on the other hand, Boykin points out that perhaps the definition of Down Low behavior is more complex that the public or media suggest. In other words, Boykin is not convinced that the definition of Down-Low should be relegated to only men, only African American and only working class individuals. Such a definition of the phenomenon creates a narrow approach to understanding how and why such a lifestyle exist in what is considered one of the most democratic nations in the free world.

Causes of the Down Low Phenomenon

The primary reason for the disconnect between lifestyle and identification is that Down Low men interpret being gay or bisexual as an "upper class white male" lifestyle. In other words, African American men on the Down Low do not compare themselves to white men who are openly gay or bisexual, because they (white gay men) still benefit from white privilege, regardless of their sexual orientation. Furthermore, the media (television and movies) continues to depict many white gay men as effeminate or jokes. Black masculinity is robustly connected with identity within the African American community. "Hyper" masculine behavior exhibited by some black men has roots worldwide, but can especially be seen in African and African-American cultures. The black community embraces men who are perceived as being very masculine and denounces those who are not. Cornel West (1993) describes the consequences of hyper masculinity:

> This situation is even bleaker for most black gay men who reject the major stylistic option of black machismo identity, yet who are ostracized in white America and penalized in black America for doing so. In their efforts to be themselves, they are told they are not really "black men," not machismo-identified. Black gay men are often the brunt of talented black comics like Arsenio Hall and Damon Wayans. Yet behind the laughs lurks a black tragedy of major proportions: the refusal of white and black Americans to entertain seriously new stylistic options for black men caught in the deadly endeavor of rejecting black machismo identities (p. 26).

A third explanation for the Down Low phenomenon involves attitudes related to class and race. African American men on the Down Low generally see themselves as working class individuals-working in historically underpaid jobs such as construction or messenger service, without a great deal of flexibility in their employment. Many African American men on the Down Low fear the loss of their employment if someone at work discovered their secret. Conversely, openly gay or bi-sexual white men appear to have much more financial security (Denizet-Lewis, 2003). These types of images can be confirmed in modern day television shows such as *Will and Grace* and *It's all Relative* and *Queer Eye for the Straight Guy*. The white gay men in all of these shows are depicted as having financial resources and professions that are congruent with their lifestyles, and in some cases their professions may be perceived as very effeminate

A forth explanation of the Down Low is associated with the fear of being stigmatized for being openly gay or bi-sexual. According to King (2004), African American men are afraid of the rebuff that comes along with being gay or bi-sexual.

> DL men cannot and will not be associated with anything that would raise any questions about their sexuality. They will not say they are gay, because those three little letters evoke fear. These three letters have them afraid of being ostracized by their community, by their church, by their family. If they tell the truth and say they're gay or bisexual, they will be called a fag. That's the worst word you can call a black man. When a man is called a fag, it

hurts. It basically strips away your manhood. You're saying I'm less than a man. You're saying I'm soft, that I want to be a woman or that I act like a woman (pp .23-24).

King argues that the fear of being called anything other than a man is unimaginable to black men on the Down Low. And the population is even willing to risk their health or the health of a wife or female partner, in order to maintain their heterosexual identity.

Down Low African American men are also critical of other African American men who identify openly as gay or bisexual. African American men who "come out" are typically seen as well educated and like their white counterparts have professions that are accepting of their lifestyles (Denizet-Lewis, 2003).

HIV/AIDS and the Black Community

The Centers for Disease Control and Prevention (2006) indicates that despite the increasing attention to the Down Low phenomenon, there is an absence of empirical data confirming the correlation between Human Immunodeficiency Virus (HIV) and Down Low behavior. Some black heterosexual women have been infected by bisexual men, but it is unclear if men who identify as Down Low are particularly responsible for the increased transmission of HIV. Clearly, HIV has had a stronghold in the black community for many years now, and there is a disproportionately high prevalence of HIV among black women who identify as heterosexual. One explanation regarding the transmission of HIV by many men who identify as Down Low is that because they fear the stigma associated with their lifestyle, they may not seek out medical attention until their health is greatly compromised.

Historically, the black community has not embraced gay and bisexual lifestyles. Waters (1999) argues that homophobia within the black community has always been a strong force of oppression. African Americans as a whole have been less accepting of men and women who label themselves gay or bisexual because it is considered a religious abomination. She concludes her research by arguing that the Christian religion served Africans Americans well in dealing with oppression stemming from days of slavery. Unfortunately, the same faith that has helped African Americans to remain strong in the face of oppression has also led to oppression of gays within the community (Coyne-Beasley and Schoenback 2000). Lewis (2003) argues that blacks and whites differ when it comes to issues of sexuality and religion. Lewis suggests that blacks were much more likely than whites to be very religious and disapproving of the gay lifestyle. Furthermore, blacks were much more likely to believe in a God who "sends misfortunes as punishments" for sins, including homosexuality.

Conversely, Rosin (1995) does not fully agree with the findings of Waters and Lewis. Instead, Rosin postulates that the African American community has been accepting of homosexuality as long as it was *closeted*: "The black community has always accepted homosexuality. There is always a gay person in church or who lives down the street or a cousin, and that's perfectly fine. It's only when that person defines himself as a gay, you know, adopts the gay white culture, like doing the rainbow flag thing, that the community reacts negatively. For a black man, family comes first (pp 24)."

In the face of this controversy regarding acceptance of gays in the African American community is the indisputable fact that HIV/AIDS infection continues to be a problem. Healthcare providers and educators continue to be frustrated by their inability to reach target populations who at are at high-risk or high prevalence for HIV/AIDS. One of these populations is men who have sex with men (MSM) but don't identify themselves as being gay or bisexual, the Down Low "brothers." These men may represent a significant reservoir for the transmission of HIV/AIDS not only to other men, but also to their female sexual partners (Malebranche, Peterson, Fulliblove, and Stackhouse 2004).

What is clearly needed is further investigation into and understanding of this recently described phenomenon referred to as the Down Low. The importance of the down Low phenomenon for social equity policy lies in its connection to public health, as a vector in HIV/AIDS transmission. The Down Low phenomenon can only be completely understood as an interaction between race, class, sexual orientation and gender .

Responding to the HIV/AIDS Crisis: The Black Church

Once considered a "white gay male" disease, AIDS has now become a black community pandemic and in some cases a black woman's greatest nightmare, particularly in some of the urban centers such as New York, Atlanta, Miami, and Chicago (Foston, 2002; Lichtenstein ,2000; Peterson,

Bakeman, Roger, and Stokes, 2001). In some of these cities the rate of HIV/AIDS for black women is alarming

But even so, it is no secret that the African American church remains one of the most conservative institutions in the community. Unfortunately, this conservatism has led to a low response in addressing the AIDS epidemic. As mentioned earlier, Lewis argues that historically African Americans generally are more religious than whites. Thus the black church has been and is still considered to be the cornerstone of the African American community. Brown and Hunter (1999; Brown, 2003) suggest that the black church was low in responding to the AIDS crisis due to conflicting messages. There were reports that AIDS was a white gay man's disease, and came from Haitian workers or African monkeys. However, what researchers have known since the mid 1980's is that AIDS can infect anyone regardless of race, gender, class, or sexual orientation. And despite the origins of the AIDS epidemic, it remains a leading cause of death within the black community. Brown and Hunter point out in their research that entire families within the African American community were eliminated due to AIDS. Their research suggests that the black community and the black church did not respond to AIDS due to the shame and embarrassment associated with the disease. In other words, very few African American churches wanted to admit that their members were engaging in pre-material sex or same-sex activities.

Baker (1999) postulates that the African American church started to respond slowly to the AIDS epidemic not because of compassion, but because of sharp criticism coming from outside the African American community. The lukewarm response of the black church was evident, despite the fact that black men were dying of the disease by the dozens and now black women as well.

Case Study

Jordon is a 25-year-old African American male, employed by a moving company. He resides with a 23-year-old woman, Jessica, with whom he has been in a relationship for four years. Jordon was raised in Denver by adoptive parents since infancy. He describes his adoptive parents as "traditional and strict," but maintains a close relationship with them. He never knew his biological parents, but believes they had substance abuse problems, which contributed to their inability to care for him. He indicates that others view him as a "proud, powerful, Black male."

Jordon states that he became involved in the Down Low subculture three years ago, and stated he learned about it on the Internet and chat rooms. He recalled the excitement and validation he experienced by being able to "connect with another universe…where I do not worry about the stigma."

Jordon describes routinely have unprotected sex with anonymous men in "public sex environments". PSEs are environments typically associated with gay male sex, but are sometimes used by men on the Down Low. Jordon often anonymously meets other men on the Down Low in private bathroom stalls or public parks for sex. He also frequents "straight" nightclubs after work to meet other men. He describes a committed relationship with Jessica, and his cognitive distortions have allowed him to believe that he is not placing her at risk, e.g. for HIV transmission (he admits to never have been tested for HIV, or that she might feel betrayed. He acknowledges that sometimes he feels "bad" about his dishonesty in their relationship.

Jordon has close ties to the black community, and feels that it would "embarrass" his adoptive parents and church congregants (despite the fact that he is not religious per se) if they knew he was having sex with males. In fact, he openly denounces homosexuality as "wrong." Consistent with the literature that homosexuality and bisexuality have historically not been considered topics for open conversation in the Black church, Jordon indicates that it was in order to maintain his identity and standing in the black community, he would have to keep his sexual interests secret. He feared that his sexual preferences and lifestyle would conflict with his community and societal values and he would be viewed as a "faggot" and ostracized. He acknowledges that he never discussed his sexuality at all with his adoptive parents, and that they have always been uncomfortable with the topic.

Jessica recently discovered that Jordon had been having sex indiscriminately with other males, and demanded a separation, although she was conflicted about this decision due to his apparent loyalty and affection toward her. Jordon states that he "loves Jessica…most of the time" and desires to remain in a relationship with her.

Case Analysis

Although Jordon engaged in what appeared to be homosexual activity, he displays anti-gay attitudes. This is a result of the intersection between sexuality and race, that is, the construction of sexuality in the black community and a history of combating racial exclusion. Additionally, Jordon developed a split self, and an elaborate defensive and justification process in order to alleviate feelings of guilt. He created a fragmented life in which he did not conceptualize the Down Low behavior as betrayal in relationship with Jessica. His hyper-masculine defense allowed him to separate himself from his behavior as being labeled homosexual, in which he was also able to dismiss any concerns about transmitting HIV. It appears that the coveting of hyper masculinity associated with the Down Low may not be about the outright degradation of women, but there is the disavowal of his relationship with her by engaging in unprotected sex acts with men on the Down Low.

Certainly, there is the issue of Jordon's lack of accountability for having sex with men, and discounting the gay lifestyle. Like any protective defense, the psychological manifestation of the Down Low is one of elusiveness and compartmentalization of harmful behavior. From the perspective of anti-oppressive approaches, oppression and racism has the effect of increase protective responses for survival and may diminish capacity for concern for others, e.g., his girlfriend, and increase agency or the capacity to act (pursue sex with other men) to address the historically marginalized subject. In essence, the Down Low may be viewed as form of psychological splitting, as a coping response to avoid discrimination in both the white and African American communities.

Action Plan Based on Anti-Oppressive Practice

Anti-oppressive practice, at its heart, calls for the development of a critical consciousness regarding the way structural inequalities create specific social phenomena (Dominelli,1988, 2008 ; Healy, 2005). An examination of the way racism, social injustice, and power differentials affect the development of individual behavior, reveals that African American who engage in Down Low behavior may be attempting to resolve internalized expressions of inequality and oppression. Such individuals may experience fragmented and contradictory aspects to a sense of self, which vary by the discourse and the social context. Indeed, there are contradictory myths about sexuality about AfricanAmericans, as noted in Johnson and Rivera's (2007) study, which contributes to the emergence of hyper-masculinity.

It should be noted that the limitations of anti-oppressive approaches stem from the combining anti-racist and anti-oppressive approaches. Ambiguity results from questioning whether or not the goals include the complete eradication of power differentials bound to racism, sexism, etc., whether or not certain forms of oppression as more significant than another, e.g., racism vs. sexism, and/or whether or not equal power relationships are even possible (and therefore truly anti-oppressive) (Sakamoto & Pitner, 2005). Despite the limitations of these approaches, they have important implications for social justice education.

The integration of content about race issues, sexuality issues, including the Down Low phenomenon, and social justice in the classroom and in practice environments has been a challenge. Unlike basic multicultural education, the goals of anti-oppressive practice should include not only empathetic regard for the *other*, but also introspection, as more than a way of thinking about oppression and marginalization of the *other*, in addition to understanding a mode of action for grasping the essence of another person's experience.

The contemporary struggle for students in a university environment is to be cognizant of power differentials based on the divisions created by race, social class, and sexual orientation, and help bridge gaps (i.e. through dialogue and critical consciousness, and relationships created by these divisions).

The discussion in this chapter of the causes and consequences of the Down Low highlights the importance of challenging racism and discrimination in the classroom and practice settings. An important component to challenging oppression in this case is to critically examine the role of gendered power relationships, and understanding the meanings behind African-American's perceptions of masculinity, largely responsible for the emergence of the DL subculture. Alternative understandings about masculinities should be developed.

Conclusion

This chapter discusses the Down low phenomenon, and an anti-oppressive framework is applied to understand the possible causes and consequences of the Down Low, including possible negative public health outcomes, such as HIV which can be passed on to female partners and/or other male partners. Additionally, an action plan is proposed, that highlights the importance of, and an awareness of power differentials and alternative masculinities. Moreover, a case was presented illustrating the structural causes, and the possible interpersonal and manifestations of DL. In summary, the Down Low is associated with a population of African American men who lead ostensibly heterosexual lifestyles, marrying or dating women, but secretly have sex with other men. The difference between Down Low behavior and bisexuality is that the Down Low men are identified specifically as African American men from working class backgrounds, as opposed to bisexuality, which cuts across gender and all socioeconomic lines. One of the arguments of this chapter is that the Down Low behavior emerges from societal inequalities. The anti-oppressive approach provides a perspective for understanding and addressing the complex relationship between various forms of oppression including race, social class sexual orientation, and gender.

Bibliography

AIDS Weekly (2003). *Failure to disclose sexual orientation leads to high AIDS incidence among African Americanm men.* Retrieved April 15,2008,from http://www.accessmylibrary.com/coms2/summary_0286-2776267_ITM.

Baker, S. (1999). HIV/AIDS, nurses and the black church: case study. *Journal of the Association of Nurses in AIDS Care,* 10(5), pp. 71-79.

Behn, R. D. (1985). Policy analysts, clients, and social scientists. *Journal of Policy Analysis and Management,* 4(3), pp. 428-432.

Boykin, K. (2000, April 30). *A poem for the Millennium March.* Millennium March On Washington, Washington, D.C.

Boykin, K. (2005). *Beyond the Down Low: Sex, lies, and denial in Black America.* New York: Caroll & Graf Publishers.

Brown, G. (2003). HIV./AIDS among African American and US Women: Minority and young women. *Minority Nurse Newsletter.*

Brown, M. & Hunter, L. (1999). Epidemic faith. *Sojourners* . v28 i2 (1) pp. 110.

Cabrerea, N. & Elizabeth, H. P. (2000).*Public polices and father involvement.* Marriage & Family Review (Spring) v29 p295

Centers for Disease Control and Prevention (2006). *Questions and answers: Men on the down low.* Retrieved December 31, 2007, from http://www.cdc.gov/hiv/topics/aa/resources/qa/downlow.htm.

Coyne-Beasley, T. & Schoenback, V.J. (2000). The African American church: A potential for adolescent comprehensive sexuality education. *Journal of Adolescent Health,* 26, pp. 289-295.

Dalrymple, J., & Burke, B. (1995). *Anti-oppressive practice: Social care and the law,* Buckingham: Open University Press.

Denizet-Lewis, B. (2003, August 3). Double lives on the Down Low. *The New York Times*.

Dominelli, L. (1988). *Anti-racist social work: A challenge for white practitioners*. Basinstoke, Hampshire [England]: Macmillan.

Dominelli, L. (2008). *Anti-racist social work (3rd edition)*. New York: Palgrave Macmillan.

Foston, N. (2002, November). Why AIDS is becoming a Black women's disease and what we can we do about it. *Ebony*, pp. 174-177.

Freire, P. (1970). *Pedagogy of the oppressed* (M.B. Ramos, Trans.). New York: Herder and Herder.

Harris, L. E. (1991). *Invisible life*. Atlanta: Consortium Press.

Healy, K. (2005). *Social work theories in context: Creating frameworks for practice*. New York: Palgrave Macmillan.

Johnson III, R.G. & Rivera, M. (2007). Refocusing graduate school education: A need for diversity competencies in human resource management. *Journal of Public Affairs Education* 13(1), pp. 15-27.

King, J.L. (2004). *On the Down low: A journey in to the lives of "straight" men who sleep with men*. Broadway Books/New York.

Lewis, G. (2003). Black-white differences in attitudes toward homosexuality and gay rights. *Public Opinion Quarterly*, 65, pp. 59-78.

Lichtenstein, B. (2000). Secret encounters: Black men, bisexuality, and AIDS in Alabama. *Medical Anthropology Quarterly*,14, pp. 374.

Malebranche, D.J., Peterson, J.L., Fulliblove, R.E., &Stackhouse, R.W. (2004). Race and sexual identity: Perceptions about medical culture and health among Black men who have sex with men. *Journal of National Medical Association*, 96(1),pp. 97-107.

McBride, Dwight (2005). *Why I hate Abercrombie and Fitch*. New York: New York University Press.

Millar, M. (2008). Anti-oppressiveness: Critical comments on a discourse and its context. *British Journal of Social Work*, 38, 362-375.

Murray, S.O., & Roscoe, W. (1998). *Boy-wives and female husbands-studies in African homosexualities*. New York: Palgrave Macmillan.

Peterson, J., Bakeman, L., Roger. L., & Stokes, J. (2001). Racial/ethnic patterns of HIV/AIDS sexual risk behaviors among young men who have sex with men. *Gay and Lesbian Medical Association*, 5(4), pp.155-162.

Rosin, H. (1995, June 5). The homecoming: Paranoia and plague in Black America. *The New Republic*, 212 (23), pp. 21-31.

Sakomoto, I., & Pitner, R.O. (2005). Use of critical consciousness in anti-oppressive social work practice: Disentangling power dynamics at personal and structural levels. *British Journal of Social Work*, 35, pp. 435-452.

Villarosa, L. (2001, April 3). AIDS education is aimed "Down low." *The New York Times*, pp.A5.

Villarosa, L. (2004, April 5). *AIDS fears grow For Black women*. The New York Times, pp.A1.

Waters, S. (1999). *Steel away to Jesus*. Georgetown University Master's of Art Thesis. Washington, D.C.

West, C. (1993). *Keeping faith: Philosophy and race in America*. New York: Routledge.

II. SOCIAL JUSTICE ACROSS THE ACADEMIC DISCIPLINES

BEYOND THE KNOWLEDGE/ACTION DIVIDE

Studying Race, Gender, and Social Justice in American University's Department of Anthropology

*Audrey Cooper, Elijah Edelman, Kathleen J. Grant,
Noor Johnson, Khari La Marca, William L. Leap,
and Michelle A. Marzullo*

Race, Gender and Social Justice (RGSJ) is an area of concentration for PhD students in Anthropology at American University in Washington D.C. This concentration was created in 1999 as department faculty sought to foreground areas of common interest among faculty and students, while simultaneously responding to the requirements of a university-wide review of graduate programs. Once created, the concentration became *a space for doing* that linked administration goals, faculty ambitions, and student interests in groundbreaking ways.

To be effective, a curriculum in RGSJ studies cannot be limited to the canonical terrain ("history of theory," "big ideas," "great books," etc.) that has traditionally structured graduate education in anthropology. We understood that students of RGSJ need to engage current conversations in sociology, political science and activism, philosophy, history, and literary criticism and related fields as well as those in anthropology. They need training opportunities in film/video production (for documentaries or advertising); basic survey research and analysis; program/policy evaluation; text analysis (for unpacking meanings in print and other documents, for preparing effective speeches, opinion pieces, or reports); strategies for organizing petition drives, demonstrations and other techniques of protest; as well as approaches to community and guerilla theatre, and performance art. Finally, the provocative orientation of RGSJ studies attracts participants from a variety of backgrounds who are diversified along the axes of gender, sexuality, race, ethnicity, nationality, age, class, ability, and linguistic repertoire. In this chapter, six students and one professor from American University's Department of Anthropology comment critically on these and other aspects of the PhD program's RGSJ concentration. From that basis, we discuss what we think effective training in RGSJ studies might entail. Because we chose to incorporate a broad range of ideas and perspectives, our approach to writing was experimental and evolved as the chapter took shape.

All seven authors contributed to the writing of this chapter through a shared electronic message board. We then collectively composed a unified narrative from a combination of our individual contributions. The chapter is presented in five parts. It begins with a description of the concentration from the perspective of one of its faculty architects, William Leap, which is then followed by a discussion of the concentration and its implications as seen by graduate students. The third section then delves further into an area of common concern for social justice training, the theory/practice divide. This leads to an exploration of the uses and effects of "academic language" in the fourth section, which we view as one way anthropologists become distanced from the publics and public concerns towards whom our work is oriented. The fifth and final section culminates in a discussion of where American University's RGSJ concentration and public anthropology might be headed.

Building an Agenda for Training:
The Race, Gender & Social Justice Concentration

In 1973, the Department of Anthropology at American University was the second department in the U.S. to create a Master's program (MA) specifically dedicated to graduate training in Applied Anthropology. We continued to offer this training in two tracks: "applied" and "traditional" anthropology until 1998. As a result of university-wide program review, we decided to merge the two programs into a single MA degree offering training in public anthropology.

The "public" focus of the MA program responded to two faculty concerns. First, department faculty saw the distinction between "traditional" and "applied" anthropology as artificial and misleading; committed anthropologists always do research and engage social problems wherever they work, and the sentiment was that faculty should be training our MA students to unite theory and practice. Second, for many faculty the term "applied anthropology" was too closely connected with government agencies and international organizations, whose policies were disrupting quality of life for local constituencies worldwide. We wanted to underscore our MA program's alignment with the ongoing struggles of those constituencies, rather than governmental agencies or agendas. *Public* anthropology expressed this alignment more precisely than did the older, more conservative reference to "applied" work (Lassiter et al., 2005; Lamphere, 2004).

So where did this move leave students in the PhD program? From the program's inception in 1967, our doctoral students have been concerned with the application of anthropological method and theory to real-world issues, and more than half of them seek (and obtain) full-time employment outside of academic circles after graduation. Even so, the PhD program was defined in terms of the traditional anthropological (sub)fields: social/cultural anthropology, archaeology, linguistics and physical anthropology. Under this arrangement, "applied" work could embellish doctoral student training in one of the traditional subfields, but it could not serve as an area of doctoral training.

Shifting the MA focus to public anthropology prompted the need to unify theory and practice at the doctoral level. Faculty considered creating a PhD "track" in public anthropology, but decided against doing so; faculty wanted instead to underscore the idea that topical interests within anthropology could—and should—have close alignments with real-world peoples and their struggles. Rather than continuing to base the program on the four subfields, faculty began searching for topics which were of greatest interest to doctoral students (as reflected in application essays, coursework preferences, and dissertation topics) and to faculty (as reflected in research interests, grants/contracts submissions, and publication records). This search sparked considerable discussion among faculty and graduate students already enrolled in the PhD program regarding program priorities. Our decision to create a PhD concentration in Race, Gender and Social Justice (RGSJ) was, in part, a product of this inquiry. Linking discussions of "race" and "gender" in terms of discussions of "social justice" placed the concerns of public anthropology in the foreground of this concentration, but did so with language reflecting the concentration's multidisciplinary as well as anthropological commitments.

Since 1999, the RGSJ concentration based in the Department of Anthropology has gradually begun to acquire a very different profile from that envisioned during the initial planning. The concentration in "gender," for instance, has been shaped by foregrounding analysis of the construction of gendered subjects through examining such practices as: "transgressive" acts, participation in labor markets, political and economic influences, and socio-historical contexts. Moreover, while race, 'gender' and 'social justice' are listed separately in our program title, this is not to reify these as disparate, or even separable, categories but rather to highlight common sites of political, social and institutional mobilization. Student research is based as often in the Middle East, South Asia, West or Central Africa, or Central America as they are in rural or urban U.S. settings indicating that the global/cross-cultural perspectives that have long been characteristics of anthropological inquiry are also maintained in the RGSJ concentration.

Many social engineering projects in late-modern U.S. settings are guided by assumptions of "redistributive justice" (Young, 1990). That is, they propose ways to make such intangibles as health care, employment, safety or prosperity available to individuals and groups for whom these quality of life resources are currently not available. Fundamental questions of why some people are denied access to quality of life resources, while other people enjoy unimpeded access to those resources, are often not examined in such projects. Redistributive justice initiatives address the symptoms of inequality but they do not engage its underlying sources.

The department's goal in the RGSJ concentration is to prepare students to ethnographically examine and publicly critique those underlying sources. Central to such an engagement are skills in critical inquiry, many of which cannot be learned within the traditional classroom setting or through training within a single academic discipline. For this reason, students in the RGSJ concentration complete 15 of their 42 graduate hours in coursework outside of the anthropology department. Classroom activities in anthropology's RGSJ-related courses usually include some form of action-oriented research projects.

Students are also encouraged to participate in a wide range of conferences, according to student interest, and research foci rather than some external criteria regarding the academic or applied nature of the conference event. In addition to attending such events off campus, our department now regularly hosts events on campus that are orchestrated around race, gender and social justice themes. This is so that students and faculty may join colleagues and speakers from other universities and outside agencies in critical discourse and community-building activities. During academic year 2006-2007, for example, three such conferences took place in our department: our third annual daylong workshop on Public Anthropology, the 14th annual Lavender Languages Conference (an event exploring lesbian, gay, bisexual, transgender and queer language and linguistics), and a two-day conference offering international perspectives on diversity, surveillance and policing.

To date (spring 2008) three RGSJ students have graduated with PhDs, and 27 are presently working on RGSJ-related dissertations projects in our department. Current RGSJ-related dissertation topics include: neighborhood resistance to gentrification; queer Latina/o resettlement in Washington, DC; changing U.S. ideologies about marriage; community self-determination through film-making; violence and carnival in Trinidad; promoting educational achievement in a slum school in Nairobi, Kenya; state formation and deaf social movements in post-socialist Viet Nam; and the "private space" of DC area Black lesbian strip clubs.

What Brought Me Here?: Students Discuss Reasons for Choosing RGSJ

Audrey, Elijah, Kathleen, Khari, Noor, Michelle: We were all drawn to the RGSJ program based upon a range of interests. Pursuing anthropological training in which *social justice* is a central and guiding component figured prominently in all of our narratives. In particular, we found that in the context of both RGSJ coursework and departmental conferences, we are continually challenged to consider the issues of whether or not our work is accessible to a broader public, what our responsibility is as the scholars, researchers and collaborators within the groups we work with, and how we might contribute to shaping matters of social justice, policy, and activism. In this section, students describe the distinctiveness of the RGSJ program as well as the diverse interests that brought us to the program.

Khari: American University's race, gender and social justice concentration provides the avenue for using anthropology in "good ways." I also felt that it would draw other students with diverse interests who wished to utilize the skills of our discipline toward positive social change, to discuss tough issues, think critically, and to struggle towards thinking in ethical and innovative ways to transform the discipline and ourselves.

Kathleen: What brought me to the RGSJ program at American University was my prior interactions with Dr. Leap over many Lavender Language conferences as I witnessed how he provided a space for multivocalities. I hoped to research deaf women, like myself, but I knew that I could only do so after I received formal training and guidance in Anthropology. What I find in the RGSJ program is coursework that puts theory into practice in a way that allows me to return to my community with a strong feminist understanding of social justice work.

Elijah: I struggled with whether or not to enter graduate school. As a high school dropout, it had been a long and arduous process just to get accepted into an undergraduate program. I anticipated that the "academy" would be twice as difficult to negotiate. My ambivalence was not simply an issue of whether or not I wanted to pursue higher learning. Rather, it was rooted in what I thought to be my exclusively activist, social justice goals. Additionally, as my research interests were to study members of my own 'community,' female-to-male trans-people, many programs did not exactly laud my incentive. The "public" element of American University's Anthropology program, as well as its clear dedication to queer research, is a rare and perfect fit for me.

Noor: I came to American University with a background in development studies and non-profit work in order to study development and conflict resolution, while pursuing a degree that would offer opportunities to explore careers in teaching, research, or public advocacy and administration. Initially, I was attracted to American University's inclusive approach to scholarship. Conversations with my advisor helped me understand that there was room in a program focused on social justice to bring in tools from other disciplines and so in addition to my anthropology coursework, I have pursued coursework in peace and conflict studies in other schools at American University. I believe that increasingly, the most interesting and relevant academic work is interdisciplinary, I was pleased to find a program that would allows me to incorporate perspectives from classes outside of anthropology. Our program's emphasis on public anthropology challenges me to consider issues such as whether or not my work is accessible to a broader public, what my responsibility as a scholar and researcher is to the groups that I work with, and how to contribute to shaping public opinion on matters of policy.

Michelle: I came to the RGSJ program for both its location and its focus. After receiving my MA degree in Human Sexuality Studies and work in epidemiological research for seven years, I realized that I wanted to pursue PhD training that held as equal a mix of qualitative and quantitative methods, allowed me to focus on translating research for policymakers, and would provide opportunities for learning about how policy and programs are experienced by people on-the-ground. This program does that. It also allows me to bring in my 20 years of activist work in ways that allow me to integrate this learning with my research. The public focus of the program also allows me to include the people I am doing research with into the process of analyzing and reporting on study findings, which is crucial for the "production of knowledge." Such community-based research techniques are integral in doing research that is concerned with social justice.

Social Justice Training: Addressing the Theory/Practice Divide

Khari, Noor, Michelle: Prior to entering the academy, each of us struggled in different ways with how to reconcile activism with scholarship generally, and with anthropology's specific participation in colonial and other imperialist projects. Of real concern was whether or not we might be able to bridge academic frames to the lived experience of the persons and communities we study. Put plainly, we questioned the relevance and compatibility of theory to practice. In this section, we reflect on some strengths of social justice training as they relate to addressing a theory/practice divide. Several of us named the process of becoming inculcated in the use of discipline-specific specialist language as a (elitist) marker of separation and a barrier to communicating our ideas clearly to non-academic audiences. The practice of publicly engaged anthropology recommends certain activities: identifying and critically evaluating social concerns; identifying one's own value-laden viewpoints and understanding one's own position relative to social issues and communities of practice; and using social justice methods of dialogue, co-construction of knowledge, and reciprocity to support interventions through social action, including intervening in the "academy-as-usual."

Elijah: During my first months in the PhD program, I had ample opportunity to engage with the politics and the negotiations of space, authenticity and legitimacy of the "ivory tower" from the "inside." In the academy, space is something we vie for. Whether this is verbal space in a classroom or at a conference, or the physical space we take up in a graduate student cubicle, we must fight for it. If we are deemed worthy enough (or are loud enough) our name goes onto a program or our raised hand is recognized and we are guaranteed our moment in the spotlight. This is not to situate "professors" or those higher up in the hierarchy of the academy as singularly responsible for the delegation of space. This recognition can be the work of our colleagues, cohorts and/or undergraduates. With all eyes on us, we read our scholarly interpretations of other people's lives (e.g., our "research") and hope that our position in the academy is secure.

Put simply: the academy, and those within it, need to engage more with what those outside of the academy (particularly the "subjects" of our research) want, need, say and understand. This engagement includes research design and methodology, write up and analysis and, even, the presentation of "our" research (instead of "my" research). If one of our goals is explicitly towards social justice, then it is even more critical that we actively recognize our elitism and desires for personal recognition. The goal should not be getting our names on the program; it should be getting the point across, regardless of whose mouth it comes from.

Audrey: Elijah's discussion of the tension between being "inside" and "outside" the academy speaks to my own experience. I was a member of a dance company when I decided to go to graduate school to study dance-movement therapy and social work; and, I vividly recall the moment I told the choreographer that I had been accepted to graduate school. She replied, "So you are not going to be a dancer anymore?" Activist friends expressed similar sentiments. These responses to my announcement and my own resulting sense of surprise are with me still. Why would I no longer dance, or do social justice work? Why would academic training stop me from participating in political, community, or aesthetic concerns?

Ultimately, what I discovered was that it wasn't the academic training per se that would work against my continued participation in other areas of practice, but the specific area in which I had chosen to do my professional work *and* my own accommodation to structures that preceded me. Trained as a clinical social worker and dance-movement therapist, I worked in mental health settings where the medical paradigm dictated a search for deficit and maladaptation. Using diagnostic matrices foundational to mental health work left me cold, while simultaneously leaving a problematic system untouched. I became convinced that I was complicit in creating the very categories that were said to naturally reflect human individual and group experience. So, I went in search of a broader container for the human experience, one that would help to deepen my questions rather than providing ready answers. This search led me to anthropology and to the RGSJ concentration specifically. Now as a student in the RGSJ program, I am still visited by the pressure to have answers, to assume a position of knowing, of explanation, and even of authority. This pressure, the accommodation to knowledge and power that is so central to the academic enterprise and to credentialing, is at the heart of my own experience of a theory-practice split.

Kathleen: As a deaf feminist lesbian student in the Race, Gender, and Social Justice program, I learned the meaning of social justice through my everyday experiences as I interacted with professors and students in the program. It encouraged me to link anthropology with the community I study that, some twenty years ago, would never have been invited to "speak back" to anthropology. But most importantly, the tools I learned from the RGSJ program helped me to understand how knowledge is power, and unpacking the workings of power is what this program is about.

Michelle: As a social justice student, I found that most social justice classes do attempt to teach critical thinking and integrate an experiential aspect: but they must do more. Training students toward social justice aims must be approached from a variety of angles and should be experientially informed, theoretically rigorous, and practically oriented. The process of engaging with social justice aims is one that must continually respond to changing political-economic and social events. There must be a critical component built into training to give students the space to engage their interests, while reflecting on what has driven that interest for themselves and for others over time. And students should be taught transferable skills beyond basic critical thinking and writing, so that they have tangible products or sets of data that are presentable to a broader public. But more importantly, so they can quickly propose projects and solutions that are based in solid skill sets.

Noor: I was in a class recently where a student suggested that what we are learning here is "how to be critical." I believe this was meant in the positive sense of "critical"—as in, how to unpack and analyze issues and events so that the broader economic and historical context becomes part of the discussion and can be incorporated into plans for social justice and social action. On the other hand, at times I believe that higher education and training could benefit from broadening out beyond just focusing on these analytical and (often) deconstructive approaches to incorporate other tools. Learning to critique is important, but equally important is learning to envision and suggest new possibilities something that training in anthropology does not always encourage. The biggest question that I often encounter from people outside of academia when I offer critiques of policy or current events is: "Okay, so if that approach isn't working, then what do you suggest?" It is not enough to simply say that a policy is privileging those who already have power—we need to envision positive and proactive alternatives that try to do better.

So there are many challenges that I think we all face to make our work "speak" on multiple levels to ourselves and our own life trajectories, to others outside the academy who may not understand the "value" of academic explorations, and to those who may have a specific perspective of what "social justice" entails. From the perspective of designing an academic program that incorporates a "social justice" lens, it is important to consider these struggles perhaps in creating an advising system that acknowledges that students will have to address this on an ongoing basis. But in part, I think we gain skills from struggling to find a voice in different arenas. If the value and authenticity of our experience as academics and practitioners were simply assumed, we would miss a valuable opportunity to hone our communication skills about the value of what we have to offer, and perhaps might even miss the opportunity to reflect for ourselves on these issues.

Michelle: Pushing the problem is particularly important for social justice training because no political solution is ever final. Instead, the solutions which social justice students will be tasked to generate are constantly up for debate, refinement, and reassessment. Training has to incorporate exercises that build a tolerance for critique as well as an ability to respond to that critique and possibly alter the solution to fit the problem in ways not originally anticipated. Importantly, integrating the tangible effects of such theories–in–practice allows students to see how theories might be practically applied and, even more crucially, to understand the possible outcomes (anticipated or otherwise) of its application.

Audrey: I like the argument for building solution-focused assessment and planning into the social justice curriculum—this seems key. Not only is solution-focused assessment a necessary tool of the social justice thinker/worker but, through real-world application and writing for a non-specialist audience, it forms a bridge between classroom and direct-action work. Academic training in social justice must do more to build ongoing dialogue with and participation in activist organizations, initiatives, and movements. If academics also learned their craft in concert with organizations and communities of action, not only would they bring their specialist knowledge to, as hooks (2000, p. 111) aptly says, "the masses of women and men" but participate in co-development of knowledge with them and through such dialogue mitigate the problems of translation."

What We Say and What It Means: Reinventing Academic Language

Audrey, Elijah, Kathleen, Khari, Noor, Michelle: Academic language is often parodied as inaccessible, lengthy and confusing. Indeed, writing for the academy is so well established it is like a prescription, containing specific ingredients, forms, styles, expectations, and cues. In this section we consider what it means to confront this challenging and often problematic interactional-discursive field and how we negotiate its demands. In particular, we consider how a publicly engaged anthropology can productively address accessibility of research through language.

Kathleen: I view academia in the U.S. as a privileged site of prescribed discourses wherein English is the language that academic citizenship prefers. The RGSJ program offers the tools necessary to knock on citizenship's door with different discourses. It also allows the student an arena to interact with other marginalized students and professors whom have also suffered from those in power as based on their own race, gender, ethnicity, sexual orientation, and/or abilities.

Audrey: If we accept, for purposes of this discussion, that the academy is a site of privilege, generally exclusivist, hierarchical, and oriented toward the promotion of internal (institutional and disciplinary) ideals of achievement and knowledge advancement: then it is important to consider what social justice programs must do differently to accommodate not only the activities of its activist-scholars, but of their counterparts, such as community activists. This is centrally a problem of language—of speaking only to or too frequently to other academics. We have many audiences.

Elijah: I have been told multiple times that part of the process of becoming an academic is learning the language. Well, what is the language? And how does this language differ from other languages? From my experience thus far, course-texts are full of high theoretical terms, jargon-laden rhetoric and sentences with more clauses than this entire paragraph. I would also argue that much of it is painfully apolitical. Identities become reductive descriptions of other's experiences that are thrown around thoughtlessly. Those that have done a little research, or perhaps just read a book, suddenly become the 'experts' about a particular subjectivity, community, or identity and feel entitled to speak/mock/act for or like them. We, the academy and academics, need to be aware that every note we take and analysis completed is our translation: it should not and cannot be used in the place of the words or knowledge of a member of that community. When we juxtapose such community-informed knowledge with academic jargon, the resulting product becomes conveniently inaccessible to the very community we are concerned with, thus shielding us from having our interpretations disputed.

Khari: Those who are serious about social justice and in seeing lasting social change happen—whether as an individual, a discipline, or as an organization—need to get very serious about storytelling. I'm not talking about public relations or in getting good press for what you are attempting to do (though training in both of these areas should be part of any master plan). The storytelling I am talking about is strategic and it needs to build in capacity as you go. Learn more about this by reading the book entitled *Extraordinary Minds* by Howard Gardner (1997). There Gardner argues that the major influencers throughout time relied on storytelling. He demonstrates that a set of exchanges need to take place for influence to occur. A must read for those committed to achieving social justice aims. Storytelling isn't simply a message or a vision of what you are trying to do: it is the drama, or "the glue" that holds everything together and sustains a concern all the way through. Such storytelling must continue.

Michelle: In my social justice work, I have been developing an applied linguistic strategy that helps advocates understand how to communicate effectively in debate situations. This work will most likely not count towards a tenure track professorship position, yet every organization I speak to about it says that it is sorely needed. This work relies heavily on George Lakoff's *Thinking Points: Communicating Our American Values and Vision* (2006). In this book Lakoff argues that most progressives get mired down in talking about the possible programmatic and policy solutions for social problems before they articulate their basic core values. In line with Khari's comments, I believe we should communicate our basic values and do so through stories. It is in narrative that we find mirrors of ourselves, as many ethnographers, writers and storytellers say, "the universal is in the particular." We are served well by working to convey our values through a storytelling medium (visual, performance, etc.) that will convey the depths and urgency of the problems that social justice work seeks to ameliorate.

Audrey: One of the areas of academic rigidity that seems most in need of intervention within the discipline of anthropology is returning *feeling* to the purview of the analytic. In much academic training, self-knowledge and affective experience in the world is devalued, squelching the impulse to responsiveness, to feeling, and to immediacy of action. Social justice work demands that our analyses be engaged not only at the level of criticism and of doing but at the level of feeling. Pedagogy aimed at helping students make links and, importantly, distinctions between personal experience (reflection), feeling (or, to paraphrase Michelle, both empathy and the identification of core values), and social justice action would help ensure that our analyses respond meaningfully to concerns of life (human and otherwise) and experience.

Kathleen: I have presented at public forums through guest speaker engagements within three different disciplines and seventeen classes. Such work exposes students outside of Anthropology to a deaf voice that signs passionately about race, gender, and social justice issues and intersectional analyses. By becoming a participant, I not only added to important research agendas but I was able to spend time with our next generation of educators by contributing the realworld experiences and point of view of a deaf woman.

Khari: We are, whether completely cognizant of it or not, doing anthropology in unconventional times and as anthropologists. So, perhaps we need to become more unconventional too by reaching out in areas, settings, and to people who don't normally hear our voices. There are wonderful opportunities for anthropologists to engage in public discourse. Consider how anthropology might be actively brought into daily life by:

1. Speaking in public forums.
2. Writing for newspapers, magazines, popular presses, blogs and video-logs.
3. Participating in interview opportunities using your knowledge base.
4. Hosting a radio show.
5. Calling in to NPR, CSPAN, and other venues, to expand the dialogue.
6. Joining a community organizing activity, the PTA, serve on the board of an agency, or an activity group with strangers who may not think like you and offer to speak about your work and perspectives whenever and wherever you can.

Audrey, Elijah, Kathleen, Khari, Noor, Michelle: Student run conferences and colloquia have been an important place for building the practical skills of organizing critical responses to topical public concerns. For instance, RGSJ graduate students organized a conference whose broad purpose was to interrogate the notion of diversity. In its first year, a focus on policing and surveillance drew community activists, interest from local news media, and the participation of anthropologists from a number of distinguished institutions. In its second year, the *Interrogating Diversity* conference expanded the draw of variously situated constituents by coalescing topical areas around language as social action, media and representation, health and displacement, and climate and environment. It has been our experience during these conferences, as much as during our annual one-day Public Anthropology Workshop, that with both academic and community-based counterparts present, analytic dialogue is better informed, better grounded in and responsible to people's attested material realities, and better available to creative approaches.

How the RGSJ Program Sets the Stage for Ongoing Praxis

Audrey, Elijah, Kathleen, Noor, Khari, Michelle: We have noted that one area of emphasis cross-cutting both RGSJ coursework and various departmental activities is bringing anthropological perspective to public issues and debates *and* a simultaneous concern with bringing public perspectives to anthropological analysis and work. To be of use to the broader public, it is vital that anthropologists are relevant and responsive, meaningfully resonant with everyday concerns, and able to communicate about such concerns in using common idioms.

Bill: The students' remarks offer a vision of the RGSJ concentration that is very different from that provided by the discussion of degree requirements and course offerings in the opening section of this chapter. For them, the concentration provides a space for critical reflection on social justice themes that is not available in other settings. If anything, student voices suggest this space needs to be expanded, to ensure that a broader, more diverse range of voices be included in the reflective conversation. To do this, RGSJ-related learning activities need to move further outside of the academy, while topics—and subjects—from real-world settings need to become more closely aligned with the work we are doing inside academe.

Admittedly certain logistics, recruitment, admissions and financial aid needs must be addressed in order to meet these goals. A good starting point in that regard may be to ask the question: Should race, gender and social justice continue to be one of three concentrations in the Anthropology department's PhD program? Instead, paralleling the public anthropology focus of the MA program, we might consider positioning race, gender and social justice as the anchoring theme of doctoral work in anthropology, whatever the student's area of interest in archaeology or cultural/social anthropology.

Noor: As a student who has not chosen to "concentrate" in RGSJ, I feel that I have nevertheless benefited from this focus through the courses that the department has to offer. I see that by delineating this as a particular departmental strength and interest, faculty and students with research interests that in some way relate to this theme have been drawn to our department. Although the technical course requirements for concentrators and non-concentrators in RGSJ differ, many of us (non-concentrators) still elect to participate in the courses that are defined as "core" to this concentration. Even within the core anthropology curriculum, faculty have woven in readings and assignments that address this theme. From my perspective and for my own purposes, the label "RGSJ" does not particularly matter. What does matter is how the label translates into a curriculum that offers a particular lens through which to engage with and understand contemporary social issues. In that sense, I would agree with Bill's suggestion that perhaps our learning community might benefit from conceptualizing this theme as cross-cutting all of our coursework, and not merely as a "concentration" that some students choose to participate in and others do not.

Michelle: I chose to concentrate in RGSJ through my work in public health and sexuality studies. In pursuing this work, I realized that much research is conducted in a way that uses researcher's concerns divorced from those of their subjects. The projects are often created from reviews of the literature, from funding priorities, for academic concerns with job retention, etc. This is far from what I went into research for. I have always wanted my research to be directly responsive to community needs and pressing problems. In the U.S., which is my area of study, examining inequities along the lines of race, sexuality and gender are vitally important. This program provides the theoretical grounding and practical support for me to craft a very specialized career that is respectful of the communities in which I work, while also remaining close to my ethical commitment for doing engaged research.

Elijah: While I would hope to see all students and academics, regardless of discipline, engage with issues of race, gender and social justice (as well as sexuality, class and so on), there is something to be said for a concentration to explicitly label itself as such. Naming this program as an element of my degree reflects something about my own politic in a way that simply stating I am in a 'Public Anthropology' program would not fully communicate. I would say that if/when we get to a point where it is the expectation of each student of public anthropology to seriously confront these issues then we no longer need such a concentration. But this focus is critical at this juncture: it sets a model for academia to draw on for responding to new concentrations that concerns with social justice might generate.

Khari: There are three steps that need to be incorporated into any training related to achieving social justice aims: visualize a result, think backward, implement forward. There is a saying that I learned through my work with the Echoing Green Foundation which is, "Every battle is won or lost before it is fought." It is critically important that those being trained in social justice understand this. In other words, you get the result you planned for (or did not plan for). Begin with the assumption that change is possible. Decide what the core principles, values, and ideas are in a social change you want to address and then learn to narrate them in everything else that you are doing. One of the most vital aspects of social justice training may be not only an emphasis on critical thinking, but also the creation of a space from which innovation can occur. Great things are usually built on the foundations of earlier efforts—find ways to incorporate that work.

Audrey, Elijah, Kathleen, Noor, Khari, Michelle: Effective participation in social justice efforts may be facilitated by a variety of preparatory activities, some of which anthropology colleagues, faculty and students, can practice together within the academy. These include:

1. Encourage students to organize conferences on topics of local or broad public import.
2. Invite community based organizations or action groups to participate in or co-organize panels, presentations, or other forums.
3. Collaborate with other departments on shared colloquia.
4. Establish a laboratory for practicing writing and speaking for social justice.
5. Produce projects (articles, books, documentaries, performances, events, etc.) featuring community members, activists, and graduate students

Race, Gender, Social Justice and You: Concluding Comments

This chapter identified and discussed some of the major themes of import to participants in the Race, Gender, and Social Justice concentration at American University. Our discussion is by no means comprehensive nor have we sought to write an entirely cohesive account of our department's approach to preparing students for social justice work in and outside of the Academy. As a group, we found the experience of writing about the concentration to be a valuable opportunity for reflection and a space in which to envision, individually and collectively, areas for future development. We hope that what we have offered here will, at a minimum, prompt others invested in social justice training to engage in similar efforts to dialogue on and document social justice teaching and learning initiatives as sites of reflexive praxis. No doubt, we each came to the RGSJ concentration with our own ideas of what composed anthropology as a discipline and how we might engage the broad-minded methodological basis that foregrounds anthropological inquiry. We found this space within anthropology for its specific holistic approach and tolerance of multiple methods of investigation. We are attempting to continue this tradition by furthering this disciplinary engagement through a social justice ethos. Politically we have orientated ourselves differently and, at times, felt the overwhelming weight of the many voices and opinions expressed. It is through this conflict, whether of the internal questioning of our own epistemological anchors, challenges from our discipline or outsiders for our explicit concern with justice, or from our analyses of the shifting terrains of power, that productive ideas and actions are born.

The Race, Gender and Social Justice concentration at American University serves as a signal to a particular field of common affect and disquiet. As such, it agitates towards mobilization. In the final analysis, what this program is called should not matter. That this particular concentration exists is informative as it glosses a particular ethos that is defined by its process, not necessarily its product. In our consumer-oriented, product driven society, finding oneself in such a program begs explanation. The particular curriculum fostered at American University allows an engagement with, not just an understanding of, contemporary social issues. In this era of the powers-that-be doggedly questioning academic freedom, social justice programs are themselves a critical model for academic responsibility. They are useful for the infusion of different perspectives into intractable social problems by opening up novel strategies and solutions that heretofore have eluded us. Programs like this hold out hope by boldly creating spaces, opening up knowledge towers, allowing the entrance of local voices and multiple modalities, and begging the innovations that come from such synergies. It is up to you, the reader, to continue to hone, implement and inspire through such programs and work. We hope you do.

Bibliography

Gardner, H. (1997). *Extraordinary minds: Portraits of exceptional individuals and an examination of our extraordinariness.* New York: Basic Books.

hooks, b. (2000). *Feminist theory: From margin to center.* Cambridge, MA: South End Press.

Lakoff, G. (2006). *Thinking points: Communicating our American values and vision.* Rockridge, CA: Rockridge Institute.

Lamphere, L. (2004). The Convergence of applied, practicing and public anthropology in the 21st Century. *Human Organization, 63*(4), pp. 431-443.

Lassiter, E.L., Cook, S., Field, L., & Jaarsma, S.R. (2005). Collaborative ethnography and public anthropology. *Current Anthropology,* 46(1), pp. 83-106.

Young, I.M. (1990). *Justice and the politics of difference.* Princeton, NJ: Princeton University Press.

CHAPTER 5
ACTING JUSTLY

Irvin Peckham

When political progressives enter a professional field, they may be surprised by the degree to which their field is complicit in sustaining oppressive social conditions in the macro culture. Nowhere is this more surprising than in higher education, in spite of its reputation of being the gadfly to oppressive social structures. English departments, occupying a central role in the liberals arts, are especially noted for their tilt toward egalitarian social policies in the United States, but progressive-oriented professors might find themselves in trouble if they do not appreciate the degree to which English departments are predicated on social relationships naturalizing exploitive social mechanisms, or, less generously, the degree to which the department itself is sustained by those mechanisms.

To be effective within covertly oppressive institutional structures, social activists should seriously investigate the working conditions within which they are embedded and their own complicity in social reproductive mechanisms. Although my focus in this chapter is the institutional structure in English departments, the question of how social progressives negotiate the conflict between their belief systems and their working conditions is generalizable beyond English departments.

Activist committed to social justice have many paths to follow, ranging from radical resistance on the outside to subversion from within, the poles bracketing a continuum of possible positions any of us decide to occupy. Where we position ourselves may not be so much a decision as a consequence of our life stories and a multiplicity of mini-decisions we make as we move from our early years to stances dependent upon factors such as our parents and their belief systems, the social classes into which we were born, who we marry, who our are friends are, what professions we follow, and our own needs for social approval. What paths we follow is not as important as a commitment to the same end, a community committed to the welfare of the whole as opposed to the social Darwinism driving contemporary American culture.

No matter what position or sets of positions we occupy, effective action depends on knowing, in Paulo Freire's terms, the limit-situations, the untested feasibility, and perhaps what feasibility has already been tested and found wanting. Freire used limit-situation to refer to any situation limiting the actor's options. Untested feasibility refers to actions actors might successfully engage in but haven't done so because they have been convinced through the socializing process that for them, those kinds of action are off-limits. In a dictatorial regime, they will be shot; in our capitalist culture, they will be fired. One's humanity, Freire maintains, lies in challenging limit-situations, in testing the untested feasibility, pushing against imagined restrictions that constrain those of us who work within the dominant social structure from acting against social policies we know are wrong.

I can imagine many social/occupational positions that place people in situations in which they have to choose to challenge unjust policies or give way, rationalizing their malleability as momentary concessions to gain purchase for future gains in the utopian project. As Audre Lorde has memorably noted in "The Master's Tools Will Never Dismantle the Master's House," the danger in conceding lies in being seduced by the privileges that attend co-option, forgetting one's ideals as one becomes a member of the establishment that maintains its privilege by the exploitation of others.

As a writing program administrator, I have found myself in this kind of situation. I am a mid-level manager of labor who gains privileges from the exploitation of that labor. I have nevertheless maintained my commitment to egalitarian politics, although I make more money than I need and live in a house too large for my purposes. Perhaps stained by co-option, I imagine I am still contributing toward the larger purpose of a social structure that emphasizes community over individual achievement, that marks its progress by a lack of poverty and people who are not in jail. My story here could be framed as resisting non-resistance. I think of it as jujitsu, using one's opponent's inertia to one's advantage. In Freire's terms, I am an educator masking as a teacher. I hope that my position can be generalized by others who are wondering how they might fit as a square peg in a round hole.

I start from an assumption that an important function of educational institutions is to reproduce the macro social structure. This is neither a new nor surprising claim, tracking from Marx (1846) through Durkheim (1915), Gramsci (1971), Althusser (1984), Freire (1995), Berger and Luckmann (1967), Clark (1960), Bowles and Gintis (1976), Bourdieu and Passeron (1990), and a host of other writers in 1980s and 1990s (Anyon, 1980; Apple, 1982; Gee, 1996; Giroux, 1983; Katz, 1975; Macedo, 1993; McLaren, 1989; Shor, 1980, to name some of the more widely cited). The thesis behind social reproduction theory seems fairly commonsensical. Societies are framed by social structures that define and maintain the relationships among various groups within the society. These relationships determine systems of privilege and exploitation.

Although glibly summarized, social reproduction is far from straight forward, particularly in advanced industrial countries marked by a radically differentiated distribution of wealth, status, and privilege. The dominant social groups, who have benefited from the macro-structure, have most to gain from its perpetuation and the most to say about the social structures and institutions that perpetuate it. Consequently, we have modes of resistance from members of dominated social groups who see through the game. The dominating social groups, in turn, develop covert strategies to overcome this resistance.

This narrative makes social structure reproduction seem like a chess game with players deciding moves. Certainly, some of the strategies may be the consequence of conscious intent from important players, but there is a sense in which the game plays itself by hiding the reproductive mechanisms from the players. It could also be called the pea and thimble game, with the game itself as the huckster.

Many of the school reproductive mechanisms are overt. The overt purpose of educational institutions, for instance, is to pass on our knowledge and ways of thinking. On a micro level, this social reproduction works with engineers, botanists, and literary critics, who work to bring new people into the field. David Bartholomae (1985) notably made this mode of social reproduction explicit in "Inventing the University." When younger people know what we know and think like us, we see ourselves reproduced in them and are as pleased as if we had outwitted death. Of course we don't want them to be just like us—or at least not unambiguously. We claim we want them to learn how to think for themselves, which is what we have been trained to imagine we do.

Other school reproductive mechanisms are covert, countering resistance to overt social reproduction. The bell curve grading system is a good example of a covert mechanism, functioning on the surface to maintain quality control; but beneath the surface, the grading system naturalizes a radically asymmetrical distributions of privileges and resources such that very few at the top (the upper 3-5 percent) get most of the community's resources with the great mass (the Bs and Cs) getting the rest, and with a smaller group (the Ds and Fs) getting little or nothing. This bell curve has become so ingrained in our collective psyche that many of us accept it as a natural phenomenon and respond accordingly, reacting, for instance, with moral outrage at the erosion of standards.

Social reproduction mechanisms like the grading system mask the underlying logic governing the structure and asymmetrical distribution of resources in English departments. Pierre Bourdieu called homologous formations like this "structuring structures" (1990, p. 53; see also 1991, "On Symbolic Power"). The structure of the English department covertly radiates outward to shape perceptions of social relationships in the macro culture and is dialectically acted upon by outside forces to structure the English department, very much as James Berlin (1987) described the relationship between the speaker and the language within which one speaks (p. 167). The overall effect—and this is the strength of symbolic power—is to mask the covert action as a simple reflection of the natural order of things, ensuring the continuation of the social structure.

This masking effect supports, for example, the exploitation of instructors in the English department, just as social structures in democratic capitalism mask the exploitation of the working classes. Consequently, agents fail to recognize the causes of their actions, frequently disguising self-interest in terms of contributions to the global community. Bourdieu (1984, p. 142) calls this transformation of motivations misrecognition, or allodoxia. Allodoxia is a primary mechanism for reproducing social relations. Misrecognized actions may salve guilt, but they fail to mitigate the exploitation; instead, they perpetuate the social relationships dependent on exploitation.

Although I will be referring in this analysis of English departments to broad social classes, I understand that social class relationships come in a variety of shades and colors. Bourdieu (1984) has described a sophisticated way of understanding the dynamic relationships of how social groups are constituted. I will be making use of his notions of different kinds of capital: social (who you know), cultural (what you know), economic (what you have), and symbolic (control of symbolic systems) being the most frequently cited. In general, people belong to social groups on the basis of the distribution of these various kinds of capital. In addition, cultural and economic poles are in opposition to each other within any social class fraction. Professors, for example, gravitate toward the cultural pole of the middle-middle or upper-middle classes. Executives or small business owners would belong to the same social class fraction but would be located toward the economic pole. These relationships are dynamic. People use cultural capital to gain economic capital, and vice versa. In addition, people within a social class fraction and with different distributions of cultural and economic capital are always trying to trump and co-opt each other. In our field, we like to imagine that those with cultural capital hold sway—thus, the dominance (for us) of the intellectual over the CEO (see Bourdieu, 1991, p. 168) . The CEOs, on the other hand, know that money buys art.

Finally, I will be making use of Bourdieu's central thesis of social class struggle as a struggle for distinction. Distinction (which is a setting apart, asserting one's rarity) depends on establishing one's distance from necessity. With a couple of transformations, this becomes establishing one's distance from labor. The symbolic world trumps the world of labor. In essence, it's more prestigious to work with words than hammers. In the English department, it's more prestigious to theorize than to teach.

English Studies Groups as Social Classes

The upper class in English studies are those who work with literature, interpreting texts like priests interpreting the word of God. The devoted elitists flocked to modernism as a way of firmly setting their world apart from the world of necessity. Literature in the modernist narrative was removed from life, establishing a field within which the work of art was judged apart from its link to lived realities; one can see the social class dynamic functioning even within the field of literature—in general, the more obscure, abstract or theoretical the discourse, the higher the social class position of the writer and reader; the more concrete and straightforward the narrative, the lower the social class of the writers and readers (Bourdieu, 1984, p. 45, p. 200). Pollack counts more than Rockwell,

Phillip Glass more than Tammy Wynette, Thomas Pynchon more than Danielle Steele.

Rhetoric and composition professors are the middle class in English studies. As James Sledd and Cary Nelson have noted, rhetoric and composition is hell-bent on obtaining the status of its partner in crime by removing itself from labor, in particular from the labor of teaching a service course. The attraction of cultural studies in our field is symptomatic of our struggle for distinction through gaining control of the symbolic. Cultural studies has gained its status by transforming the interpretation of literature into the interpretation of culture, thus maintaining its distance from labor.

Near the bottom of our rhetoric and composition social class hierarchy lies technical and professional writing with its focus on the production of texts that do work in the world. The respective distance from labor in these two poles of the rhetoric and composition field is an index of their social positions. As technical and professional writing developed, it predictably turned toward a cultural studies approach to workplace writing, notably by applying Stuart Hall's interpretation of articulation theory to its subject.

The non-tenure-track professors, generally called instructors or lecturers, are the working-class members of English studies. They have less social, symbolic, cultural, and economic capital than members of the professoriate. I realize that some readers will bristle at this generalization, but it seems obvious that the higher one's salary and the more one's symbolic capital (e.g., how many degrees one has and books one has published), the more one will be welcomed in rarified circles. It seems equally obvious that the more money and leisure time one has, the more cultural capital one gains. Tickets for the symphony, opera, and drama series can be expensive, and it's easier to go out in the evening when you pay others to take care of the housework, plumbing, cooking, and kids.

What counts as social and cultural capital is relative to who is counting. Members of the different class fractions have different notions of legitimate cultural and social capital. But beyond this relativism lies an absolute: the social and cultural capital that counts is determined by the social groups in power. They determine people's access to symbolic and economic capital through educational institutions, which are predicated on the dominant classes' determination of what constitutes cultural and social capital.

As a consequence of their relative lack of symbolic capital, instructors have to do the labor in English departments. They teach four classes a semester in contrast to the one class a semester taught by the stars and the two or three classes taught by the rest of us. In addition, they teach the service courses, primarily first-year writing. Hardly any professors— even rhetoric and composition professors—teach those classes. Professors like to work with graduate students. They want seminars, and not very many of those because you get more economic, social, cultural, and symbolic capital by writing books, not by teaching. No news here.

The Contradiction in Rhetoric and Composition

Rhetoric and composition is characterized by egalitarian values—one could say, poses. These egalitarian poses may in part be the consequence of who we are and what we teach. A higher percentage of rhetoric and composition scholars than literature scholars come from dominated social groups. In a survey of 791 professors in English studies that I completed several years ago (1988), 16% of the rhetoric and composition respondents came from the lower two classes (lower-working and middle-working class) and 49% came from the upper two classes (middle-middle and upper-middle class). In literature, 12% came from the lower two classes and 57% came from the upper two. While my confidence level of 3.5% makes these differences negligible (Asher and Lauer, 1988), they show that members of the professoriate with working-class origins gravitate toward composition more than literature.

The differences between men and women are, however, striking. Women constituted 61% of the total in rhetoric and composition but only 46% in literature. If we can consider women a dominated social group, then their presence might account in some way for the more egalitarian tendency in rhetoric and composition. This tendency might be abetted by the slightly greater percentage of working-class academics in composition than in literature. Interestingly, a greater percentage of women in rhetoric and composition (14%) than in literature (9%) came from the working classes. But among men, 13% in both fields came from the working classes. It is possible that women, being a historically dominated social group, gravitate toward the lower social order in English studies, just as members of the working classes who go to college gravitate toward less prestigious fields in academia (Bourdieu, 1988, pp. 78-84; Bowan & Schuster, 1986, p. 32).

Rhetoric and composition's subject area may also contribute to our field's egalitarian disposition. Rhetoric and composition in its second incarnation pays more attention than literature to the material circumstances of writing, thus aligning itself with labor. And finally, rhetoric and composition's own marginalized history inclines us to identify with other marginalized workers in society. Bourdieu (1984) explains this logic of homology through an analysis of the relationship of dominating and dominated within a relatively autonomous field (he uses the examples of a village and a factory setting): "other things being equal," he claims,

> "this logic predisposes members of the oppositional classes to vote either left or right as a consequence of generalizing from their own position in the restricted field [the factory] to the whole society [the village]" (p. 459).

But in rhetoric and composition, we are caught in a highly visible contradiction: although we may want to undermine non-egalitarian social structures, we are ourselves engaged in a struggle for distinction that defines the social structure we attempt to disrupt—a consequence of our having been socialized into a institutional structure that has as part of its purpose social class reproduction. Some of us may acknowledge our role in the struggle for distinction outright and in fact glory in it (particularly if we have gained distinction in our field); some may live with it like a splinter underneath our nails; and others may develop strategies to drive it underground only to have it re-emerge in disguise.

Allodoxia

I am not letting myself off the hook. I could expand at length the ways in which I have been trying to improve my social space location. One of my more obvious gambits lay in my decision to return to graduate school after teaching high school for thirteen years. I could pretend to various socially acceptable motivations, but I was basically looking for better working conditions and more prestige. Others who have shifted from high school to college know what I am talking about. I have moved from the labor of teaching 160 students a day to spending half my workday reading and writing. I do some teaching and I direct a large first-year writing program, but I know that publishing is what this job is all about. Every word I write is in some sense is an attempt to gain more purchase in my personal struggle for distinction in the academic market place. The struggle over words and ideas is the struggle for control of the symbolic, which is different from raising pigs.

We working-class academics, in particular, have learned to mis-recognize our social scramble for distinction as a disinterested search for knowledge. The common trope among us has been "we were different. We were always in the library. We liked to read. We were smart. We weren't concerned with who won the game or the kind of car so and so has." In most of our working class narratives, you will find some version of this trope. In books, it is generally somewhere in the second chapter — if not in the opening salvo. In articles, it is usually on page three. Check it out. Look at *This Fine Place So Far from Home* — a collection of narratives from working-class academics (Dews & Law, 1995). Look at *Writing on the Bias* (Brodkey, 1994), *Bootstraps* (Villanueva, 1993), *Lives on the Boundary* (Rose, 1989), or *Limbo* (Lubrano, 2004) — the newest entry into the genre of working class narratives.

Perhaps we were smart, but other things may have drawn us toward libraries as well; in my case, it was my mother, who adamantly wanted her children to escape the working-class condition. The truly interesting thing about the escape theme of working-class academics lies in our denial of it, which is really a denial of social class betrayal. We go to some lengths to insist that we are still working-class, rejecting the middle-class label for which we have ironically been struggling. But most of us are dominantly middle-class, and as middle-class writing program administrators (WPAs), many of us have found ourselves in the middle of a social class struggle between our working-class instructors and the literature studies elite. So you might say we are twice middle-class — once within the larger social hierarchy and once within the field of English studies. That's why James Sledd (1991) called us "boss compositionists." We are middle-class managers of working-class labor.

Marc Bousquet (2002) has taken on Sledd's rhetoric with a vengeance. Bousquet argues that we assuage our guilt by imagining ourselves as heroic WPAs (p. 496), ironically resituating Richard Miller's (1998) earlier claim that teachers were playing "teacher-hero" to disguise their complicity in social class reproduction (p. 26). Unwittingly using Miller's rhetoric against him, Bousquet indicts Miller and his fellow/sister travel-ers as functionaries who accept their managerial status under the illusion that they will be able to change the rules from the inside. The problem with playing the insider game, Bousquet argues, is that as one learns the rules and accrues the privileges that come along with being an insider, one is tempted to become an insider. He has a point. Within this frame-work of social transformation, working-class WPAs' gestures toward dis-rupting the hierarchy within English departments are a trace only, in memory, perhaps, of their social group origin.

Bousquet's argument could be reframed within Bourdieu's analysis of symbolic violence, based on misrecognizing and misrepresenting self-interest as disinterest. As David Swartz (1997) describes Bourdieu's the-sis,

> The logic of self-interest underlying all practices—particularly those in the cultural domain—is misrecognized as the logic of 'disinterest.' Symbolic practices deflect attention from the interested character of practices and thereby contribute to their enactment as disinterested pursuits. This misper-ception legitimizes these practices and thereby contributes to the reproduc-tion of the social order in which they are embedded. Activities and resources gain in symbolic power, or legitimacy, to the extent that they become sepa-rated from underlying material interests and hence go misrecognized as rep-resenting disinterested forms of activities and resources. (p. 90)

Like other intellectuals, we WPAs don't want to admit, especially to ourselves, the degree to which our privilege to be an intellectual depends on the labor of the non-tenure track teachers, whose high class loads give the us the leisure to read, research, and write. I expect that many of the positions we take can be traced to our uneasy association with manage-ment and the benefits we receive by having instructors teach four classes a day at half our salary. We pretend, for example, to be unambiguously on the side of exploited labor; in the meantime, we use our release time to negotiate for professional traction by publishing our insights and our new and effective solutions to age-old WPA problems.

At a higher level, we could outline what the elite in English studies gain by the labor of WPAs, who run the game underneath them. You could argue that the work of rhetoric and composition scholars, which occasionally has some pragmatic value, deflects a critique of literary scholarship, which relatively speaking has none. But our pragmatic ir-relevancy doesn't stop any of us from claiming value in our work, and in particularly unreflective moments, justifying our "research" time, our fancier computers, our larger office space, our windows, and our higher salaries. I acknowledge the irony of my writing about this application of symbolic violence this morning while my instructors are teaching.

Self-Deception

Since I am acknowledging the WPA's complicity in social reproduction, I am not going to let instructors off the hook either. Like members of the professoriate, most of them have fetishized books over labor, and like us, they privilege theory over practice. Most of the instructors at LSU really want to be teaching literature, not "composition." They like to have their students interpret texts; thus, the popularity of readers. But because the majority of instructors are women (70% at Louisiana State University; see also NCTE, 1997) and I suspect a significant proportion from the working classes, they have unequal chances of gaining the symbolic capital of the doctorate. So they try to gain access through the backdoor of composition just as we doctoral compositionists, on another level, have tried to become pseudo literary theorists.

Instructors are beguiled by the allure of "the university." In their comparison of labor practices of two California universities, Jennifer Trainor and Amanda Godley (1998) cite Eric, an instructor at one of the universities: "'When you first get hired, you think it's such a boon. You have a mailbox. You teach at the college level. Everybody's impressed.'" A little bit later, they find out they have been tricked into accepting tertiary social status, marginal working conditions, and humiliating wages. "'You find out,'" Eric continues, "'how easy it is to get a job, how they take anybody … . I used to feel really proud when I'd tell people that I teach college, at a State U. Not anymore'" (p. 166).

Eric is suffering from what Bourdieu (1984) calls hystereisis, or the lag effect. This is what happens when the individual perceives that the prize is no longer worth the game (p. 142). In a less complimentary fashion, we can compare hystereisis to the carrot dangled in front of the donkey. The dominant classes under-reward labor by convincing workers that the carrot is real (or as Bousquet [2002] put it when describing the delusions of middle-class managers, that the boat shoes are the boat [p. 497]). Bousquet refers to a particularly embarrassing example of instructors buying into the game in his summary of Jill Carroll's (an instructor) article, "How to Be One of the Gang When You're Not" (p. 501). The essence of Carroll's article is that by hanging around with professors (and deferring to them), instructors will seem like professors.

I doubt that any of us who are middle-class managers ever articulate the degree to which we dangle carrots in front of instructors, but I suspect most of us have some awareness of the game. The professoriate has tricked instructors into additional labor and marginalized status through the promise of incipient status. Encouraging this misrecognition for our own profit leads to complicity that needs to be veiled through gestures like the Wyoming Resolution, which fleetingly gave some promise of redress for instructors. It ultimately fell flat, transformed into the "Statement of Principles and Standards for the Postsecondary Teaching of Writing" (CCCC Executive Committee, 1989). James Sledd (1991) and James Sleven (1987) wrote particularly scathing accounts of why the Wyoming Resolution had to fail, tangled as it was in the politics of who gets paid what, who has to do most of the teaching, and who gets research time to write and think about theory. At another level, the question that bedeviled the Wyoming Resolution, written by a coalition of professors and instructors putatively on behalf of the instructors (Robertson et al., 1987), troubles middle-class social activists like myself. How much of my salary should I give to organizations that fight non-egalitarian social policies? Why do I need such a big house? How much of my time should I spend on social action rather than on writing articles and books so that I can become a full professor? One can strike too close for comfort when one starts asking questions like these. It's much better to imagine we are scholars pushing for truth or middle-class managers trying to create good working conditions for our teachers and learning situations for their students as we all lumber forward into an uncertain future with little evidence that anything is gained by the drops we contribute to the bucket.

Balancing

I seem to have painted myself into a bleak picture. I wonder whether the dark colors are a consequence of my social class origin and what I have learned about myself and various social structures as I have crossed several social classes to become an associate professor in a tier three, doctoral extensive university. The trip hasn't been easy, and I know I have had to tell myself several stories to make sense of what I am doing. I am quite certain that if I had been born to this middle-class, academic world, the picture would have different colors. One simply can't disentangle what one sees from what one has seen.

But regardless of my personal history, the story I have narrated above is the one I have seen in English departments. It reflects the macro culture, filled with people who want to do good but are also engaged in their personal struggles for distinction, for being noticed, for being counted, for being more than zero. We all find our ways of making our interested actions, as Bourdieu has noted, seem disinterested through symbolic action. I have described the conundrum of the English department because I am certain it is repeated elsewhere and that true social progress depends on agents recognizing the covert details of the social structures within which they exist and how they have been structured by those "structuring structures" (Bourdieu, 1990, p. 53). I, for instance, know perfectly well that I write what I write so that I can get a few more publications, which allow me to be recognized by my colleagues as a productive intellectual. In high school, I was an athlete, and I know the link between a letter and letters and how we allow our peers to shame us into a race for both. I can't tell you how obvious this link is when we discuss in department meetings why we should hire candidate one and forget about candidate two. I am frequently embarrassed in these discussions by my colleagues and good friends.

Within this structure, as I see it, and within the concomitant way I have been structured, I have to find ways to act that reflect my beliefs without inordinately jeopardizing my own struggle for distinction—or at least my employment. Being aware of the nature of the struggle helps—although I still wake up at 2:30 in the morning wondering why I can't finish the book I have been working on for several years. I work for a balance between motivations that I know are stupid and my personal need to have people say hello to me when I walk into a room. I struggle for the same balance in my negotiations for better working conditions for my teachers and my ability to maintain a working relationship with my dean. I struggle for the balance as I recognize the rights of my teachers that are sometimes in conflict with the rights of students. And finally—and very much to the point of this book—I balance the student's right to social mobility in favor of social justice.

I suspect that most of us who have contributed to this book have a variety of positions from which to balance the imperatives of employment, professional satisfaction, family responsibilities, and social action. Rather than blueprints, what we offer are complicated ways of balancing our personal needs against the call to challenge an obviously creaky superstructure. I would like readers leave this book with a sense of the complications involved in choosing career paths and linking those choices to our commitment to leaving the world a little better off than when we entered it.

I have described here the underbelly of English departments, the facades of their putatively disinterested intellectual projects underwritten by exploitive social class mechanisms. I have focused on English departments because they are my hometown. They are where I live. If I wrote about other hometowns, I don't think the stories would be radically different. Hometowns are probably very much like people: structured by the environments within which they exist, telling acceptable stories about themselves to strangers, neighbors, and themselves but with lingering suspicions that many of these stories mask socially unacceptable motivations—the kind of suspicions that surface in dreams. I have known several social reformers who are never compromised. They follow clear paths, in contrast to the thicket that has been mine. The rest of us have to do what we can to wipe some of the cobwebs from our eyes so that we not only can see the deceptions that constitute our social and professional environments but also the self-deceptions that make up our stories. When we see clearly, we are more likely to do good. I think this is what Marcus Aurelius had in mind.

Bibliography

Althusser, L. (1984). *Essays on ideology*. London: Verso.

Anyon, J. (1980). Social class and the hidden curriculum of work. *Journal of Education*, 162 (2), 67-92.

Apple, M. (1982). *Education and power*. Boston: Routledge & Kegan Paul Ltd.

Asher, W. J., & Lauer, J. (1988). *Composition research: Empirical designs*. New York: Oxford University Press.

Aurelius, Marcus. (167 C.E.) *The Meditations*. (G. Long,Trans). Retrieved April 18, 2008 from http://classics.mit.edu/Antoninus/meditations.html.

Bartholomae, D. (1985). Inventing the university. In M. Rose (Ed.) *When a writer can't write* (pp. 134-65). New York: Guilford Press.

Berger, P., & Luckmann, T. (1967). *The social construction of reality*. New York: Anchor Books.

Berlin, J. (1987). *Rhetoric and reality: Writing instruction in American colleges, 1900-1985.* Carbondale: Southern Illinois University Press.

Bourdieu, P. (1984). *Distinction: A social critique of the judgement of taste.* (J. B. Thompson, Ed., & G. Raymond & M. Adamson, Trans.). Cambridge: Harvard University Press.

Bourdieu, P. (1988). Homo academicus. Palto Alto: Stanford University Press.

Bourdieu, P. (1991). *Language and symbolic power.* (J. B. Thompson, Ed., & G. R. Adamson, Trans.) Cambridge: Harvard University Press.

Bourdieu, P. (1990). *The logic of practice.* (R. Nice, Trans.). Palo Alto: Stanford University Press.

Bourdieu, P., & Passeron, J. C. (1990). *Reproduction in education, society, and culture.* (R. Nice, Trans.). Newbury Park: Sage.

Bousquet, M. (2002). Composition as management science: Toward a university without a WPA. *JAC, 22,* 493-526.

Bowan, H., & Schuster, J. (1986). *American professors: A national resource imperiled.* New York: Oxford University Press.

Bowles, S., & Gintis, H. (1976). *Schooling in capitalist America.* New York: Basic Books.

Brodkey, L. (1994). Writing on the bias. *College English* , 56, 527-47.

CCCC Executive Committee. (1989). Statement of principles and standards for the postsecondary teaching of writing. *College composition and communication* , 40, 329-326.

Clark, B. (1960). The cooling out function in higher education. *American Journal of Sociology,* 65, 569-76.

Delpit, L. (1990). *Other people's children: Cultural conflict in the classroom.* New York: The New Press.

Dewey, J. (1938). *Experience and education.* New York: Collier.

Dews, C. B., & Law, C. (1995). *This fine place so far from home: Voices of academics from the working class.* Philadelphia: Temple University Press.

Durkheim, E. (1915). *Elementary forms of the religious life.* London: Allen and Unwin.

Durst, R. (1999). *Collision course: Conflict, negotiation, and learning in college composition.* Urbana: National Council of Teachers of English.

Freire, P. (1995). *Pedagogy of the oppressed* (20th Anniversary ed.). (M. B. Ramos, Trans.). New York: Continuum.

Gee, J. P. (1996). *Social linguistics and literacies* (2nd ed.). Bristol: Taylor & Francis.

Giroux, H. (1983). Theories of reproduction and resistance in the new sociology of education: A critical analysis. *Harvard Educational Review,* 3 (53), 257-93.

Gramsci, A. (1971). Selections from the prison notebooks of Antonio Gramsci. (Q. H. Smith, Ed., & Q. H. Smith, Trans.). New York: International Publishers.

Katz, M. (1975). *Class, Bureaucracy and schools: The illusion of educational change in America.* New York: Praeger.

Kuhn, T. (1970). *The structure of scientific revolutions* (2nd ed.). Chicago: University of Chicago Press.

Lorde, A. (1984). The master's tools will never dismantle the master's house. In *Sister outsider* (pp. 110-13). Berkeley, CA: The Crossing Press.

Lubrano, A. (2004). *Limbo: Blue-collar roots, white-collar dreams.* Hoboken: John Wiley & Sons.

Macedo, D. (1993). Literacy for stupidification: The pedagogy of big lies. *Harvard Educational Review* , 63, 183-206.

Marx, K. (1846). *The German idology*. Retrieved Feb. 15, 2008, from http://www.marxists,org/archive/marx/works/1845/german-ieology/ch01b.htm

McLaren, P. (1989). On ideology and education: Critical pedagogy and the cultural politics of resistance. In H. Giroux, & P. McLaren (Eds.), *Critical pedagogy, the state, and cultural struggle* (pp. 174-204). Albany: State University of New York Press.

Miller, R. (1998). The arts of complicity: Pragmatism and the culture of schooling. *College English*, 61, 10-28.

Mueller, C. (1973). *The Politics of communication*. New York: Oxford University Press.

NCTE. (1997). Statement from the conference on the growing use of part-time and adjunct faculty. Retrieved Feb. 17, 2005, from http://www.ncte.org/about/over/positions/category/profcon/107662.htm?source=gs

Nelson, C. (1988). English, vanguard of the fast food university: What hath English wrought? Retrieved Feb. 17, 2005, from Against the Current: http://solidarity.igc.org/solidarity/atc/cary74.html

Robertson, L. R., Crowley, S., & Lentrichhia, F. (1987). The Wyoming conference resolution opposing unfair salaries and working conditions for post-secondary teachers of writing. *College English*, 49, 274-80.

Rose, M. (1989). *Lives on the boundary*. New York: Penguin Books.

Sackrey, J., & Ryan, C. (Eds.). (1984). *Strangers in paradise: Academics from the working class*. Boston: South End Press.

Shepard, A., McMillan, J., & Tate, G. (Eds.). (1998). *Coming to class: Pedagogy and the social class of teachers*. Portsmouth, New Hampshire: Boyton/Cook.

Shor, I. (1980). *Critical teaching and everyday life*. Chicago: University of Chicago Press.

Sledd, J. (1991). Why the Wyoming resolution had to be emasculated: A history and its quitxoticism. Retrieved March 4, 2003, from JAC: http://jac.gsu.edu

Slevin, J. (1987). A note on the Wyoming resolution and ADE. *ADE Bulletin*, 87, 50.

Sullivan, P. (1998). Passing: A family dissemblance. In Shepard et al. (pp. 231-251).

Swartz, D. (1997). *Culture and power: The sociology of Pierre Bourdieu*. Chicago: University of Chicago Press.

Tate, G. (1998). Halfway back home. In Shepard et al., (pp. 252-261).

Toulmin, S. (1958). *The uses of argument*. Cambridge, England: Cambridge University Press.

Trainor, J. S., & Godley, A. (1998). After Wyoming: Labor practices in two university writing programs. *College composition and communication* , 50, 153-81.

Villanueva, V. J. (1993). *Bootstraps: From an American academic of color*. Urbana: National Council of Teachers of English.

CHAPTER 6

LEADING BEYOND LABELS
The Role of the Principal in Leading through a Social Justice Framework for Students with Disabilities

Susan Hasazi and Katharine Shepherd

Leaders of public schools have the responsibility to ensure that all students have the opportunity to learn and succeed regardless of their backgrounds, abilities, and experiences. Simply put, leaders of public schools need to lead within a social justice framework. While we acknowledge that this framework applies to children and youth from a variety of traditionally marginalized groups, our concern in this chapter is to discuss leadership and social justice in the context of educating students with disabilities. For the most part, discussions of social justice in public school settings have focused on issues such as race, socioeconomic status, gender, and sexuality; however, more recent literature has begun to acknowledge disability as defining factor among children and youth who are often marginalized (Meekosha, & Jakubowicz, 1996; Slee, 2001).

In examining the imperative to bring students with disabilities into the dialogue about social justice and leadership, we see a need to describe what it means to be a school leader who acts on behalf of all students. In this chapter, we propose a social justice framework for understanding leadership and disability within the context of schools. We focus on the role of the school principal in operationalizing the framework through an approach to leadership that fosters the development of an inclusive school culture, effective instructional practices, professional learning communities, and family and community-centered practices.

From Managers to Caring Visionaries: Changing Views of School Leadership

Traditional conceptions of school leadership have, for the most part, equated the principal's role with management and the maintenance of a smoothly functioning system (Giroux, 1997). Principals were regarded as the primary instruments of authority and power, whose responsibilities included the supervision and evaluation of teachers, maintenance of the school's physical plant, compliance with bureaucratic requests, and control of student behavior. Over the past two decades, however, more contemporary views of leadership and the role of the school principal have acknowledged that the increasing diversity among students in our public schools requires a less managerial and more collaborative and visionary approach to leadership (Riehl, 2000). At the heart of this approach is the school principal's commitment to social justice as both a means and an end to bringing about greater equity and opportunity to students and families who have been devalued as a result of disability, race, language, poverty, gender and sexual orientation (Dantley, 2002; Delpit, 1992; Hallinger & Leithwood, 1998; Murphy, 2002; Pounder, Reitzug, & Young, 2002; Riehl, 2000; Riester, Pursch, & Skrla, 2002).

Defining Social Justice in Schools

Recognizing the multiple definitions surrounding the concept of social justice, we focus in this chapter on its meaning in the context of public schooling and in relation to leadership: in this case, the school principal. As such, we find that a commitment to social justice in schools is evidenced by the presence of principals who value the unique aspects of all students and promote equal access to opportunities for high achievement and social inclusion for all students, including those with disabilities. Much of the recent research on approaches to educating students with disabilities has   identified leadership as a key component to successful inclusion (Furney, Hasazi, 2003; Pounder, Reitzug, & Young, 2002; Thousand & Villa, 2005); however, there is a need to more clearly articulate how a social justice framework can guide principals' actions and approaches to leadership.

Beyond Labels: Reframing Disability Through a Social Justice Perspective

Historically, persons with disabilities have been characterized as having internal deficits or impairments that must be overcome in order for them to participate more fully in life (Christiansen & Dorn, 1997). The negative stereotypes accompanying such labels, as well as the ensuing lack of opportunities for students with disabilities (Meekosha & Jakubowicz, 1996; Slee, 2001) have led many to form alternative perspectives in which disability is recognized to be socially constructed by the dominant culture

(Bogdan & Taylor, 1994; Kliewer & Biklen, 1996). Schools' initial attempts to make schools more hospitable and accommodating places for students with disabilities have been replaced by a deeper understanding of what it means to educate students with disabilities alongside of their nondisabled peers. Some schools have begun to understand disability as one aspect of a social justice perspective that includes the whole range of human experience. In this more holistic view, schools are called upon not to "rehabilitate" students, but to ensure that they have equal access to the opportunities and educational outcomes promised to all.

Applying the Social Justice Framework

The remainder of this chapter draws on the literature on leadership and social justice, including findings from the authors' previous research in these areas, to describe four components of a social justice framework that can be enhanced through the principal's leadership. These include: 1) developing school cultures that recognize the needs and contributions of students with disabilities, 2) promoting instructional practices that are effective for students with and without disabilities, 3) creating professional learning communities characterized by collaboration, reflection, and empowerment, and 4) ensuring that the perspectives of students with disabilities and their families are central to the mission of the school.

Developing School Cultures that Recognize the Needs and Contributions of Students with Disabilities

School leaders who play a central role in fostering school cultures attentive to the needs and contributions of students with disabilities need to be skilled in developing a shared vision and culture, understanding special education policies and practices, and ensuring that the structure and organization of the school reflects a commitment to inclusion. Each of these skills and dispositions is explored in greater detail below.

Developing a shared vision and culture. It is critical that leaders committed to social justice take an active role in helping to articulate a belief and a vision that emphasizes the attributes and potential of all students, including those with disabilities (Hallinger & Leithwood, 1998; Scheurich, 1998). Moreover, the vision needs to emphasize the rights of students with disabilities to have access to the full range of opportunities available to all students. In our own research on effective school leaders (Furney,

Aiken, Hasazi, & Clark/Keefe, 2005), one teacher spoke for many when she described the ways in which her school principal used stories of children with disabilities to reinforce the school's commitment to shaping the school's vision in ways that address the needs of all children:

> Each time we meet, our principal begins with a story about one of our kids, how he or she struggles to be successful in school given particular challenges he or she faces. Over and over, she will ask us: "What more can we do? How will this goal relate to the kids we know and have in our school?" (p. 553)

In addition to developing a shared vision, school leaders need to set a context for participatory leadership that includes multiple opportunities for reflection and dialogue (Pounder et al., 2002). The school leaders we have encountered through our research have emphasized the need to ensure that the school's vision is carried out in the context of a democratic approach to decision-making and change. These leaders recognize that "change may be resisted if it is perceived as a top-down mandate" (Godek, Furney, & Riggs, 2005 p. 84). They understand the need to keep visions vital by re-visiting them often to engage teachers in discussing and debating various perspectives and practices. One teacher noted her principal's skills in this regard:

> He creates forums and processes that encourage this kind of open communication...He seems to want and expect diverse viewpoints and then creates ways for all of us to take a new look at our own beliefs and assumptions, especially about students at risk. He helps us think differently about how we approach these kids, and what we do and why (Furney et al., 2005, pp. .555).

When schools engage in practices that are not in keeping with such a vision, leaders need to be skilled in identifying and addressing resulting inequities and moral dilemmas (Wong, 1998). As Sergiovanni (1992) notes, leaders must at times lead through "moral outrage" taking steps to engage their teachers and school communities in difficult conversations about what is and is not working in terms of their school's policies, practices, and procedures. Establishing a vision within a social justice framework is important, but the vision needs to be revisited often to ensure that its underlying premises resonate throughout the school community.

Understanding special education policies, inclusive practices, and their link to social justice. School leaders who are successful in fostering inclusive cultures understand and apply special education policies to ensure that the intent of relevant laws is realized in the school's vision as well as its practices. They need to be familiar with the principles and regulations associated with federal and state laws and regulations pertaining to both general and special education, including the Individuals with Disabilities Education Improvement Act (IDEIA, 2004) and the No Child Left Behind Act (NCLBA, 2000). These laws serve to reinforce school leaders' attempts to co-create a vision as well as effective structures and practices that benefit all students. A principal in one of our studies (Godek et al., 2005) described how "it may be helpful to emphasize the moral and ethical aspects of inclusion, the degree to which inclusion is part of existing laws and regulations, and the positive, research-based outcomes for students with and without disabilities" (p. 84). A teacher in another school talked in similar terms about the ways in which her principal helped teachers to understand how new supports and services for students with and without disabilities "grew out of state and federal mandates" (Furney et al., 2005, p. 561).

Along with knowing how to implement state and federal mandates, school principals need to demonstrate an understanding of specific disability categories and their instructional implications. At the same time, leaders play a central role in ensuring that schools do not use the disability labels as a way to organize and deliver instruction. Leaders of inclusive schools need to reject a deficit view in which disability is regarded as a medical or organic condition that rests within the individual and must therefore be "fixed" through technical and categorical approaches (Slee, 2001). Instead, principals can help to foster a broader conceptualization of disability and low achievement in which the goal of the school is to create an instructional context that meets the needs of all learners within a common framework of high expectations and accountability (McLaughlin, Artiles, & Pullin, 2001). In doing so, they help to build cultures in which diversity and disability are recognized as interrelated and socially constructed phenomena that need to be addressed through the schools' articulation of values and the creation of learning environments that are responsive to all students (Meekosha & Jakubowicz, 1996).

Ensuring that the Structure and Organization of the School Reflects the Underlying Commitment to Inclusion

School principals must also ensure that the moral and cultural conversations they promote in schools lead to a reshaping of school structures and processes that promote social justice and inclusion. Dillard's (1995) comment that "effective leadership is transformative political work" (p. 558) has implications for principals engaged in restructuring their schools. Ultimately, principals and their staff must move beyond a view of cultural assimilation to one in which school structures are true vehicles of social change for students from diverse cultures and backgrounds, including those with disabilities (McLaughlin et al., 2001).

One issue of great concern within special education is that of the over-representation of African-American males in specific disability categories (Harry & Anderson, 1994; McLaughlin, Artiles, & Pullin, 2001). While the reasons for this are complex and beyond the scope of this chapter, some do in fact relate to the intersection of the perspectives and potential biases of general and special education teachers around such students, and the degree to which special education structures and processes are operating in the context of fairness and justice. It is important to recognize the ways in which over identification of particular populations of students creates its own inequities, particularly when large numbers of students from minority backgrounds are grouped in special education classes that do not provide the equal access to the general education curriculum. Such practices are not uncommon and hearken back to early arguments around segregated educational settings. Clearly, the interplay of race, disability, and gender that results in over-representation in specific disability categories is one that needs further exploration and attention by both researchers and practitioners concerned with a social justice framework.

Structural changes and issues are also related to resource allocation. Principals who adopt a social justice framework understand the critical need to maintain a level of flexibility in funding that deemphasizes categorical approaches and the sorting and differentiating of students and staff (Furney et al., 2003; McLaughlin & Verstegen, 1998). More open systems assure that services are provided on the basis of student need, rather than on the basis of the availability of individual school personnel or categorically-based services (Thousand & Villa, 2005). In short, school leaders need to look across their school systems to create structures that will distribute financial and human resources in ways that are commensurate with the school's vision to enhance the education of all students. An interviewee in one of our studies of effective leadership described it this way:

> We used to work in such silos. But now, (the principal) really has created opportunities where we can work with other professionals in the school. At first, it was hard; we speak different languages. But after awhile, we really found that by so many people coming to the table, we were able to come up with more creative and new ways of supporting students. We also learned much more about their situations: their challenges and their families (p. 554).

Promoting Instructional Practices that Are Effective for Students with and without Disabilities

Over the past 20 years, the literature on school leadership has emphasized the importance of principals as instructional leaders for all students (Blase & Blase, 1999a;1999b; Schmoker, 2004; Sheppard, 1996). Pressures related to high-stakes testing and increased school accountability, as well as the range of managerial and bureaucratic tasks that confront principals on a daily basis, make it difficult for many to fully adopt this role (Pounder et al., 2002). Still, the literature on the current challenges and context of school leadership is clear about the need for principals to understand effective curricula and instructional practices, and the use of assessment practices and data-based decision-making in efforts to improve schools for all students (Brock & Groth, 2003; Janisch & Johnson, 2003; Munoz & Dossett, 2004).

Understanding Effective Curricula and Instructional Practices

Leaders who are fully engaged in understanding effective curricula and instructional practices visit classrooms on a regular basis, praise and give feedback to teachers, discuss assessment results in relation to curriculum and instruction, and seek teachers' advice about instructional matters (Blase & Blase, 1999a; Blase & Blase, 1999b; Southworth, 2002). They support teachers in finding ways to promote student engagement in learning, and to implement research-based strategies designed to enhance the inclusion of students with disabilities in general education classrooms (Quinn, 2002; Slee, 2001). The latter include strategies such as peer tutoring, cooperative learning, positive behavioral supports, school-wide approaches to literacy and numeracy, and effective use of individual accommodations (Sapon-Shevin, Ayres, & Duncan, 2002; Tomlinson, 1999; Tomlinson& Allan, 2000).

Principals also need to ensure that the specific curricula and instructional strategies used in their schools are a good match for students' cultural and individual needs (Harthun, Drapeau, Dustman, & Marsiglia, 2002; Janisch & Johnson, 2003). Pounder et al. (2002) caution that in the current era of educational reform, principals may feel pressured to engage in superficial approaches to improving student performance. These include "teaching to the test," excluding students with learning challenges from taking tests, or failing to publicly report the scores of students with disabilities. Leaders utilizing a social justice framework seek instead to implement an "authentic pedagogy," in which students learn in a culturally responsive environment about things that really matter to them (Finnan, Schnepel, & Anderson, 2003).

Using assessment practices and data-based decision-making as the basis of efforts to improve schools for all students. School principals also need to have a deep understanding of the link between assessment, curricula, and instruction, and the use of data-based decision-making for school improvement. An emerging body of literature describes the success of school leaders in engaging teachers and community members in conversations about using assessment data for the purposes of improving instruction and student outcomes (Furney et al. 2003; Janisch & Johnson, 2003; Shepherd, 2006). School principals committed to social justice support their teachers in utilizing individual and classroom performance data in order to provide effective instruction for all students, as well as to guide professional development and resource allocation (Brock & Groth, 2003; Morrocco, Walker, & Lewis, 2003; Reister, Pursch, & Skrla, 2002).

Creating Professional Learning Communities Characterized by Collaboration, Reflection, and Empowerment

In recent years, the research on leadership and change has moved away from approaches utilizing external consultants for strategic planning (Kouzes & Posner, 1995; Schmoker, 2004) to a focus on creating change by building schools' capacity to function as professional learning communities. In these learning communities, change is viewed as a collaborative enterprise closely tied to the realities of classrooms and the core purpose of individual schools (DuFour & Eacker, 1998; Fullan, 2002; Fullan, 2003; Huffamn & Jacobson, 2003; Sckmoker, 2004; Senge, 1990). The professional learning community model rejects the idea of externally developed staff development efforts, replacing them with action research models and similar opportunities for teachers to engage in dialogue and reflection on actual student work (Huffman & Jacobson, 2003).

The professional learning community places teachers at the center of change efforts; however, it is clear that principals play an essential role in the community's establishment and continued growth. Effective leaders understand the importance of collaborative teaming and action oriented inquiry, and the ways in which these processes help to ensure the success of students with disabilities (Schmoker, 2004). The literature has identified a number of related effective principal behaviors, including empowering teachers through talking openly and freely with them about teaching and learning, providing time and encouraging peer connections, and leading in ways that motivate and facilitate growth among teachers (Blase & Blase, 1999a).

As principals implement professional learning communities, they need to promote an expectation within the school that both general and special education teachers are responsible for students with disabilities (Morrocco, Walker, & Lewis, 2003; Southworth, 2002). One strategy for establishing this expectation is to create problem-solving teams with high levels of principal involvement and support (Furney, Hasazi, Clark/Keefe, & Hartnett, 2003; Furney et al, 2005; Shepherd, 2006). These teams bring general and special educators together for the purpose of developing and monitoring plans to support students with disabilities as well as those at risk of educational failure. Our research indicates that teachers value the efforts of principals to provide the time, structure and training needed to make problem-solving teams successful, noting that:

> As a result of our principal's efforts, our meetings are really productive. We know how to listen better, how to engage in finding new ways to support students and teachers, and have really learned how to work as a team (Furney et al., 2005, p.556).

In addition to creating problem-solving teams, principals can be influential in promoting models such as co-teaching and joint professional development that enhance the capacity of general education teachers to address the needs of students with disabilities within their classrooms (Frey, Fisher, & Henry, 2005). Each of these changes needs to occur in the context of a collaborative approach to leadership that recognizes the unique culture of the school. In the words of one principal, "particularly when resistance is likely, change may need to start not with leaders in positions of authority, but with individuals throughout the system who are willing to try something new" (Godek et al., 2004, p. 84).

Ensuring that the Perspectives of Students with Disabilities and Their Families Are Central to the Mission of the School

Principals who lead from a framework of social justice ensure that school personnel understand, respect, and value the unique experiences, strengths and challenges of students with disabilities and their families. Leaders play a key role in helping teachers to examine their own assumptions about disability and diversity, and to reflect on how those assumptions positively or negatively affect their interactions with families. In a classic study of the interactions between special education professionals and Puerto Rican families who had children with disabilities, Harry (1992) articulates the ways in which school personnel failed to understand the cultural context of the families, and in turn, misinterpreted parents' actions and participation in educational planning meetings. Rao's (2000) case study of "Rose," an African-American mother of a child with disabilities, portrays a similar lack of cultural understanding on the part of school and agency personnel. They used language and labels that held negative connotations for Rose and conflicted with her more positive construction of her son's challenges. Over time, she lost a sense of trust in the service providers and systems that she had expected would offer her support and her team lost its ability to be provide effective support for her and her son.

Stories such as these emphasize the need for principals to examine the degree to which a school's understanding of and investment in families of diverse backgrounds is reflected in its overall culture, classrooms, team processes, and daily operations (Lopez, Scribner, & Mahitivanichch, 2001; Scheurich, 1998; Shapiro, Monzo, Rueda, Gomez, & Blacher, 2004). With respect to children with disabilities and their families, principals need to ensure that all special education processes are family-centered. For example, parents need to receive information on legal and educational issues in their first language and prior to any formal meetings scheduled with school personnel. Educational planning meetings need to take into account a range of family needs, including families' preferences for meeting times, child care, and transportation issues. Moreover, they need to be conducted in a manner that demonstrates cultural sensitivity and promotes trust, open communication, and respect (Harry, 1992; Rao, 2000; Salembier & Furney, 1997).

Principals play a vital role in ensuring that schools demonstrate a commitment to bringing families into the community and the community into the schools (Dryfoos & Maguire, 2002; Scheurich, 1998). Principals need to take the lead on connecting families of children with disabilities to appropriate supports and activities within the school, as well as to supports and services available in the community. Leaders can promote school and community collaboration by stressing the need for integrated school and community services, collaborative partnerships that place parents at the center of planning efforts, and seamless connections between the school and community (Hasazi, Furney, & DeStefano, 1999).

How can leaders acquire the dispositions and skills they need to address the needs of students with disabilities and their families within a social justice framework? Academic course work and educational internships are important; however, a recent study in which aspiring principals participated in family internships suggested that more intensive, family-based experiences helped to "make real life connections with families with diverse needs" (Alonzo, Bushey, Gardner, Hasazi, Johnstone, & Miller, 2006, p. 134). Students participating in the internships spent 25 hours in one family's home over a week's period. During this time, they engaged with parents and their children in the daily activities of the family. The interns reported a variety of benefits associated with the internship, including opportunities for both the interns and family members to learn about one another and to grow in their understanding of each others' worlds. They described the "humanizing effect" of gaining "an insider perspective on what it means to have a child with a disability" (Alonzo et al. 2006, p. 135). A parent provided her perspective on the need to provide similar experiences for future principals:

> I hope we move toward a curriculum that includes an understanding of the challenges of the personal lives of individuals with disabilities as well as their families, and even further, what the family has to offer school leadership in pursuit of successful education. We need to prepare educational

leaders for their role of leading not only formal education, but also to be responsible for initiating open dialogue with families. Leaders need to set a tone of inclusion not just for the child in the system, but the family as well. Future leaders should be guided in how to recognize the individuality of these families, yet at the same time, their desires to live a typical life like anyone else. Ultimately, this process will teach leaders to empower families, resulting in the most successful education of the children (Alonzo et al 2006, pp. 134-135).

Conclusion

In the present educational context, we need to prepare principals who embrace and can operationalize a social justice framework for the purpose of promoting the inclusion of students with disabilities and their families in the full life of the school. Four components of a social justice framework that can guide a principal's practice are described, including 1) developing school cultures that recognize the needs and contributions of students with disabilities, 2) promoting instructional practices that are effective for students with and without disabilities, 3) creating professional learning communities characterized by collaboration, reflection, and empowerment, and 4) ensuring that the perspectives of students with disabilities and their families are central to the mission of the school. Throughout this chapter, we have attempted to articulate the ways in which students with disabilities need to be viewed beyond their special education labels and within a social justice framework. Recent literature on the preparation of educational administrators has advocated for building a curriculum around a framework of social justice (McKenzie & Scheurich, 2004; McLaughlin, Artilles, & Pullin, 2001; Murphy, 2002; Pounder et al., 2002; Riehl, 2000; Riester, Pursch, & Skrla, 2002).

In addition to integrating this information into the formal preparation of principals, we recommend that school systems and universities collaborate to develop a structure for mentoring potential leaders and principals who are in the early stages of their career. Approaches to mentoring might address topics such as collaboration with families from diverse backgrounds, the basic legal rights of children with disabilities and their families, and frameworks for understanding diversity in the context of social justice. This information could be offered through informational workshops, as well as through on-site mentoring and the use of group problem-solving approaches in which new leaders are brought together to work collectively on real issues that confront them in their work with children with disabilities and their families.

Our final thoughts on the families of children with disabilities suggest that their voices need to be heard and addressed in our continuing efforts to improve schools for all children. By reconceptualizing the role of principals in our increasingly diverse world, it is our hope that the tenets of social justice will lead to more positive outcomes for all students, including those with disabilities.

Bibliography

Alonzo, J., Bushey, L., Gardner, D., Hasazi, S., Johnstone, C., & Miller, P. (2006). 25 hours in family: How family internships can help school leaders transform from within. *Equity & Excellence in Education, 39* (2), 127 – 136.

Blase, J., & Blase, J. (1999a). Effective instructional leadership: Teacher's perspectives on how principals promote teaching and learning in schools. *Journal of Educational Administration, 38* (2), 103 – 141.

Blase, J., & Blase, J. (1999b). Instructional leadership through the teachers' eyes. *The High School Magazine,5,* 17 – 20.

Brock, K.J., & Groth, C. (2003). "Becoming" effective: Lessons learned from one state's reform initiative in serving low-income students. *Journal of Education for Students Placed At Risk, 8* (2), 167 – 190.

Christensen, C.A., & Dorn, S. (1997). Competing notions of social justice and contradictions in special education reform. *The Journal of Special Education, 31* (2), 181-198.

Dantley, M. (2002). Uprooting and replacing positivism, the melting pot, multiculturalism, and other important notions in educational leadership through an African American perspective. *Education and Urban Society, 34* (3), 334 – 352.

Delpit, L.D. (1992). Education in a multicultural society: Our future's greatest challenge. *Journal of Negro Education, 61* (3), 237 – 249.

Dillard, C.B. (1995). Leading with her life: An African American feminist (re) interpretation of leadership for an urban high school principal. *Education Administration Quarterly, 31* (4), 539 – 563.

Dryfoos, J.G., & McGuire, S., (2002). *Inside full service community schools. Thousand Oaks:* Corwin Press.

DuFour, R., & Eaker, R. (1998). *Professional learning communities at work: Best practices for enhancing student achievement.* Bloomington, IN: National Educational Service.

Finnan, C., Schnepel, K.C. , & Anderson, L.W. (2003). Powerful learning environments: The critical link between school and classroom cultures. *Journal of Education for Students Placed at Risk, 8* (4), 391 – 418.

Frey, N., Fisher, D., & Henry, D.P. (2005). Voices of inclusion: Collaborative teaming and student support. In R.A. Villa, & J.S. Thousand (Eds.), *Creating an inclusive school* (pp. 124 – 133). Alexandria, VA: Association for Supervision and Curriculum Development. .

Fullan, M. (2002). The change leader. *Educational Leadership, 59* (8), 16 – 25.

Fullan, M. (2003). *Change forces with a vengeance.* New York: Routledge Falmer.

Furney, K.S., Aiken, J., Hasazi, S., & Clark/Keefe, K. (2005). Meeting the needs of all students: Contributions of effective school leaders. *Journal of School Leadership* 5,(15), 546 – 570.

Furney, K., Hasazi, S., Clark/Keefe, K., & Hartnett, J. (2003). *Exceptional Children,* (1), 81 – 94.

Furney, K.S., Hasazi, S., & Clark/Keefe, K. (2005). Multiple dimensions of reform: The impact of state policies on special education and supports for all students. *Journal of Disability Policy Studies,* 16(3), 169-176.

Giroux, H. (1997). *Pedagogy and the politics of hope: Theory, culture, and schooling.* Boulder, CO: Westview.

Godek, J., Furney, K.S., & Riggs, M.L. (2005). Voices of inclusion: Changing views from the porch. In R.Villa & J. Thousand (Eds.), *Creating an inclusive school* (2nd ed.) (pp. 81 – 88). Alexandria, VA: Association for Supervision and Curriculum Development.

Hallinger, P., Bickman, L., & Davis, K. (1996). School context, principal leadership, and student reading achievement. *The Elementary School Journal, 96* (5), 527 - 549.

Hallinger, P., & Leithwood, K. (1998). Unseen forces: The impact of social culture on school leadership. *Peabody Journal of Education, 73* (2), 126 – 151.

Harry, B. (1992). An ethnographic study of cross-cultural communication with Puerto Rican-American families in the special education system. *American Educational Research Journal, 29* (3), 471 – 494.

Harry, B., & Anderson, M.G. (1994). The disproportionate placement of African American males in special education programs: A critique of the process. *Journal of Negro Education, 63* (4), 602 – 619.

Hasazi, S., Furney, K.S., & DeStefano, L. (1999). Implementing the IDEA transition mandates. *Exceptional Children, 65* (4), 555 – 566.

Huffman, J.B., & Jacobson, A.L., (2003) Perceptions of professional learning communities. *International Journal of Leadership in Education, 6* (3), 239 – 250.

Janisch, C., & Johnson, M. (2003). Effective literacy practices and challenging curriculum for At-risk learners: Great expectations. *Journal of Education for Students Placed at Risk, 8* (3), 295 – 308.

Kouzes, J.M., & Pozner, B. (1995). *The leadership challenge.* San Francisco: Jossey-Bass.

Lopez, G.R., Scribner, J.D., & Mahitivanichcha, K. (2001). Redefining parental involvement: Lessons from high-performing migrant-impacted schools. *American Educational Research Journal, 38* (2), 253- 288.

Meekosha, H., & Jakubowicz, A. (1996). Disability, participation, representation, and social justice. In C. Christensen & F. Rizvi (Eds.), *Disability and the dilemmas of education and justice* (pp. 79 – 85). Buckingham: Open University Press.

McKenzie, K.B., & Scheurich, J.J. (2004). Equity traps: A construct for departments of educational administration. *Educational Administration Quarterly, 40*(5), 601-632.

McLaughlin, M.J., Artiles, A.J., & Pullin, D. (2001). Challenges for the transformation of special education in the 21st century: Rethinking culture in school reform. *Journal of Special Education Leadership, 14*(2), 51 – 62.

McLaughlin, M.J., & Verstegen, D.A. (1998). Increasing regulatory flexibility of special education programs: Problems and promising strategies. *Exceptional Children, 64,* 371 – 384.

Morrocco, C.C., Walker, A., & Lewis, L.R. (2003). Access to a schoolwide thinking curriculum: Leadership challenges and solutions. *Journal of Special Education Leadership, 16* (1), 5 – 14.

Munoz, M.A., & Dossett, D.H. (2004). Educating students placed at risk: Evaluating the impact of success for all in urban settings. *Journal of Education for Students Placed at Risk, 9* (3), 261-277.

Murphy, J. (2002). Reculturing the profession of educational leadership: New blueprints. *Education Administration Quarterly, 38* (2), 176 – 191.

No Child Left Behind Act of 2001. 20 U.S.C. 6301. et seq. (2001).

Quinn, D. (2002). The impact of principalship behaviors on instructional practice and student engagement. *Journal of Educational Administration, 40* (5), 447 - 467.

Pounder, D., Reitzug, U., & Young, M.D. (2002). Recasting the development of school leaders. In J. Murphy (Ed.), *The educational challenge: Redefining leadership for the 21st century* (pp. 261- 288). Chicago: National Society for the Study of Education

Rao, S.S. (2000). Perspectives of an African American mother on parent-professional relationships in special education. *Mental Retardation, 38* (6), 485 – 488.

Riehl, C.J. (2000). The principal's role in creating inclusive schools for diverse students: A review of normative, empirical, and critical literature on the practice of educational administration. *Review of Educational Research, 70* (1), 55 – 81.

Riester, A.F., Pursch, V., & Skrla, L. (2002). Principals for social justice: Leaders of school success for children in low-income homes. *Journal of School Leadership, 12,* 214 – 249.

Rusch, E.A. (1998). Leadership in evolving democratic school communities. *Journal of School Leadership, 8,* 214 – 249.

Salembier, G., & Furney, K.S. (1997). Facilitating participation: Parents' perceptions of their involvement in the IEP/transition planning process. *Career Development of Exceptional Individuals, 22* (1), 29 – 42.

Sapon-Shevin, M., Ayres, B., & Duncan, J. (2002). Cooperative learning and inclusion. In J.S. Thousand & A.I. Nevin (Eds.), *Creativity and collaborative learning: The practical guide to empowering students, teachers, and families (2nd ed.)* (pp. 209 – 222). Baltimore: Paul H. Brookes.

Schmoker, M. (February, 2004). Tipping point: From feckless reform to substantive instructional improvement. *Phi Delta Kappan,* 424 – 432.

Schuerich, J.J. (1998). Highly successful and loving, public elementary schools populated mainly low-SES children of color: Core beliefs and cultural characteristics. *Urban Education, 33* (4), 451 – 491.

Senge, P. (1990). *The fifth discipline: The art and practice of the learning organization.* London: Random House.

Sergiovanni, T.J. (1992). *Moral leadership.* San Francisco: Jossey-Bass.

Shapiro, J., Monzo, L.D., Rueda, R., Gomez, J.A., & Blacher, J. (2004). Alienated advocacy: Perspectives of Latina mothers of young adults with developmental disabilities on service systems. *Mental Retardation, 42* (1), 37 – 54.

Shepherd, K. G. (2006). Supporting all students: The role of principals in expanding general education capacity using response to intervention teams. *Journal of Special Education Leadership 19* (2), 30 - 38.

Sheppard, B. (1996). Exploring the transformational nature of instructional leadership. *The Alberta Journal of Educational Research, XLII* (4), 325 – 344.

Slee, R. (2001). Social justice and the changing directions in educational research: The case of inclusive education. *International Journal of Leadership in Education, 5* (2/3), 167 – 177.

Southworth, G. (2002). Instructional leadership in schools: Reflections and empirical evidence. *School Leadership and Management, 22* (1), 73 – 91.

Starrat, R.J.,(1999). Moral dimensions of leadership. In P.T. Begley & P. Leonard (Eds)., *The values of educational administration .pp. 15-20.* London:Falmer Press.

Thousand, J., & Villa, R. (2005). Organizational supports for change toward inclusive schooling. In R.Villa & J. Thousand (Eds.), *Creating an inclusive school* (2nd ed.), (pp. 57 – 80). Alexandria, VA: Association for Supervision and Curriculum Development.

Tomlinson, C.A. (1999). Leadership for differentiated classrooms. *The School Administrator, 56* (9), 6 – 11.

Tomlinson, C.A., & Allan, S.D. (2000). *Leadership for differentiating schools and classrooms.* Alexandria, VA: Association for Supervision and Curriculum Development.

Wong, K. (1998). Culture and moral leadership in education. *Peabody Journal of Education, 73,* (2), 106 – 125.

HOW DOES IT FEEL TO HAVE YOUR SKIN COLOR?

Uncovering Children's Inquiries About Race

Efleda Preclaro Tolentino

Introduction

"How does it feel to have your skin color?" a five-year old child asked me one day. I was a guest speaker in a kindergarten class and had just introduced myself and asked the children if there was something they wanted to know about me before I started. All eyes were on me. I paused for a moment before I responded to the question. The child's question was, without a doubt, an invitation to a conversation. It was just the question I needed to get us started talking about race. I have always perceived children's questions as stems of inquiry that support their meaning-making process. Because children are active seekers of knowledge, they engage in dialogue with others, giving meaning to events by making connections between them (Wells, 1986). This particular question revealed one child's awareness of skin color as well as curiosity about a *lived* difference. Although I have always been aware of privileges and disadvantages associated with my race and ethnicity, I never fully explored what race meant from the perspective of young children.

The increasing cultural, racial, linguistic and ability diversity of students in K-12 schools especially in the last three or four decades has made a profound impact on the field of education. As a result, there has been a significant shift in our ways of thinking about teacher education and the ways we prepare future teachers to teach in diverse multicultural contexts. The move towards a more global approach to education and the emphasis placed on ways that we address diversity in learning contexts indicate an awareness or consciousness on the part of teacher educators for the need to provide education that is inclusive, equitable, and democratic for all children. Children develop concepts about diversity in many forms: race, ethnicity, ability, gender, social class, age, sexual orientation, and culture. Just as children have questions about intersecting identities, they also have inquiries about race and ethnicity. In its most complex form, race is socially constructed (Frankenberg, 1993; Weis, Fine, Weesen & Wong, 2000). Within this schema, race has "connotations that reflect culturally constructed differences that maintain the prevailing distribution of power and privilege in a society" (Rothenberg, 2007, p. 8). Ethnicity, on the other hand, is a form of identity that embodies the cultural and social experiences shared by a group (Rothenberg, 2007). Ethnicity is rooted in a group's "history and ancestral geographical base" (Wijcyesinghe, Griffin, & Lowe, 1997, p. 88). In other words, ethnicity implies common ground among members of a group and a common heritage. Although it is worth noting that a child's concept of race is developmentally different from that of an adult's, skin color is a physical attribute that children associate with race and ethnicity. Unfortunately, children in American society learn early on that the color of one's skin influences and shapes the dynamics of interaction as well as the life opportunities of an individual. As children are socialized into society, they internalize the messages about race that are conveyed by adults within their immediate environment. Children quickly pick up messages through the language of others, the attitudes of their family members, caregivers, relatives and friends, through books and media, and from personal encounters with the real world (Harro, 1982).

Our schools are socializing agents. Through the curriculum, school structure, policies, and relationships with teachers, as well as interactions with peers and personnel, schools convey messages about race (Orfield & Lee, 2005). Our teachers are socializing agents that come in direct contact with children. Through daily encounters and social acts, teachers project their dispositions, their beliefs and their values. Our current teaching force is composed of monocultural, White and middle class teachers (Banks, 2000; Ladson-Billings, 2000; Sleeter, 1992). The National Center for Education Statistics (2004) indicates that eighty- five percent of American school teachers in K through 12 schools are White. It is an alarming contrast to the steady growth of a racially and culturally diverse student population. As of 2005, forty- two percent of the U. S. student population was comprised of children of color (National Center for Education Statistics, 2005). Rather than celebrating the growth of diversity, however, teachers seem unprepared to meet the challenges of an increasingly diverse student population. Research reveals that there is a lack of awareness among teachers about racial and cultural diversity (Garmon, 1996; Ukpokodu, 2004). Researchers stipulate that the limited experience of White teachers with individuals and groups from diverse backgrounds can be a disadvantage for children (Downey & Cobbs, 2007, Herbeck, 2003). Because of racial and cultural differences between teachers and children, there is a greater tendency on the part of the teacher to misinterpret, misunderstand, ignore, disregard, and disqualify social acts and forms of communication by children whose background is diverse, whose cultural values and worldview are different. Long before they graduate from teaching colleges and universities, preservice teachers possess biases, assumptions and prejudices toward children whose race, ethnicity, and culture are different from their own (Sleeter, 2001). These are conveyed through social acts, words, and nonverbal ways of communicating. Being in the early stages of their teacher education programs, preservice teachers are considered apprentices in teaching who develop knowledge, skills, qualities, and dispositions that are necessary to teach children (Schwebel et al., 2002). Under the guidance of teacher mentors, preservice teachers are socialized into the field of teaching. Unfortunately, however, studies reveal negative dispositions and preconceived notions about race on the part of preservice teachers toward students from diverse backgrounds (Parajes, 1991; Marx, 2006; Smith, 1998; Zimper & Ausburn, 1992). Unfortunately, such dispositions and beliefs permeate in the curriculum, the teaching and learning process, as well as in the classroom dynamics. Marx's study (2006) reveals the racial attitudes and misperceptions of White preservice teachers toward their students of color. Her study documents the tendencies of White preservice teachers to perceive themselves as saviors and models for children of color with whom they work and their tendency towards setting low expectations for children from diverse backgrounds (Marx, 2006). Studies reveal how teachers tended to underestimate the literacy abilities of their Native American students, evaluating their performance based on White ethnocentric construct (Noll, 1998). In other words, the lack of sociocultural congruence in the beliefs and dispositions between children with diverse backgrounds and their White middle class teachers can have grave implications in the teaching and learning process, the classroom dynamics, and the potential of both the learner and the teacher. If unad-

dressed, the gap between teachers and children widens, and the opportunities to have meaningful learning experiences diminish.

Because American society in the 21st century continues to become
more racially, ethnically, linguistically, and culturally diverse, educational institutions, schools, and early child care educational environments need to reexamine ways in which they can be more inclusive in
responding to the needs of a more diverse population. Being that educational environments such as public schools have opportunities to reconstruct definitions of identity and to raise children's consciousness about
race and ethnicity, it is of great value for teachers and care providers to
pay attention to children's inquiries and articulations about diversity and
difference. Children's questions and articulations are an invitation to reexamine dispositions about identity so that teachers can teach respon-
sively and develop a caring and sensitive pedagogy.

Research Question

Teachers can create inclusive and democratic classrooms by developing
an "equity pedagogy" (Banks, 1994). This entails modifying teaching "in
ways that will facilitate the academic achievement of students from diverse racial, cultural, ethnic, and gender groups" (Banks,1994,
p.14). To provide "equity pedagogy", teachers must create learning opportunities that are made accessible to all children, regardless of their
background. In doing so, teachers will acknowledge the importance of
hearing other voices, especially those of underrepresented groups and
this can be achieved through developing a pedagogy of listening. A
pedagogy of listening invites teachers to step back, reflect upon their
practice, and question the ways that they are empathetic towards the
needs of all learners (Dahlberg & Moss, 2006). This research seeks to contribute to the existing literature on social justice in the context of teacher
education by bringing children's perspectives on race at the forefront of
critical discourse. The questions that fuel this research are: What do
children's questions and articulations reveal about perceptions of skin
color? How can we create contexts that respond to children's inquiries
about diversity and difference? This chapter is an invitation for readers
to examine what children's articulations reveal about diversity and reflect upon the ways that adults, as socializing agents, play a role in helping children develop not only cultural sensitivity but more importantly,

human sensitivity. The field invites teachers to be more intentional in their practice by creating contexts that are inclusive and democratic, and by becoming change agents within their schools. One way this can be achieved is to listen to children's inquiries about diversity and difference.

Research Context, Data Collection, Analysis

This study was an attempt to capture children's questions and thought constructions about diversity and difference within a safe, familiar context: their classroom. The study emerged from a series of conversations between myself and the school's guidance counselor about multicultural awareness and diversity in the school setting. Because I wanted to provide descriptive information on the nature of children's inquiries and dispositions about race, I decided to use the constructivist research paradigm (Guba & Lincoln, 1989). The qualitative method is based on the premise that events can be better understood if they are seen in context (Bogdan & Biklen, 1982; Lincoln & Guba, 1985; Lofland & Lofland, 1984). Researchers in the constructivist paradigm build grounded theory based on the conceptual relationships constructed from data (Glaser & Straus, 1967).

The study took place in a K- 5 public school with a population of 323 children, located inan urban setting that is socio-economically, culturally, linguistically, and racially diverse. The racial diversity of student population within the school's county indicated that eighty-two percent of the students were White and the remaining eighteen percent were composed of Black, Asian, Hispanic or Latino, American Indian or Alaskan, Native Hawaiian or other Pacific Islander, and multi-racial children. Within the school, eight languages other than English was spoken by the children whose country of origin was not the United States and twenty four percent of the school population participates in the English as a Second Language (ESL) Program.

Participants in the study were children from first through fifth grade. Typical class size ranged between eighteen to twenty-five children. In total there were eleven classes that participated in the study: two sections in the fifth grade; two sections in the fourth grade; two sections in the third grade; three sections in the second grade; and two sections in the first grade. Participation of the children was in the form of class discussion under the school's Guidance Program, with the researcher serving as facilitator of the group. Under the supervision of the guidance counselor, discussions were held for thirty minutes in the children's classroom during their Guidance period. The school's guidance counselor was present throughout every class discussion. Participation in the discussion was voluntary and the children's identity was not revealed in the documentation of responses.

Because the nature of my work as a teacher educator entails observation of student interns in classrooms, the public school context was a familiar place. I was aware of the approach and philosophy of the school; its commitment to diversity as well as its efforts to build community. Since I was entering the field as a researcher, it was important for me to write field entries as I described the context observed. Field notes served as reference to help me understand the wholeness of the context and the relation of the parts to the whole. Visits to the school prior to data collection were essential as a way to become acquainted with the culturally acceptable ways of meaning within the school community.

The children had been informed by their teacher and guidance counselor that they would have a guest. I was introduced to the children as Mrs. T. After giving some background about myself, I started every class conversation by sharing a prompt: "What comes into your mind when you see a person whose skin color is different from your own?" The open-endedness of the question did not inhibit the children from responding. I wrote the children's responses in verbatim on an easel pad. I also re-read their response out loud to ensure that I was able to accurately capture their words. Children appeared to be receptive throughout the conversation and willingly shared questions and points of view.

One of the goals of the constructivist research paradigm is to richly describe and interpret social phenomena in natural settings (Schwandt, 1994). Since the main source of data in this study was children's narratives, I used qualitative content analysis (Simpson & Nist, 1997). I coded and categorized children's utterances, highlighting the patterns and themes that resonated. I also used field notes to reflect upon and challenge my interpretations of the children's utterances. Data in the form of questions, statements, and opinions emerged from discussions with children about their feelings and dispositions toward race. Children's responses were transcribed, coded, and analyzed for patterns and themes. To establish trustworthiness, research assistants reviewed and counterchecked the analysis of data. It was necessary to deliberate over terms that seemed ambiguous before finalizing the terms used for analyses. Research assistants enabled me to view data with a critical eye and enabled me to reexamine my analyses more carefully. Using the qualitative mode of analysis enabled me to examine data from various angles and enabled me to preserve the integrity of children's responses.

Children across the grades appeared to associate skin color with race, ethnicity, and culture. Among the utterances collected from the discussions with children, three distinct themes emerged: uncertainty about race, ethnicity, and culture; curiosity towards people of another race, ethnicity, and culture; and an awareness of privilege and disadvantage based on race.

Children Express Uncertainties about Race, Ethnicity and Culture

During class discussions, children expressed varying levels of awareness with regards to diversity and difference but the theme that resonated across grade levels was that of uncertainty. Children in the primary grades shared differences that they noticed in terms of physical attributes among individuals and groups of another race. They also revealed an awareness of cultural, linguistic, ethnic, and religious diversity. What follows are statements shared by the children about their perceptions of people whose skin color is different from their own.

"They might talk differently."
"If they spoke a different language, would they understand you?"
"They might wear different clothes."
"They might be from a different religion."

The responses among children in the early grades revealed tendencies to associate individuals of another race with different clothing, a different language, a different religion, and foreign attributes. The words "might," "if" and "could" emerged in statements shared by the children. An underlying theme, that of uncertainty, seemed to intersect among the children's statements as they spoke of the race, culture and ethnicity of individuals whose skin color was different from their own, viewing them as "other," apart from themselves. This implies social distance and lack of connection with individuals or groups that are different from one's own. The tendencies toward "othering" appeared to be stronger among children who have had minimal interactions with individuals of another race. This finding is consistent with what the literature reveals about the experience of children of color being seen as "other" (Copenhaver-Johnson, 2006). Just as the younger children expressed uncertainties about diversity, the older children also manifested dissonance as they expressed their opinions. In the transcript that follows, fourth graders associated skin color with race and ethnicity. Some of their peers, however, were quick to point out the diversity within their community, acknowledging that individuals and groups of a different race actually lived in their neighborhood.

Tyler:	They must not be an American.
Sean:	They must be from a different country.
Tina:	Just because their skin color is different than yours, they can still be American like you.
Trisha:	They could be from America and Vermont.
Tina:	They don't have to be in a different place.
Trisha:	They're just like everybody else.
Tina:	I just see a human being.

Children were co-constructing the image of race with their peers. Using their own schema, children were addressing their peers' uncertainties about race. In other words, children were not only *informing* each other of race; they were *transforming* each other's construct of race. Tyler and Sean's statements served as catalyst for exploratory talk among the children. Tyler appeared to make a distinction between being American and being a person of a different race. Sean, on the other hand, traced racial difference to foreign origins. It is interesting how both children, who happened to be Anglo-American, seemed to perceive racial difference as dissociated from being American. From their points of view, being American made one distinct from ethnic groups. Hurtado and Stewart (1997) have argued that "in the United States, national identity has been construed as White" (p. 305). Because of the pervasiveness of social connotations that relate to race, culture and ethnicity, children can be vulnerable to internalize racial and cultural stereotypes. For instance, through institutional and cultural socialization, children of immigrants associate Whiteness to power and privilege and being nonwhite and immigrant, to second-class citizenship (Hurtado & Stewart, 1997). Tyler and Sean's constructs, however, are challenged by Tina and Trisha. While Tina's concept of race transcends skin color, Trisha takes it further by acknowledging the existence of biracial, multiracial, bicultural and multicultural communities, thereby expanding Sean and Tyler's schema of race. The conversation revealed that older children also have uncertainties and varying levels of awareness about diversity and difference. They experience disequilibrium as their mental construct of race is challenged when in dialogue with others. As demonstrated in the conversation above, children can be a source of information to each other and are capable of correcting misconceptions of their peers about diversity and difference. Through dialogue, children worked within each other's zones and served as scaffolds for each other to bring their peers to a higher level of understanding (Bruner, 1978, Vygotsky,1978). It is interesting to note that during class discussions, children directed their responses initially to the facilitator, but as ideas were shared, children began to address their peers.

Children Have Lingering Curiosities toward Individuals of a Different Race, Ethnicity and Culture

Throughout the grade levels, children appeared to express a natural curiosity for people whose racial, ethnic, and cultural identity differed from their own. An overwhelming number of children acknowledged that there were differences among *all* of us as individuals and groups. There were also a fair number of children who named things that they had in common with others whose skin color was different, expressing a desire to find common ground; and being one with *all* human beings.

"We dress differently."
"We speak different languages."
"We have a different color skin, eyes, hair."
"We all have families."
"People are different."

The use of "we" instead of "they" reveal an interesting shift in thinking about diversity: drawing commonalities among human beings regardless of skin color, acknowledging that people are different and diverse in their own ways. It is not clear whether the perceptions of the children were influenced by their level of maturity, by the influence of their family, schooling or interactions with more diverse groups or if their beliefs were schemata that they, as individuals, constructed. Children who admitted living with and among people of a different race appeared to embrace a universal disposition, identifying common ground among individuals and groups. This supports what the research stipulates: that children who have had interracial exposure are less likely to submit to stereotyping (Wright, 1998). In contrast, children who have had limited or no opportunity to interact with individuals of a different race are more likely to internalize cultural stereotypes (Logan, 2001). The experience of children of color is different. Children of color are often associated to their racial or ethnic group (Green, 2002). Hence, early in life, race and ethnicity become salient parts of their identity. Families of children of color talk to them about race. This is particularly true of African-American families, who openly discuss race-related issues with their children (Copenhaver-Johnson, 2006; Hughes & Chen, 1997; Quintana & Vera, 1999). Being targets of stereotyping and racial bigotry, children of color are socialized about race early in life (Pinel, 1999). In contrast, Anglo-American children are not socialized by their parents about race (Quintana & Vera, 1999).

With acknowledgment of differences emerged curiosity for individuals of another race. Children shared a number of questions that reflect their desire to find common ground with someone whose racial background was different.

"Are they nice or mean?"
"Will they be afraid of you?"
"Do they like the same things?"

The questions appear to reflect how children are grappling with diversity, especially in relation to individuals or groups who are different from mainstream culture.   While children appeared excited at the prospect of interracial and cross-cultural friendships, they also shared lingering questions. Their inquiries and curiosities about individuals and groups of a different race or ethnicity can be a starting point for cultivating cultural competence. A number of children expressed how there should be no reason to treat individuals of another race differently because of skin color and acknowledged the possibility of initiating friendships. There was an overwhelming response among children across the grades in their desire to initiate friendships with individuals and groups of different racial, ethnic, and cultural background.

"I want to say 'hi' because they're like everybody else."
"They want to be a friend to us."

While some children expressed how such friendships could be a means to learn from each other they also expressed the importance of mutual respect.

"Get to know about them."
"You might learn something from a different culture."
"We'll teach them different things."

Children's articulations are fertile ground for developing cultural competence as well as cultural sensitivity. First and foremost, children need to understand that they are cultural beings and that their identity is shaped by interactions with others. Using a cultural styles approach, children can develop awareness of cultural differences while still respecting the values and beliefs that individuals or groups uphold (Gutierrez & Rogoff, 2003). "There is value in talking to children about valued practices of cultural groups rather than teaching broad generalizations" (Gutierrez & Rogoff, 2003, p.20). Gary Weaver (1986) likened culture to an iceberg; like an iceberg, culture has many layers, some of which tend to be visible, while others remain hidden from one's view. The tip of the iceberg is that part of culture which is seen and felt while that which is not visible is known as deep culture, aspects of a culture that are understood only by its members (Weaver, 1986).

Children are at the cusp of defining their concept of race, culture, and ethnicity during their elementary years. This supports the research that tells of how children's awareness of differences in skin color evolve into an understanding of race as they further refine their construct (Ramsey, 1991; Wright, 1998). Through various encounters, children internalize social understandings about race and ethnicity. Unfortunately, they also uncover racial stereotypes that are blatantly or subtly communicated through social acts and meanings. From the data, it is safe to assume that children are aware of cultural differences but the true question is how comfortable are they in relating to individuals and cultures that are different from themselves? Layers of culture include language, religion, ethnicity/nationality, and social and familial practices. In what ways do teachers nurture cross-cultural competence? In what ways can teachers strengthen children's ability to respect and acknowledge sociocultural, ethnic, and linguistic diversity? Over the years, children develop empathy and awareness of the feelings of others. Inquiring into other cultures and people of a different race is a way of exploring the meaning of diversity and difference.

Children Are Aware of Privilege and Disadvantage Based on Race

Discussions with children in the older grades reveal an awareness of privilege and disadvantage, prejudice and oppression, all of which were associated with race.

> "You shouldn't make fun of them."
> "Don't judge them by skin color."
> "Just because they're different, it doesn't mean that they can't go on the playground with you."

It is interesting to note how some children define their relationship with individuals and groups of diverse backgrounds in behavioral terms, expressing the dos and don'ts of social dynamics. At this point, it appears as though children have internalized behaviors and are socialized to act in ways that are acceptable to the members of society. It also seems as though children are aware that there are disadvantages associated with being different. The term "racist" emerged as a child was responding to the question, "What comes into your mind when you see a person whose skin color is different from your own?"

> Spencer: They might not be different from you because when people judge you by your skin color, they might think that they are bad people.
> Rachel: You mean racist. Being racist is when you insult or judge someone from a different country or skin color.
> Sam: ...and when you don't like other people of different races.
> Eli: Yeah, when you call people names because of their country or race.

From the conversation, children reveal an understanding of what it means to be prejudiced towards people of another race. Children acknowledge that racism does exist in the present times and that individuals and groups who are within the minority are in a position of disadvantage. The children seemed to be fully aware that racism is wrong as it is exclusionary and oppressive. It would be interesting to see how children's perspectives about fairness and social justice translate in their social worlds. Studies indicate how children's friendships tend to be race-oriented as early as preschool (Copenhaver-Johnson, 2006). There is also convincing evidence that reveal how children who believe in treating people of a different race in a fair and equitable manner tend to exhibit exclusionary tendencies in their social worlds (Larson & Irvine, 1999). Worth noting in this conversation is how individual children worked within each other's realm of understanding to shape their construct of race. Children who were familiar with the term "racism" expanded the awareness of peers who were still in the process of shaping their definitions of race.

In one of the fifth grade classrooms, the discussion took a different turf. Children reminisced a time in history when slavery was prevalent. Responding to the same prompt, Emma provokes a number of responses from her peers.

Emma: It reminds me of slavery, because they traded people with a different skin color and they were treated differently.

Jen: ...how bad they used to be treated.

Tunisha: They got separated from their families.

Carlos: They didn't go to the same schools.

There appeared to be a somber tone as children made their associations. There seemed to be shared knowledge among the members of this particular group about slavery, segregation, prejudice and oppression. It was noticeable how a number of children in the fourth and fifth grade classes associated race with Black History and the Civil Rights Movement. While the children acknowledged social oppression as a historical reality, there was, however, no attempt to associate the concept of oppression and slavery to the present time. The results are consistent with the literature in that while children are aware of oppression and struggle to obtain equality, they associate these actions to the past and at the same time dissociate themselves from the role of oppressor (Copenhaver-Johnson, 2006). While it is of extreme value to acknowledge introduce the concept of oppression as it relates to race, it is just as important to introduce children to the richness of culture as well as the creative arts of people of different racial and ethnic groups.

The children who participated in this study were interested in exploring the concept of racism. Since racism is a learned behavior, it can be unlearned (Ladson-Billings, 2000). Teachers can help children in their process of peeling the layers of understanding about racism by opening dialogue and encouraging children to share their inquiries about race. Children may be experiencing dissonance about discriminatory acts that they witness, experience, or initiate. When there are no opportunities to share observations, raise questions, concerns, and doubts that relate to diversity and difference, children develop uncertainties and are likely to embrace prevailing stereotypes. This poses a challenge for the field of education. In what ways are schools socializing children about race? When and where do children share their questions and opinions that pertain to race? Children's openness to share their points of view about race and to participate in dialogue with others about intersecting identities is an invitation for teachers to revisit existing curriculum and classroom practice and ways that social consciousness is fostered and social justice, embraced.

Worth noting in this study is teacher presence. Because the discussions were held during the children's Guidance period, teachers had the option to stay or to leave the classroom. Some teachers opted to stay with their homeroom class and participated as listener while I was facilitating the discussion. Others remained in the classroom but did not join our group. In two or three classes, there was no teacher present. Interestingly, children carried on the conversation without their teacher. Because there was minimal intervention from the facilitator and the guidance counselor, children took ownership for the conversation and used the constructed space to explore their understanding of race.

Limitations of the Study

This study was an attempt to bring the children's voice into the forefront of critical discourse of race and issues of social justice. It has strengths as well as limitations. First, the sample population represents the perspectives of children from one school community. While this enabled me as a researcher to become more intimately acquainted with one school community, it did not allow me to explore other school populations. The responses of the children in this study may very well reflect the views and values of their community and may differ from school communities that may be more homogenous or more diverse in its population. It is worthy to pursue a more large-scale study that does explore this. Second, since the responses drawn were within a large group, it may have excluded the perspectives of children who may not feel comfortable speaking in such a context. While the large group seemed a familiar venue for the children to engage in dialogue, it also limits children from disclosing perspectives that may not be viewed as appropriate or acceptable by members of the group. Perhaps facilitating dialogues within small groups or one-on-one encounters might change the nature of the data collected. Third, the dialogue that unfolded in various classes emerged as a response to a question. Hence, children's responses were limited to addressing the question posed by the researcher. Worth considering is modifying the approach to data collection. How different would the data be if children's narratives were collected as they were engaged in interaction with peers?

Although broad generalizations cannot be drawn from the study, the message conveyed by the data are authentic and may be a source of reference for researchers, administrators, teachers, teacher educators, care providers and families. At best, the study draws attention to the voice of young children and their inquiries into race.

Implications for Teaching Practice

Young children are aware of differences in physical attributes, one of them being skin color. This awareness of difference in skin color evolves into an understanding of race (Wright, 1998).   Based on the results of the study, children associated skin color with race, culture, and ethnicity. The responses of the children reflect uncertainty, curiosity, and acknowledgment of privilege and disadvantage based on race.

Children recognize race as part of their identity as human beings and yet there seems to be very few opportunities in the primary and elementary classrooms for them to engage in conversations that will help them find meaning in recognizing this part of their identity. With little or no opportunity to unlock what race means, children experience dissonance and are unable to articulate and validate their working construct of race. Their lack of understanding of race makes them vulnerable to conform with social acts that promote discrimination and prejudice. There is an unsettling difference between the socialization of children of color and their Anglo-American counterparts. While children of color are socialized by their families about race and ethnicity early in life, their Anglo-American peers seem to have limited or no opportunity to uncover race and ethnicity (Quintana & Vera, 1999). There also seems to be some tension as children of color grapple with issues that directly affect their identity and what it means to retain one's multicultural identity while their Anglo-American peers seem to be distanced, albeit far removed from race-related issues. Teachers do children a disservice when tensions such as those mentioned above are unaddressed. Teachers play a key role in creating a climate of inquiry, a space that will welcome children's observations as well as questions; a space that will encourage peers to co-construct emerging understandings about intersecting identities.

Children's understanding of race is an amalgam of messages conveyed by members of the growing child's environment and their personal construction of race. Analysis of the qualitative data reveals curiosity on the part of many children to know more about race, ethnicity, and culture. This summons teachers to create opportunities that celebrate diversity and acknowledge multicultural identity. For children to fully understand culture, they must first see themselves as multicultural beings. Teachers can further strengthen partnerships with families as a way to open conversations about culture. Immigrant, biracial and multiracial families can co-construct curriculum and co-facilitate dialogue that will widen children's understanding of diversity and deepen their understanding of social justice. Families can inform as well as enrich classroom curriculum and co-create spaces in the classroom that value every child's culture.

When children in this study associated race with privilege and disadvantage, they were making visible their awareness of racism and other forms of social oppression. Their observations are potential starting points for critical dialogue into race. When children's questions can find no room in the classroom curriculum and their ideas about race are silenced, it is easy for them to assume that race-related issues are unimportant and that racism is a natural part of life. When discriminatory acts such as racial bigotry and prejudice are unquestioned, we raise a generation of citizens who are numb to the realities that are experienced by underrepresented groups, who are content in keeping things the way they are. When we allow this to happen, children will be deprived of opportunities to raise their consciousness about race, to acknowledge each other as multicultural beings, and to strengthen cultural competence. It will be to the disadvantage of our society to silence issues that relate to social injustices. This is a golden opportunity to educate children with more intentionality and with a firm commitment to social justice.

Teachers can be change agents. They can open doors of possibilities and build bridges that will emancipate generations of children from a state of not knowing. Teachers can make visible real dilemmas that abound within communities and challenge children to engage in dialogue that promotes critical inquiry into identity. Because teachers play a crucial role in the education of young children, there is a critical need for them to engage in introspection and to challenge their current practice. To create a climate of respect and appreciation for diversity, teachers need to consider how their environment reflects the culture of the children that they teach as well as opportunities that enable children to express themselves as cultural beings (Tolentino, 2007). Part of the process of introspection is critically questioning one's pedagogy and questioning one's influence in shaping the dynamics of classroom interactions. Teachers can question the ways that they tend to be inclusive or exclusionary. In doing so, teachers become aware of voices that are silenced and stories that remain unheard. In order to develop a caring and sensitive pedagogy, teachers need to create spaces in their classroom that will invite diverse ways of meaning making and celebrate difference (Tolentino, 2007). Becoming change agents demands transformation within. Self-reflection and critical questioning of one's practice can be the first steps.

Conclusion

Creating a climate of that embraces social justice requires teachers to reconstruct their approach to teaching; reframe their research questions, and become more intimately connected with the children that they teach. Working within this revolutionary context demands a change in the roles of teachers and teacher educators, a shift in ways of thinking about teaching, and an intentional approach to creating contexts that invite inquiry and honor diversity. John Mayher, one of the greatest scholars of our time expressed his vision of teacher education:

> "If teacher education has a single theme, it is that schools must be dramatically changed if they are to fulfill their educational mission in a democratic society. Teachers are the only people who have the power, the commitment, the desire, and the capacity to be leaders in the process of change. But to take on such leadership roles, we must substantially change our conceptions of the nature and processes of schooling. Doing so will not be easy, since these conceptions have not been the subject of professional scrutiny and analysis. Questioning such assumptions requires both examining and reinterpreting the meaning of our learning experiences in and out of school by looking at them through new theoretical lenses" (1990, p. 119).

Questioning happens now, within classrooms, among students, in partnership with schools and communities. Teacher education can be liberating as well as transformative, responsive to the needs of a growing diverse population. Listening to children is the first step towards achieving social justice.

"So how does it feel to have your skin color?" the child asked me once more. I looked at her with fondness and said, "I don't feel so different. The only time I do feel different is when people treat me differently because of the color of my skin." The child smiled apparently satisfied with the response I had given her. Deep inside, it felt good that she asked this question. In doing so, she created a space to construct and build upon her working definition of race. As adults, children's questions about race, ethnicity, and culture remain invisible until we create a space within our environments for them to articulate their inquiries and to explore their working theories of race. The children are listening. How are we, as members of society, responding to children's questions about diversity and difference?

Bibliography

Banks, J. A. (1994). *Multiethnic education: Theory and practice* (3rd ed.). Needham Heights, MA: Allyn & Bacon.

Banks, J. A. (2000). *Cultural diversity and education: Foundations, curriculum, and teaching.* Boston, MA: Allyn & Bacon.

Bogdan, R. C. & Biklen, S. K. (1982). *Qualitative research for education: An introduction to theory and methods.* Boston, MA: Allyn & Bacon.

Bruner, J. S. (1978). The role of dialogue in language acquisition. In A. Sinclair, R. J.,Jarvelle, & W. J. M. Levelt (Eds.); *The child's concept of language.* New York: Springer-Verlag.

Copenhaver-Johnson, J. (Fall, 2006). Talking to children about race: The importance of inviting difficult conversations. *Childhood Education, vol. 83, no.* 1 pp \. 44-49.

Dalberg, G. & Moss, P. (2006). Introduction: Our Reggio Emilia. In Rinaldi, C. (Ed.) *In Dialogue with Reggio Emilia: Listening, researching and learning.* New York, NY: Routledge.

Downey, J. A. & Cobbs, G. A. (January, 2007). "I actually learned a lot from this": A field assignment to prepare future preservice math teachers for culturally diverse classrooms. *School Science and Mathematics, vol. 107, no.* 1 pp. 24-60.

Frankenberg, R. (1994). Whiteness and Americanness: Examining constructions of race, culture, and nation in White women's life narratives. In S. Gregory, & R. Sanjek (Eds.), *Race* (pp. 62-77). New Brunswick, NJ: Rutgers University Press.

Freire, P. & Macedo, D. (Fall, 1995). A dialogue: Culture, language, and race. *Harvard Educational Review, v. 65,* n. 3, pp. 377-402.

Garmon, M. A. (April ,1996). *Missed messages: How prospective teachers' racial attitudes mediate what they learn about diversity.* Paper presented at the annual meeting of the American Educational Research Association, New York.

Glaser, B. & Strauss, A. L. (1967). *The discovery of grounded theory: Strategies for qualitative research.* Chicago: Aldine.

Green, M. R. (May, 2002). *Maiming the spirit: The journey of Brown children through White Schools.* Master's thesis, University of Vermont.

Guba. E & Lincoln Y. (1989). *Fourth generation evaluation.* Newbury Park, CA: Sage Publications.

Gutierrez, K. D. & Rogoff, B. (June/July, 2003). Cultural ways of learning: Individual traits or repertoires of practice. *Educational Researcher, vol. 32, no.* 5, pp. 19-25.

Harro, B. (1982). *Cycle of Socialization.* Amherst, MA: Diversity Works.

Herbeck, J. (Winter, 2003). Awakening preservice teachers' awareness of privilege. *Academic Exchange Quarterly,* vol. 8. pp. 189-193.

Hughes, D. & Chen, L. (1997). When and what parents tell children about race: An Examination of race-related socialization among African-American families. *Applied Developmental Science, vol. 1,* pp. 200-214.

Hurtado, A. & Stewart, A. J. (1997). Through the looking glass: Implications of studying Whiteness for feminist methods. In M. Fine, L. Weis, L. C. Powell, & L. M. Wong (Eds.) *Off white: Readings on race, power, and societ;.* London and New York: Routledge,(pp. 297-311).

Ladson-Billings, G. (2000). Preparing teachers for diversity: Historical perspectives, current trends, and future directions. In L. Darling-Hammond & G. Sykes (Eds.) *Teaching as the learning profession: Handbook of policy and practice.* pp. 86-87. San Francisco, CA: Jossey-Bass.

Larson, J. & Irvine, P. D. (1999). "We call him Dr. King": Reciprocal distancing in urban classrooms. *Language Arts, vol. 76,* pp. 393-403.

Lincoln , Y. & Guba, E. (1985). *Naturalistic inquiry.* Beverly Hills, CA: Sage.

Lofland, J. & Lofland, L. H. (1984). *Analyzing social settings: A guide to qualitative observation and analysis.* Belmont, CA: Wadsworth.

Logan, J. (2001, April 3). *Ethnic diversity grows, neighborhood integration lags.* Presented at The National Press Club. New York.

Marx, S. (2006). *Revealing the invisible: Confronting passive racism in teacher education.*New York, NY: Routledge.

Mayher, J. S. (1990). *Uncommon sense: Theoretical perspective in language education.*Portsmouth, NH: Heinemann.

National Center for Education Statistics (2005). The condition of education 2005. Indicator 4. Racial/ethnic distribution of public school students. Retrieved August 25, 2007 from http://nces.ed.gov/programs/coe/2005/section1/indicator04.asp.

Noll, E. (1998). *Experiencing literacy in and out of school: Case studies of two American Indian youth. Journal of Literary Research,* vol. 30, no. 2, pp. 205-232.

Orfield, G. & Lee, C. (2005). *Why segregation matters: Poverty and educational inequality.*The Civil Rights Project at Harvard University. Cambridge, MA: Harvard University.

Parajes, F. (Fall, 1991). *Teachers' beliefs and education research: Cleaning up a messy construct. Review of Educational Research.* Vol. 62, no.3

Pinel, E. (1999). Stigma consciousness: The psychological legacy of stereotypes. *Jour nal of Personality and Social Psychology, vol. 76,* no. 1, pp. 114-128.

Quintana, S. M. & Vera, E. M. (1999). Mexican-American children's ethnic identity, understanding of ethnic prejudice, and parental ethnic socialization. *Hispanic Journal of Behavioral Sciences, vol. 21,* no. 4, pp. 387-404.

Ramsey. (1991). The salience of race in young children growing up in an all-White community. *Journal of Educational Psychology, vol.83, no 1. pp 28-34.*

Rothenberg, P. (2007). *Race, class, and gender in the United States: An integrated study.* New York, NY: Worth Publishers.

Schwandt, T. A.(1994). Constructivist, interpretivist approaches to human inquiry. In N. Denzin, and Y. Lincoln, (Eds.). *Handbook of qualitative research.* (pp. 118-137) Thousand Oaks, CA: Sage Publications.

Schwebel, S. L., Schwebel, D. C., Schwebel, B. L., & Schwebel, C. R. (2002). *The student teacher's handbook.* Mahwah, NJ: Lawrence Erlbaum Associates.

Simpson, M. L. & Nist, S. L. (1997). Perspectives on learning history: A case study. *Journal of Literacy Research, vol. 29,* no. 3, pp. 353-396.

Sleeter, C. E. (2001). Preparing teachers for culturally diverse schools: Research and the overwhelming presence of whiteness. *Journal of Teacher Education, V. 52,* pp. 94-106.

Sleeter, C. E. (1992). *Keepers of the American dream: A study of staff development and Multicultural education.* Washington, D. C.: Falmer Press.

Smith, P. G. (Spring, 1998). Who shall have the moral courage to heal racism? *Multicultural Education, v. 5,* n. 3, pp. 4-10.

Tolentino, E. P. (July, 2007*). Why do you like this page so much?*: Exploring the potential of talk during preschool reading activities. *Language Arts, vol. 84,* n. 6, pp. 519-528.

Ukpokodu, N. O. (Winter, 2004). The impact of shadowing culturally different students on preservice teachers' disposition toward diversity. *Multicultural Education, vol. 12,* n. 2, pp. 19-28.

Vygotsky, L. S. (1978). *Mind in society: The development of psychological processes.* Cambridge, MA: Harvard University Press.

Weaver, G. R. (1986). Understanding and coping with cross-cultural adjustment stress. In R. M. Paige (Ed.).. *Cross cultural orientation: New conceptualizations and applications.* pp. 23-36Lanham, M.D.: University Press of America.

Wells, G. (1987). *The meaning makers: Children learning in language and using language to learn.* Portsmouth, NH: Heinemann.

Weis, L., Fine, M..Weseen, S. & Wong, M. (2000). Qualitative research, representations, and social responsibilities. In L. Weis & M. Fine (Eds.). *Speed bumps: A student's friendly guide to qualitative research.* pp. 32-66. NY: Teachers College Press.

Wijeyesinghe, C. L., Griffin, P. & Love, B. (1997). Racism curriculum design. In Adams, M., Bell, L. A. & Griffin, P. (Eds.), *Teaching for diversity and social justice: A sourcebook.* New York, NY: Routledge, (pp. 82-109).

Wright, M. A. (1998). *I'm chocolate, you're vanilla: Raising healthy Black children in a race-conscious world.* San Francisco, CA: Jossey-Bass.

Zimpher, N. I. & Ashborn, E. A. (1992). *Countering parochialism in teacher education: New expectations.* San Francisco, CA: Jossey-Bass.

TEACHING ABOUT RELIGION IN RELIGIOUSLY PLURALISTIC CONTEXTS

Sensitivity, Academic Rigor, and Justice

Jeffrey A. Trumbower

The academic field of Religious Studies in Western universities is a relatively recent phenomenon. It evolved largely from theological and seminary studies, and its earliest practitioners were usually people who had been trained in those realms, but who wanted to expand their horizons into a non-confessional approach to the study of religion. In more recent decades it has become common to find religion scholars, even at church-related institutions, who have had a thoroughly secular training. Some academics have questioned the validity of religious studies as a separate field, saying it is nothing more than a branch of cultural anthropology that focuses on religious phenomena; any claims for distinctiveness are merely vestiges of an outmoded theological paradigm (Fitzgerald, 2003). Even if one sees some merit in this point, the current scene has been shaped by the history, and religious studies departments thrive throughout North America, attracting students and faculty who want to focus on religious phenomena from a variety of perspectives: literary, political, historical, economic, aesthetic, philosophical, sociological, psychological, as well as theological. In Europe one is more likely to encounter faculties of Protestant or Catholic Theology, even at state-run institutions, but most of the scholars in these faculties are indistinguishable in method and sensibility from their U.S. or Canadian counterparts in religious studies departments. As witnessed by the variety of approaches enumerated above, the academic study of religion is inherently interdisciplinary, and is increasingly relevant to a world where many of the current conflicts have at least some basis in religion. Increased understanding of religion in all its manifestations is crucial for charting our way towards constructive engagement with one another and perhaps even our survival as a species.

The study of religion is of particular value to any curriculum that has as its aim the fostering of global social justice. A surprising number of enduring religious movements have sprung from the experience of oppression and injustice, so grappling with these traditions is a great benefit to those who might wish to prevent future injustice while understanding the resilient human spirit. One example is the Jewish apocalyptic tradition, born out of the experience of loss of sovereignty, homeland, and independence in the sixth to the second centuries B.C.E. That apocalyptic tradition eventually gave rise to a group of Jewish sectarians who believed that God was fulfilling ancient promises of restorative justice in their own day, namely, the early Christians. Other examples of religions that criticize an unjust status quo would include the famous "cargo cults" of the Pacific region and the Native American "Ghost Dance" traditions (see Trompf, 1990). In addition, since religions, sometimes even the ones born from injustice, are so often used to *promote* injustice, understanding that side of the equation is essential as well. Religion can serve to justify and reify oppressive structures as well as tear them down, and anyone who wishes to challenge those structures needs a thorough understanding of their religious aspects.

Students and faculty therefore find themselves in religious studies courses at the college level in the West (or in a Western-inspired curriculum anywhere in the world), but then what? How can the academic study of religion be undertaken to prepare students for global social justice? It would certainly be easy to design a religious studies curriculum that had the opposite aim. One can imagine a course of study that triumphantly proclaims the superiority of one particular religion while denigrating all others, emphasizes the need to bring the entire world under its thumb, and disallows critical inquiry. These are characteristics found in a great number of Christian and Muslim curricula today, and they were typical of the religious aspects of colonialist and imperialist educations of the past. Another type of curriculum that might foster injustice would be one that has as its aim the destruction of all religious belief or sentiment, or that treats all existential religious questions and answers as ridiculous or absurd. Such attitudes toward religion have been characteristic of the education found in Marxist/Leninist societies, and unfortunately are also sometimes found in Western secular education. It's one thing to study a particular religion or atheism, it's another thing to require either one as the only stance acceptable for a student or faculty member to adopt.

For the rest of this chapter I will outline what it means to chart a pedagogical course between these two poles of religious profession on the one hand and denigration of religion on the other. In my view, such a "middle way" of teaching religion is the most conducive to preparing students for global social justice, since to work for lasting justice they will need to relate to a wide variety of religious persons and approach public policy as citizens who understand religious claims and value systems. My remarks will focus only on the teaching of undergraduates at both secular and church-related institutions, because the foundational undergraduate experience should always be one of open inquiry and unmasking of presuppositions. My remarks would not apply to graduate seminary education or theological training, since those students have made a professional and confessional commitment to a particular religious tradition, and their education should appropriately reflect that choice.

The first step towards the sort of religious studies pedagogy I am advocating is an honest religious self-assessment on the part of the professor. This is not something that can be done once and for all time, since our religious outlooks are constantly evolving. A professor can be a committed Christian, practicing Buddhist, questing agnostic, convinced atheist, believing Muslim, a combination of these or anything in between and still approach an undergraduate classroom in a non-confessional way. This takes a great deal of work, however, and it is never easy. One's presuppositions always shine through in readings selected, assignments crafted, and offhand comments made to students. Often the students will want to know the instructor's religious stance right away, and for some academics such an initial self-disclosure may be valuable, but I have always found it better to wait until the end of the semester to self-disclose, if then. If students have trouble figuring me out along the way, or guess wrongly, I consider my teaching a success, since I do not want them to treat me as an oracle who has all the answers or as a model for easy emulation.

Once the professor has a good sense of his or her own religious stance, the next step is to try to mask it for a time, for pedagogical purposes. This is as true for the atheist as it is for the believer. We professors must allow ourselves to empathize deeply with our objects of study, and we should always devote some portion of our syllabus to the study of those with whom we disagree In this way, the class will be more likely to develop a spirit of true inquiry rather than indoctrination into the professor's views. This process will help to foster the religious sensitivity necessary for deeper understanding.

There are limits to this religious sensitivity, and the knottiest part of the religion scholar's job is to be sensitive to religious belief and to avoid alienating religious students while at the same time upholding academic rigor. In my years of teaching I have encountered fundamentalist Protestants who thought the Bible was inerrant, docile Catholics who did not want to question authority, Mormons who had never heard any challenges to their faith, atheists who thought all talk about religion was a waste of time, and committed Muslims from abroad who were shocked by the open inquiry about religious matters in an American classroom. If each of these students had had his or her way as expressed at the beginning of the semester, there would have been little to discuss or study during the term. Thus, when sensitivity and academic rigor are in conflict, as they often are, it is the sensitivity to religious belief that must be sacrificed in order to maintain the integrity of the academic program, but done in such a way that draws students in rather than freezing them out. I have found that it is always more effective if the students come to their own challenging conclusions based on primary evidence rather than having someone else pronounce those conclusions for them in a lecture or reading assignment. For this reason, I emphasize the reading of primary texts, while I use textbooks and secondary articles only sparingly. The typical North American undergraduate classroom is a diverse stew of religious backgrounds, beliefs, and opinions. The academic study of religion, if done correctly, is always upsetting to traditional believers of all stripes, no matter the religion, though some religious traditions have historically been more malleable and open to challenge than others. At the same time, many students are predisposed to think that religious questions and claims are always absurd. It is never easy for the professor to navigate through this minefield, especially if the goal is to prepare students for global social justice, which requires a world where religion is given the space to meet the real needs of people without aggressively dominating others or creating injustice.

How does the combination of sensitivity and academic rigor work in practice? I can only speak from my own experience and my observations of colleagues. I have been teaching biblical studies, early Christianity, and ancient Judaism at a Roman Catholic college for 19 years, and in 2005 I was named the academic Dean of that college. My graduate training in religious studies was thoroughly secular, though I was raised in the Episcopal Church and became a Unitarian Universalist well into my teaching career. I take it as a badge of honor that my students often think that I am Jewish, since I seem to know a lot about the Jewish tradition. My teaching has evolved, like that of most of my colleagues, from a lecture/testing format to a combination of interruptible lecture, interactive assignments, directed discussion, group projects, and other forms of active learning. I have had the luxury of fairly small classes (15-30 students) at my medium-sized college (about 2,000 students) to experiment with teaching techniques. My students come from a variety of religious backgrounds, with a slight majority at least nominally Catholic, but the one overriding cultural fact is that the college is located in New England, surely the most secular region of the country. I was raised and attended college in the South, went to graduate school in the Midwest, studied in Europe, and taught religious studies for a semester in central Mexico, so I know that academic discussion of contentious religious issues takes on a very different character depending on the cultural context.

A few concrete examples will serve to illustrate what I mean about treading the line in the classroom between religious sensitivity and academic rigor. Take the example of teaching the Hebrew Bible prophets like Jeremiah or Isaiah, people who were certain that Yahweh, the god of Israel, was speaking to them and giving them divine insight into human affairs. Inevitably the question arises in class, was God really speaking to these prophets? That question becomes especially acute when the students read texts in translation from other ancient cultures like Mari in Syria or Moab right next to Israel, who also had prophets and kings claiming to receive messages from their respective gods. And if that weren't enough, the Bible itself is full of accounts about Israelite prophets whom the biblical authors considered "false" because they were on the wrong side of some religious or political divide. They, too, claimed to be receiving messages from Yahweh. Well, the students want to know, what's the *real* story? Were the canonical prophets really the "true" ones and these other ones "false?" I never answer that question in class. Some Jewish, Christian, or Muslim theologians might think that such questions either shouldn't be raised or should be glibly answered in favor of the canonical prophets. Some secular skeptics think the question is easily settled since talk about God's activity in this or any other context is meaningless.

One biblical author wrestled with a version of this question, and the best he could come up with was to say, in effect, you can only tell from hindsight whether a Yahweh prophet is true or false (Deuteronomy 18:20-22). But I prefer to put it in the following way that I've found draws in both the ardent believers and committed skeptics among my students: it may be that God was speaking to or inspiring those human beings, either the "true" prophets or the "false" ones, or perhaps even both (1 Kings 22!), but if he was, he was doing so in the midst of all the messiness of human life, and that has to be understood first. I don't pretend to teach the students about what God was doing, but rather, I insist that they try to understand the social, economic, political, literary, psychological, and religious factors that help us to account for the texts and other artifacts in front of us. This approach neither excludes God nor does it necessitate him, and I think this is the appropriate stance to take in any sort of religious studies class for undergraduates, whether at a religious school or a secular one, whether the subject is one of the monotheisms or any other religious system.

Another anecdote will help illustrate this point even further. Once in a New Testament class we were studying the Gospel of John and its claim that Jesus is the embodiment of the eternal Logos—the "Word" that is somehow both with God and God at the same time. A student raised his hand and asked, "Well how do we know this isn't just some guy's theory?" What a great question! My response was: we *do* know that it was some guy's (or gal's) theory, a theory shared by others but not all others in early Christian circles. As such, it can be analyzed for the influences that led to it, the impacts it had, and the controversies it generated. But the key word in his question was the word "just," as in "*just* some guy's theory." That I can't answer. Maybe God had a hand in inspiring this theory because it is true at some metaphysical level—I can neither prove nor disprove that by studying the texts. Similarly, maybe God was responsible for calling the prophet Muhammad and delivering to him his message for the sake of humanity. I can neither prove nor disprove that claim by studying the Qur'an and the Hadith. Perhaps a divine spirit truly comes to inhabit the Haitian participant in a Voodoo ceremony; I do not limit the possibility of divine inspiration only to the worldwide, multi-ethnic, institutional religions. My interest is in understanding these phenomena in all their complexity as products of human experience. But they may not be reducible merely to human experience; the divine may be working in us and through us. Again, this approach neither excludes God or the divine realm nor does it necessitate them.

Admittedly, in these classroom episodes it was fairly easy to hew a middle ground, because divine inspiration for long-dead prophets, the metaphysical relationship between Jesus and God, or the workings of the divine in the life of an individual mystic are not things that can be either proved or disproved. But some religious claims do fall into that category, and in those cases, academic rigor must win the day. No amount of desire to be sensitive to religious beliefs can allow a scholar to give credence to the notions of creationism, intelligent design, or, for example, the Book of Mormon's claims about North American history, since all of these are easily disproved. "Theories" such as these are fascinating for students of religion to investigate how, when, and why they arose, but one does not serve the cause of global social justice by giving them even lip service as possible true explanations of reality. What I'm really talking about here is the useful distinction between science and theology as separate spheres: on one hand, there are certain questions of value and ultimate meaning that neither science nor the study of history can answer, and on the other hand, theologians cannot make pronouncements about a scientific or historical matter simply because some sacred text or tradition says it is so. One *can* say that the stories of Genesis 1-11 or the Book of Mormon's narrative shed light in some deep way about the nature of humanity and God, ethical principles, or our relationship to God, as long as such insights do not stand or fall on the historicity of the events depicted. As *literature* they may be divinely inspired (or not), but they certainly are not accurate history or science. Some sacred texts of the world's religions do provide some fairly accurate historical data, but that's different from claiming that they are necessarily accurate because they are sacred.

In both secular and church-related higher education, where the church-related school wishes to participate in the mainstream of academic life, scholars must be interested in the honest search for truth. And if it is to be a real search and not a sham, it means that no question can be suppressed, no evidence ignored, and one cannot begin one's investigation with the conviction that the results have already been revealed. That's the way Nazi and Soviet science operated, that's the starting point for many fundamentalist Christian universities, and that's the way some of the madrassas of western Pakistan operate. Going down that road in the academy is hardly a recipe for global social justice. The culture of a mainstream religious college like my own may be distinctive in terms of its course requirements, openness to religious expression, campus ministry, parietals, and other aspects of college life. But if a religious school is to avoid narrow sectarianism, its academic study of religion needs to be as free and open as that found in secular universities. And if secular schools are to avoid unjust treatment of the religious students in their midst, they need to avoid the ridicule and uncritical disparagement of religion so often heard in academic circles.

The socially just religious studies classroom, one that is preparing students for global social justice, will have a number of features: respect for religious sensitivities when possible, combined with relentless rigor in understanding the context of religious claims, with students working with primary materials in order to draw critical conclusions on their own. Preparation for global social justice also requires that students of religion learn how to make sober, reflective, thoughtful value judgments about their object of study. In most cases it will be possible and even preferable to adopt a "live and let live" approach with a variety of religious and other cultural phenomena—it certainly does not serve the cause of global social justice to insist that the "other" must always be transformed into oneself. We should never advocate the arrogant, rapacious colonial attitudes that have been the wellspring of so many of the world's current troubles. In fact, in many cases students of religion will learn surprising new things about their own cultural/religious heritage or about those of others and wish to adopt or incorporate a new belief or practice into their own lives. But at other times a preparation for global social justice will demand that a value judgment be made and certain beliefs or practices decried. To cite the most obvious example, one cannot be a feminist and a cultural relativist at the same time. Either there are minimum universal standards for the dignity and rights of all people, including women, or there are not, and when that dignity is trampled in the name of religion or some long-standing cultural practice, it is incumbent upon students of religion to speak out from both secular and opposing religious viewpoints. An example of this sort of approach may be found in the writings of Ayaan Hirsi Ali (2006, pp. 60-63) who, though at times painting Islam and Muslims with too broad a brush, is one of the clearest contemporary voices warning about the dangers of uncritical multiculturalism. But while developing a critical perspective, it is also important to recognize that no religious tradition is monolithic or unchanging, and this is especially true of large, multi-ethnic, worldwide movements like Christianity, Islam and Buddhism. Therefore, resources for self-critical analysis and the promotion of social justice can almost always be found from within these traditions, in addition to whatever valid criticisms might come in from the outside.

Some religious beliefs and practices have had pernicious effects, and this harsh reality always arises in the classroom whether one is studying the past or the contemporary scene. Other religious beliefs and practices have advanced and continue to advance the cause of social justice. There will always be debate about which beliefs and practices ought to be criticized, which should be praised, and which should invite indifference, but the notion of a value-neutral education is perverse; we are training the next generation to be human beings engaged with the world, not merely walking encyclopedias of information. Value judgments must be carefully considered and not rash, informed by a genuine attempt at deep understanding and empathy, but we should not pretend that they can be avoided or that they are somehow undesirable.

Implementing the practices I have described is no guarantee of success. There will always be students (and faculty) who will resist a critical study of their own religion, who will not be willing to engage critically with a culture distant from them in time, space or worldview, or who will mock and scoff at all religious people for their supposed simple-mindedness. But I have found most students whom I encounter are open to the combination of approaches described here, and if such training leads some of them toward a life of working for global social justice, this will be one among many ways that the academic study of religion has demonstrated its extraordinary value.

Bibliography

Fitzgerald, T. (2003). *The Ideology of Religious Studies.* New York: Oxford.

Hirsi Ali, A. (2006). *The Caged Virgin: An Emancipation Proclamation for Women and Islam.* New York: The Free Press.

Trompf, G. W. (1990). *Cargo Cults and Millenarian Movements.* Berlin and New York: Mouton de Gruyter.

THE USE OF THE INTERNET TO PROMOTE SOCIAL JUSTICE WITH LGBT INDIVIDUALS

Andrew Quinn and Bruce Reeves

Lesbian, gay, bisexual and transgender (LGBT) persons continuously fight for equality and freedom from discrimination and violence in both urban and rural pockets in the United States. In urban centers, while discrimination exists, given the population density of the urban centers LGBT individuals can find support comfortably and acceptance. However, the case is different for those living in rural areas. Rural is defined as places with less than 2,500 people (US Census Bureau, 1995). Rural areas are also defined as "not in places" (US Census Bureau, 1995). These population areas can be larger than 2,500 people but are remote pockets that are extensions of urban centers. Rural communities tend to center on a tight reliance on church and family (Lindhorst, 1997). Given this reliance, rural communities often urged conformity, thus making non-acceptance an issue (Foster, 1997). Due to this, LGBT individuals are often ostracized in the name of religion and seen as living outside the will of God (Smith, 1997). The beliefs of the church can reinforce beliefs that support homophobia (Lindhorst, 1997). In addition, rural pockets tend to provide a source of cohesion between families and the community (Lindhorst, 1997). This sense of cohesion supports closeness to traditions and supportive systems within the community. Recently, the *Washington Post* reported that census data indicated more LGBT individuals are living in rural areas (Lynsen, 2007). However, some LGBT individuals, despite the fact that they want to live in rural areas, are fearful of being labeled and stereotyped and continue to fight conformity to the dogma of rural life (Lindhorst, 1997). The non acceptance that can be present in rural communities leads to social isolation for LGBT individuals living in a rural community (Smith, 1997). In order to find like minded individuals, the LGBT person often has to go some distance for social contacts with people like, or sympathetic to themselves. Unlike urban areas where there are connections; the rural community can lack connections further perpetrating isolation.

The oppression and isolation experienced by LGBT individuals leads to a lack of social justice for this population. The idea of social justice is that all citizens, no matter their background and preferences, should be allowed identical rights, protections, opportunities, obligations, and social benefits (Baker, 1991). The human service industry is a group of professionals whose mandates include the promotion of social justice. Human service workers, include, but not limited to, individuals whose professional practice focuses on education, health, housing, employment training, and personal social services (Kahn, 1977). The human service worker can come in the form of the doctor, the teacher, the psychologist, and social worker. In rural communities it is the responsibility of the human service worker to promote social justice. Often times, LGBT individuals, due to the isolation and oppression, will seek solace by seeing a human service professional for support. In fact, using the support of a human service worker can be a healthy intervention for combating feelings of oppression. Furthermore, such support can help normalize the issues experienced by the LGBT living in the rural community (Lindhorst, 1997).

The purpose of this chapter is twofold. First is to discuss how the Internet can be used to promote social justice. Second is to demonstrate how the human service professional can help the LGBT client become aware of, assess, and evaluate the use of the Internet to promote the goals of social justice.

Promoting Social Justice with the Internet

The human service worker can assist with fostering the tenets of social justice with their LGBT clients. In fact, one way to do so is to use the Internet (Lindhorst, 1997; Hagg & Chang, 1997; Meha, Merkel, & Bishop, 2004). The Internet can provide a forum so oppressed individuals can gain access to educational information, peers to talk to, and a forum in which they can meet and discuss and find solidarity in their communications. Human service practitioners who see LGBT clients can encourage them to use the Internet so that they can gain access to information, therapeutic advice, and social support systems that involve the collaboration of ideas, concerns, and joys with other LGBT individuals. In fact, human service workers in their professional practice can rely on the Internet as an agent of change while promoting the dogma of social justice. Ultimately, the Internet is a platform for communication and knowledge dissemination where all individuals regardless of location, race, social standing, sexual orientation, religion, and economic standing can have equal access to the dissemination of information (Fitchter & Martin, 1997).

The Internet allows LGBT individuals living in rural communities the opportunity to gain access to information and other individuals when such opportunities are not physically possible in a closed rural systems. In fact, many LGBT individuals have been turning to the Internet to seek out information and contact with other LGBT individuals (Lindhorst, 1997).

The rural human service worker who uses the Internet to promote social justice is doing so by the fact that they are able to assist the LGBT clients in finding vital information about health care, partners, lifestyle, friends, and news. There are various sites designed to provide information to LGBT individuals. Examples include GayHealth (http://www.gayhealth.com) which provides medical and health information for the LGBT community, http://glaad.org or Gay and Lesbians Alliance Against Defamation which consists of publications and news releases that focus on LGTB issues, the Human Rights Campaign located at http://hrc.org which presents information focused on obtaining equal rights for LGBT individuals, and the National Gay and Lesbian Task Force located at http://thetaskforce.org which provides information related to LGBT persons along with suggestions for becoming activists.

In addition, the LGBT individual is assisted in finding a safe space in which self expression, in concert with others, can be accomplished, typically, without fear of reprisal. In fact, LGBT individuals can seek out various Internet technologies (text chat, audio/video chat, discussion groups, and forums) to communicate with likeminded individuals. For example, Meha, Merkel, & Bishop (2004) describe an electronic mailing list (listserv) dedicated to LGBT topics. Topics discussed included barriers faced by LGBT individuals while trying to seek information, support, and resources, and actions the LGBT mail list members can take to build a better community. The discussion on the list was focused in several areas including the organization of a LGBT event, how the LGBT community can communicate with the heterosexual community on subjects such as inappropriate outings of LGBT individuals, and providing psychological and social support to them and closeted members of the listserv community. Overall, the list provided LGBT members a place to socialize and bond with each other. The tenets of social justice, in this case, were accomplished by way of the listserv by giving the LGBT individual a chance to obtain support and opportunities that sometimes are not available to the rural LGBT community.

Chat rooms are also a resource for promoting social justice among LGBT. Chat rooms are virtual meeting spaces where individuals can talk online in real time. Chat rooms tend to be thematic where individuals gather under a common umbrella. They do so in the guise of privacy where expression is uncensored. Social justice is accomplished via chat rooms by affording the LGBT individual protection by allowing free expression without fear of reprisal. In fact, as early as 1997, many Internet service providers have chat rooms so that LGBT individuals can communicate (Lindhorst, 1997). A current search of the words "chat room gay" with Google's search engine turned up a plethora of opportunities.

With the Internet, LGBT individuals can explore their feelings about their same-sex attractions with others who have similar feelings or they can use the Internet to mitigate feelings of isolation caused by oppression (Shernoff, 2006). The Internet also allows the rural individual a chance to seek out information when feeling isolated and or oppressed.

One important feature of the Internet is the ability for the LGBT individual to remain anonymous (Haag & Chang, 1997). Thus a LGBT individual living in the rural community can protect their identity and remove some of the isolation they experience. Furthermore, the ability to remain anonymous can allow the LGBT individual who is thinking of coming out to practice by communicating with others without fear of being discovered. In fact, the coming out process might be made easier for rural people by providing a shield until they are comfortable being open (Haag & Chang, 1997). By remaining anonymous the LGBT individual is afforded opportunities, which in turn further promotes the Internet as an agent of social justice.

While the Internet is thriving with opportunities for promoting social justice for the LGBT individuals, using the Internet has the capacity to hinder social justice. First, not everyone has access to the Internet. In fact, broadband access can be limited in remote rural areas. This lack of access is referred to as the digital divide. The digital divide can be described as the gap that exists in most countries between those with ready access to the tools, information, and communication technologies and those who do not have such access (Cullen, 2003). Access can be limited due to socioeconomic status, disabilities, language barriers, race, gender or any other characteristics that have been linked with unfair treatment (Judge, Puckett, & Bell, 2006).

Second, there are dangers when seeking out information and communicating on line. One danger is the existence of on-line predators. These individuals who are hateful of the LGBT persons can pose as LGBT individuals and attack people seeking information or on line conversations into a relationship and provide inaccurate information, belittle them, and attack them. In addition, predators also can take advantage of vulnerable populations, such as LGBT, for their own gain. For example, the predator might find an easy date or pose as a teenager to lure LGBT individuals into sexual encounters. The second danger concerns the anonymity of individuals on the Internet. Even though one can mask their identity on line, their actions can be traced. Internet browsers tend to keep histories of sites visited. The sites that closeted individuals viewed are subjected to discovery; which can result in a premature outing.

Despite the aforementioned concerns, the Internet can serve as an agent of social justice for rural LGBT individuals by providing access to information about LGBT resources and opportunities for isolated individuals a chance to communicate without being ostracized by their community. In a sense, the Internet can be used to promote social justice with LGBT individuals living in rural areas by removing isolation, putting LGBT individuals in touch with information and creating an environment where LGBT individuals can be in touch with like-minded individuals.

This section focused on how the Internet can be used to promote the dogma of social justice. The next section will demonstrate how the human service professional can work with the LGBT client by becoming aware of, assess, and evaluate the use of the Internet to promote the goals of social justice.

Evidence-Based Practice and Evaluating the Internet as an Agent of Social Justice

The human service professional can suggest the Internet as an agent of social justice with the LGBT individual. However, while working with LGBT individuals, the human service professional needs to have a way of becoming aware of how the Internet can be used. Furthermore, the human service professional needs to be able to assess and evaluate the successful use of the Internet with LGBT individual. Evidence based practice is a step-by-step process for becoming aware of, assessing, and evaluating work with the LGBT individual. Evidence- based practice is the use of sound evidence in making decisions about the care of the client (Rubin & Babbie, 2007). Evidence- based practice consist of several steps. First, formulate the question/problem of what needs to be addressed in the helping relationship. Second, search for evidence and to critically appraise the evidence. Third, determine which approach to use with the client and apply the intervention. Finally, the intervention is evaluated and feedback is exchanged between the client and the professional. Using evidence based practice can be very empowering for the LGBT individual. They become involved in the decision-making process. In fact, evidence based practice is a "compassionate, client-centered approach to practice" (Rubin & Babbie, 2007, p. 5). Evidence based practice can be used in all human service professions. Applying interventions without evidence and evaluation can be risky and be considered unethical.

Formulate the Question/Problem. The first step is to formulate a question rooted in what the client wants to work on. For example, when the LGBT individual is closeted and isolated, living in a rural area and wants to come out, the focus might be on developing ways of coming out without risk of facing oppression or ridicule at the hands of the rural community. By talking to other LGBT individuals, one can approximate the feelings that arise when others came out in their community. Thus, the issues for evaluation become "Does seeking out information on coming out provide suggestions for the client" and "Does coming out to other LBGT individuals on line assist the client when dealing with feelings that arise when wanting to come out in their community?"

Search for and Appraise the Evidence. The next step is to search for evidence-based interventions. Evidence can typically be found in the academic literature. In addition, the LGBT individual can turn to the Internet for additional evidence. In fact, the LGBT individual can be assigned homework to search out LGBT-related information and support on the Internet. This assignment can be twofold and occur over the course of the relationship with the human service professional. First, the LGBT individual uses the Internet to seek information that focuses on coming out. Second, the LGBT individual needs to find a way of communicating with others on line. This second evidence-based practice step can be very empowering for the rural LGBT client. First, such research, especially conducted on line, allows access to a wide array of information that may not otherwise be available in the rural context. Second, the LGBT individual becomes the censor of information, picking and choosing based on what has been discovered on the Internet. Third, the LGBT individual can seek out a preferred method of communicating online with others. By allowing the LGBT individual to seek the information, a repertoire of approaches to coming out can be developed.

Evidence based practice is client centered. The human service professional provides feedback and serves as a sounding board. In the case of closeted LGBT individuals, the human service professional, along with the individual, needs to be aware of the available resources and approaches for the LGBT person who wants to come out. Finally, in the case of technology, it is helpful for both parties to recognize and understand the advantages and disadvantages of the different technologies used in on line community networks.

After the evidence is gathered it needs to be appraised. The LGBT individual and human service professional can work together to determine what evidence is worthwhile to consider. If using nonacademic evidence then the task becomes a judgment of creditability. The professional takes an active role in the appraisal by using their specialized knowledge on issues of coming out in rural area. Furthermore, the human service professional with knowledge of the Internet can assist the LGBT individual with choosing the best approach on the Internet.

Determine and Apply the Intervention. The next steps are to determine and apply the intervention. First, after the evidence has been appraised, the interventions need to be chosen. For the LGBT individual, these interventions include the resources gathered while on-line and how these resources are used while communicating with other LGBT individuals. At this point, an approach to coming out that is comfortable for the rural client has been identified. Now the individual turns to the Internet to communicate with their peers. At this point, the LGBT individual can proceed as they like. In other words, they can visit a chat room and get some ideas on their approach, or even practicing coming out to members of the chat room. Coming out on line provides a stage in which practice without fear of reprisal, prior to coming out in the community can occur. The LGBT individual works closely with the human service professional by providing updates on their progress. The professional, in turn, serves as a sounding board for the client.

Evaluate the Intervention and Provide Feedback. The final step in evidence based practice is to evaluate the intervention and provide the LGBT individual with feedback. Ultimately, the goal is to answer the questions posed in the first stage. There are many qualitative and quantitative ways of evaluating the intervention. The question "Does seeking out information on coming out provide suggestions for the client?" can be evaluated by examining the quantity of the information. The question can also be evaluated by examining the quality of the information. To do so, a matrix can be developed that can be used to assess the quality of the information. The second question "Does coming out to other LBGT individuals on line assist the client when dealing with feelings that arise when wanting to come out in their community?" can also be investigated qualitatively and quantitatively. The human service professional can allow the LGBT individual to talk openly about the experience surrounding coming out on-line. They can discuss the pros and cons of coming out. The conversation can focus on what worked and how the individual felt. The evaluation arises from examining the data generated from the conversation. The human service professional can pay attention to the words and listen for indications of success and failures; furthermore, body language can be examined when the LGBT individual talks about the exciting or negative experiences of coming out using the Internet.

The empowering nature of coming out on the Internet can also be evaluated quantitatively. Emotions prior to and after coming out can be quantified. Scores on scales designed to measure the emotions can be examined using a pre-post design. For example, the human service professional and the LGBT individual can quantify feelings of isolation and measure the feelings of isolation for the time period prior to and after the client comes out on line. This type of approach is called a single subject design. Single subject designs are typically a quantitative approach to monitoring progress of a therapeutic intervention. Single subject designs are typically used when you have one subject (Rubin & Babbie, 2007). With any intervention, the best approach is to understand how to analyze the data given the question and the variables presented. During and after the evaluation period, a feedback loop must be maintained. The reason of feedback is twofold. First, the LGBT individual can receive confirmation about his/her progress. Second, not every intervention is applicable to all individuals. By evaluating the work done with the LGBT individual, the human service worker can truly assess whether the intervention was successful would be open to the person.

Conclusion

The human service professional can utilize the Internet to assist the LGBT individual with combating issues of isolation and non-acceptance in rural communities by using the Internet to help seek out information about and communicate with the LGBT community. By doing so, an avenue to accessible information, services, and support that might not otherwise be available.

In addition, evidence- based practice can be used as an approach for becoming aware of, assessing, and evaluating the use of the Internet to promote social justice for the rural LGBT individual. Evidence-based practice can be used to assist working through the process of finding reliable information and a social outlet. Furthermore, the steps of evidence-based practice require the human service worker to evaluate the success of using the Internet to combat feelings of isolation and non-acceptance. In rural communities, the LGBT individual often has to seek solace through clandestine methods. The Internet is one technology that can be used to break down some of the barriers that exist in rural communities. While access to technology is (and will always be) an issue, what this chapter suggest is when access is available, there are ways that the Internet can promote the goals of social justice for the LGBT individual living in a rural community.

Bibliography

Barker, R. L. (1991). *The social work dictionary* (2nd ed.). Washington DC: National Association of Social Workers.

Cullen, R. (2003). The digital divide: A global and national call to action. *The Electronic Library, 21(3)*, 247-257.

Fitchter, D. & Martin, C. (1997). Community networks and health information providers: A natural partnership. *Health Care on the Internet, 1(1)*, 5-21.

Foster, S. J. (1997). Rural lesbians and gays: Public perceptions, worker perceptions, and service delivery. *Journal of Gay & Lesbian Social Services, 7(3)*, 23-35.

Gay and Lesbian Alliance Against Defamation. Retrieved March 14, 2007, from http://glaad.org/

GayHealth. Retrieved March 30, 2007, from http://gayhealth.com.

Haag, A. M. & Chang, F. K. (1997). The impact of electronic networking on the lesbian and gay community. *Journal of Gay & Lesbian Social Services, 7(3)*, 83-94.

Human Rights Campaign. Retrieved March 30, 2007, from http://hrc.org.

Judge, S., Puckett, K., & Bell, S. M. (2006). Closing up the digital divide: Update from the early childhood longitudinal study. *The Journal of Educational Research, 100(1)*, 52-60.

Kahn, A. (1977). The sixth social service system. *The Social & Rehabilitation Record, 4(2)*, 3-6.

Lindhorst, T. (1997). Lesbian and gay men in country: Practice implications for rural social workers. *Journal of Gay & Lesbian Social Services, 7(3)*, 1-11.

Lynsen, J. (2007). More Americans coming out in rural areas. *Washington Blade.* Retrieved September 10, 2007 from http://www.washblade.com/2007/1-26/news/national/rural.cfm.

Merha, B, Merkel, C. & Bishop, A. P. (2004). The internet for empowerment of minority and marginalized users. *New Media & Society, 6(6)*, 781-802.

National Gay and Lesbian Task Force. Retrieved March 30, 2007, from http://thetaskforce.org.

Rubin, A. & Babbie, E. (2007). *Essential research methods for social work.* Belmont, CA: Thomson Wadsworth.

Shernoff, M. (2006). The heart of a virtual hunter. *The Gay and Lesbian Review, January-February*, 20-22.

Smith, J. D. (1997). Working with larger systems: Rural lesbians and gays. *Journal of Gay & Lesbian Social Services, 7(3)*, 13-21.

U.S. Census Bureau (Oct, 1995). Urban and rural definitions. Retrieved September 10, 2007, from http://www.census.gov.

II. SOCIAL CLASS AND SEXUAL ORIENTATION

HELPING COLLEGE STUDENTS EXPLORE THE HIDDEN INJURIES OF SOCIAL CLASS

DeMethra LaSha Bradley and Robert J. Nash

Introduction

We are two educators, both inside and outside of the formal classroom setting, at a prestigious public university. Much of the student population is social justice minded and community service oriented. We teach, as best we can, undergraduate and graduate college students how to talk with one another about personal and sometimes controversial topics. One of the most controversial and personal topics we have engaged in with our students is social class. We teach a course that features this subject matter, "Higher Education in the United States," and there is never a dull moment as we aid our students in uncovering and sharing their stories around social class. Many of the students we teach are self-identified change agents, social justice allies and educators. Thus, they not only seek to understand the topic of social class for their own learning; they seek to understand it as it pertains to global social justice. Whenever we introduce the topic of social class as a unit for exploration in our course, there is typically an unsettling energy that enters the room.

We describe this energy, this classroom aura, as containing elements of pride, confusion, embarrassment, guilt, entitlement, enlightenment, and denial. These are just a few of the emotions present at the onset and throughout the duration of our conversations around social class. As teachers, we are charged with guiding our students in learning how to talk with each other around this and other controversial topics (such as religious and political difference, and race, gender, and sexual orientation diversity), but we must admit, the social class unit is often the most personal and controversial unit we teach.

Due to the personal and controversial nature of many of our course topics, our challenge is always the same: how to establish a safe, yet stimulating, space for discussing and writing about provocative and sometimes personal topics like social class. "We strive to create this safe space not only in our seminar room, but also in conference halls, campus offices, and any other sites where teachers, administrators, and students might come together to be fully present to one another" (Nash & Bradley, 2007, p. 137). We also strive to empower our students to have these conversations with others outside of our department, college, or university setting (Nash, Bradley, & Chickering, 2008).

As our students embark on various levels of social justice advocacy, education, and global citizenry, we hope they leave our classroom with a better understanding of themselves, their personal and tribal stories, and how each of them navigates the pluralistic world around them. As teachers, we espouse that one of the foundational elements of taking action towards greater social justice work, is the ability to understand ourselves and our narratives around various hot-button social topics. We implore our students to use their time with us and each other to perform what we call "me-search." "Me-search" is what we have defined as the intentional action of exploring oneself; of going beyond the surface self and digging deeper in an effort to extract new knowledge of one's self and one's place in the world. We have witnessed first-hand how "me-search," combined with the desire to transform their leadership, has been able to aid our students in building stronger foundations for their pursuit of global citizenry and social justice. We will talk at greater length in a following section about our "me-search" work with students.

In addition to our "me-search" investigations, we spend much of our course time together engaging with each other around controversial topics. We call this "we-search." We advocate that it is not only important to be able to discover and express our own individual stories, but it is equally as important to be able to listen to and engage with others around our stories. To this end, we promote "me-search" and "we-search" with our students. We will also talk about our "we-search" teaching around social class and social justice in a following section.

Finally, in this chapter, we will share with you our own understandings of social justice and social class. We will also introduce you to scholarly personal narrative (SPN) writing as a tool for your own "me-search" regarding social class (Nash, 2004). We will explore moral conversation as the dialogue tool we use in our course to facilitate "we-search," and we will provide you with a list of activities and/or ways to embark upon your own plan of action (be that informal or formal) to seek further understanding, or to provide education to others, around the topic of social class.

Social Justice

First, we want to acknowledge that social justice is a huge topic, and literature around the subject is ever growing and evolving. In the next few pages, we discuss our take on social justice, followed by an exploration of the intersection of social justice and social class difference. Our academic expertise on the topic of social class is based on our own writing, thinking about, researching, and teaching this material. However, we also self-identify as social justice allies, activists, and educators, with a passion for creating both classroom and cross-campus opportunities to dialogue about social class difference.

We unapologetically think of social justice in old-fashioned liberal terms (Rorty, 1999). It is our belief that social justice is what happens whenever we realize that no matter what the difference, he or she is still one of *us*. A person's needs for freedom, love, equality, justice, and human satisfactions are the same as our needs. We implore our students and colleagues to think about social justice as a way in which we *include* rather than *exclude*. Our definition of social justice has two-parts: first, there is no *us* and *them*, there is just *us*; likewise there is no *you* and *me*, there is just *we*. Moreover, no one's needs carry any intrinsic right to override some one else's needs. Adams, Bell, and Griffin (1997) assert that "social justice includes a vision of society in which the distribution of resources is equitable and all members are physically and psychologically safe and secure" (p. 1). The authors "envision a society in which individuals are both self-determining (able to develop their full capability), and interdependent (capable of interacting democratically with others)" (p. 1). They remind us that the ability to be self-determining and interdependent is an important aspect of what makes a socially just society.

We value both the distributive (distribution of goods based on equality and equity) and the procedural (decision-making influences) aspects of justice that inform the social justice discussion (Reason and Davis, 2005). In our course, we guide our students in exploring their self-determination via "me-search" and practice their interdependence via "we-search." Social justice is what Dr. Martin Luther King, Jr. spoke about on August 28, 1963 when he said:

> I have a dream that my four little children will one day live in a nation where they will not be judged by the color of their skin but by the content of their character.
>   I have a dream that ... one day right there in Alabama, little black boys and black girls will be able to join hands with little white boys and white girls as sisters and brothers.

Martin Luther King Jr.'s words spoke to his dream of a world where the right to explore one's abilities and desires was not determined by someone else's arbitrary opinion of who a person is, and where there was space for us to interact with one another in an effort to learn from one another. As teachers embarking on the journey of social justice under-standing, advocacy, and education, we hope to see a day when all of our social institutions realize at their very core that all people have an equal right to maximize their opportunities to live the good life, regardless of individual or group variation. That commitment fuels our passion around the topic of social class and its intersection with social justice.

Social Class

Social justice and social class intersect when poverty, lack of equal oppor-tunity, and inferior educational preparations keep people from dreaming big dreams and doing what they need to do in order to fulfill them. So-cial justice and social class also intersect when race, ethnicity, religion, sexual orientation, or political beliefs prevent people from having an equal right, no matter how talented or hardworking they might be. In many places in the United States and abroad, self-determination and in-terdependence (the essence of social justice) do not exist because of social class differences. Research continues to highlight that the lack of aspira-tion for many of our United States citizens is due to systems of oppres-sion and displacement, particularly of our low-income citizens (McLead, 1995). Also, social class is still considered a taboo subject to engage in conversation about in much of our society, including higher education (Sennett & Cobb, 1993; hooks, 2000; Duffy, 2007). Thus, we consider so-cial class difference to be a huge roadblock on the way to creating a so-cially just society.

At the outset, let us say that there are numerous definitions of social class, and most scholars agree that some sort of social hierarchy exists. The attributes by which that hierarchy is created and often sustained includes, but are not limited to, financial status, education, employment, social connections, and upward mobility opportunities. We suggest that social class is a way for people to sort themselves out into a kind of pecking order according to how they compare to others in regards to the attributes we listed above. This pecking order, or sorting out process, sometimes transcends other differences, but it can also be connected to race, gender, and sexual orientation factors.

We think of social class, therefore, not simply as a technical term in the social sciences but as more of an overall mind-set that is sometimes conscious and sometimes not. The French call this a *mentalite*, a worldview that includes a cluster of formal and informal learning, attitudes, beliefs, experiences, backgrounds, situations, and lifestyles that influence/shape/determine how each of us goes about our daily lives. This worldview, or *mentalite*, is one of the most powerful determinants of personal/cultural/social/professional identity, and, yet it is largely neglected in higher education as a way to understand individual and group identity. Social class is, in the words of Vance Packard regarding advertising, the "hidden persuader."

We believe that social class could very well be the predominant background story to each of our lives (although we admit that this assertion is certainly arguable). Social class explains our personal ambition or lack thereof, our hopes and dreams or lack of them, our definitions of success and failure, our lifestyles and life understanding. It often shapes our most significant beliefs, our sense of right and wrong, and our ideas about relationships, family, education, work, play, and financial standing, not to mention even our aesthetic standards. And, yet, something so essential to who each of us is as human beings, something so salient to how each of us views the world, is still considered a taboo topic of discussion (hooks, 2000; Sennett & Cobb, 1993; Duffy, 2007).

Literature addressing the lack of social class discussions on our college campuses attributes this void to the larger lack of these conversations within our society (Correspondents of *The New York Times*, 2005). There has been a swell in advocacy for bringing social class diversity to the foreground on our campuses, and much of that advocacy has come

from faculty and administrators who see social class diversity as a pivotal area of multicultural learning for our students. Faculty and administrators who are comfortable talking about social class difference serve as
role models in getting our students to talk about a topic as volatile (and
"hidden') as social class difference. We agree with Duffy's (2007) assertion that "as faculty, staff, and administrators become better educated
about the value of the working class, they can lift the veil of misunder-
standing about social class and create opportunities to discuss their own
background and personal prejudices with students both in and out of the
classroom" (p. 19).

Based on the conversations we have with our students and colleagues, we have heard over and over again how one's social class background has clear implications for how one's emotional and moral
response may contribute to issues of injustice, justice, equality, and equity. By no means are we saying that a person's mind-set around these
issues is absolutely determined by their social class background. We are
merely trying to help individuals make the links between their social
class backgrounds and their thoughts and actions concerning social justice.

In order to encourage and guide our students in making the connections between their social class backgrounds and their thoughts around
social justice, in our seminars, we invite them to engage with various authors' narratives around social class. Initially, as a group, we examine the
stories of a number of writers (e.g., Lubrano, 2004; Rodriguez, 1982), and
then we engage in our own social class-story telling via writing. All the
while, we are exploring the subject of social class together via group conversations. For many of our students this is the first time they have ever
engaged in a public dialogue about social class (inside or outside their
homes). The time that we spend together during our course unit on social
class is often the most liberating, emotional, eye-opening, tense, guilt-
inducing, and "ah-ha moment" learning experience for our students.

With the help of various authors, our students find the words for
their social class experiences. They identify with a social class concept
called "Limbo," as described by Lubrano (2004), living a dual class life
style, exploring the ever growing categories associated with social class
(e.g. working class, blue-collar, affluent class, etc.), dealing with the feelings of guilt or betrayal for advancing educationally, and the ways in

which many U.S. citizens piece together wages from multiple jobs just to get by (Ehrenreich, 2002). What we learn about our students and the stories they share regarding social class never cease to captivate us each and every year.

At this time, we want to briefly introduce readers of this chapter to five social class typologies that we see emerge over and over again with our students, both in our classroom, as well as in a number of other campus venues. One of the authors, D. L. Bradley, created these typologies after listening to numerous student narratives surrounding social class, and they exist between and among different social class groups (Nash, Bradley, & Chickering, 2008). We use these typologies in an effort to move away from the more conventional and stereotypical empirical labels often associated with social class (e.g., financial status, education, possessions) and move towards understanding social class from a *mentalite* perspective. What follows is a brief description of the types of students we have encountered whenever we listened to their narratives around social class:

Embarrassed students believe that their social class background is a cause for them to feel ashamed or guilty, and they are often silent when they are in the minority (regardless of their social class background). Their silence is negatively encouraged or reinforced by the stereotypes that swirl around them regarding people from their neighborhood, type of upbringing, or financial status. These students do not want anyone to know what their social class narrative entails, and some students go to great lengths to hide it. Details of their upbringing, especially any that would disclose their social class background, are omitted from the stories they share with most people. The main motif in the embarrassed students narrative is this: *because they often fear exposure of their social class status due to rejection, ridicule, or somehow being labeled as different from their peers, embarrassed students desire to escape any stereotypes associated with their social class status by blending in as much as possible with the majority of their peers.* Social justice through the lens of Embarrassed students is a way to be included regardless of their background. It encourages them to create connections with others, as opposed to creating distance.

Comfortable students are at ease in their social class narrative. Regardless of what that narrative entails, these students make no apologies for what was or was not available to them based on their social class standing. There is a low, if it even exists at all, level of angst in regards to their social class narrative. These students may be heard saying, "it is what it is." The "it" is their particular social class identity, and there is no cause for further explanation or dissection of this narrative. For some, the comfort in sharing their stories is due to a lack of knowledge regarding the impact of social class on who they are, but even when they begin to explore the concept of social class, their comfort levels tend to remain the same. Unlike Embarrassed students, Comfortable students enjoy sharing their narrative because it is a significant part of who they are, and they are proud of it. The same "it is what it is" mentality carries over in the Comfortable students' outlook around social justice. The main theme is this: *there may be a desire to live in a more socially just world, the world that Dr. King envisioned for us, but the fact-of-the-matter is that we do not. It is what it is.* This is not to say that these students are not social justice allies and educators, because many of them are. But in our experiences, these students tend to have a worldview that reminds them of all the work to be done in order to have a socially just society.

Straddler students are struggling to exist among and between two or more social classes. Lubrano (2004) defines the Straddler as "born to blue-collar families and then, like [him], moved into the strange new territory of the middle class" (p. 2). Many first-generation college students fit Lubrano's definition because the upward mobility of education has placed them in a strange new territory-a different social class circle from what they were raised in. Other Straddlers have endured an upbringing in one social class but feel like more of their authentic self exists in another social class. These Straddlers differ from Lubrano's definition because they *choose* consciously to associate themselves with a different social class, rather than simply finding themselves in another social class because of their collegiate associations. These students cope with feelings of abandoning the social class they were raised in, awkwardness in navigating their new social class circle, or proving themselves to their peers in order to be accepted in a social class circle that remains foreign to them. The controlling theme in the Straddler narrative is this: *A socially just society would solve their issues of not quite fitting in because the emphasis for social interaction would be to learn from, and with, one another. This would help to break down the class fences that they straddle.*

Multi-class lingual students function well in multiple social class circles. Their *mentalite* has helped them to navigate multiple social class circles with ease. Their familiarity with a wide range of experiences, coupled with their ability to access those different experiences, helps these students to navigate their way through various social class circles. To cope with the sometimes frustrating and uncomfortable realities of social injustice on the road to social justice, they rely on their ability to be social class chameleons, and they are proud of their knack for social adaptation. At the heart of the Multi-class lingual narrative is this image: *Their road to social justice contains various types of terrain and opportunities, and their ability to navigate those terrains enables them to continue on the road to social justice with few, if any, unexpected social surprises.*

"Me-Search": Scholarly Personal Narrative Writing

As mentioned earlier, we explore social class with our students via the process of discussing the narratives of various authors we assign, and then by encouraging them to share their own stories. For the majority of our students, this is the first time they have been asked to share their personal stories as a part of an academic course. To that end, our course is typically the first time they have been introduced to a formal writing method for narrating their stories. The method we teach is called scholarly personal narrative (SPN) writing. Personal narrative writing "helps us all to understand our histories, shape our destinies… [and] when done in an intellectually and emotionally respectable way, personal narrative writing can result in stunning self-insights" (Nash, 2004, pp. 2-3). We believe that the structure of SPN writing is a wonderful way to experience "me-search." In our opinion, active participants (allies and educators) in the social justice movement should not only be able to understand and interact with the stories of others, but they should also be able to tell their own stories with dignity and candor. For many people in the social justice movement, it is the mutual sharing of social-justice and social-class narratives in a safe yet robust conversation space that most effectively enables us to find our commonalities and understand our differences.

SPN is a special way of thinking, and writing, about very controversial issues. This kind of writing begins with the inner life and consciousness of the writer and radiates outward. It places subjectivity on a par with (but does not replace) objectivity. It is both concrete and abstract;

particular and universal; private and public. When done well, SPN writing moves from "me-search" to "we-search." (In the next section, we discuss moral conversation as a collective, meaning-making process by which the "me" in scholarly writing gets shared with the "we" in moral conversation.) In no time at all, with lots of encouragement and examples, most students learn how to write about social justice and social class by exposing their personal views and by sharing their various experiences within the five typologies we develop earlier. Our aim is to teach our students to see themselves as the pivotal variables in their social class narratives, without whom there would be no social class narrative at all.

Students begin to understand that SPN writing gives them permission to identify themselves as as central to any rigorous investigation of social class and social justice. They arrive at the same conclusion as the eminent anthropologist, Ruth Behar (1996), does. She calls this kind of writing "an act of personal witness," a kind of "self-ethnography." Other like-minded scholars, such as many feminist, social justice, and postmodern thinkers, refer to this way of writing as "autobiographical scholarship" or "personal scholarship" (e.g., Holdstein & Bleich, 2001). Like them, we believe that SPN writing helps students to re-vision their scholarly inquiries, because it looks to the lived lives of students as the major source of questions, perspectives, and methods around the burning issues of social class and social justice.

Whenever our students investigate their own social class statuses in their SPN free-writes, personal reflections, and longer scholarly papers, they tend to take more risks and dig more deeply into the complexities of social class and its intersection with social justice issues. As they become more proficient in using a writing methodology that effectively blends personal stories, interpretation, theory, and universalizable themes, most arrive at the place Diane P. Freedman and Olivia Frey describe in their own use of SPN with their classes. Students produce "beautiful, evocative writing that connects with readers and serves as a trusted, enlightening source" (Freedman & Frey, 2003, p. 13).

Because we believe that, at some level, all writing is autobiographical, we want to encourage our students to be as candid, up-front, and self-disclosing as possible about their challenges with social class and social justice. For these purposes, therefore, SPN writing is not merely another interesting research option for all of us to play with during a 15-

week semester. Rather, we feel that it is the *only* way-at this particular time in our students' lives-that they can communicate the raw personal truths of their social class experiences to others. We offer the following excerpts from some of our most memorable SPN writings during the social class unit:

- "I am thankful to have had a chance to read *Limbo*, and finally be able to put words to the feelings I have when I go home, but don't *go home*... . Now, perhaps, I can figure out where I belong, and why I feel like I do not belong"
- "I realize that even talking about economic class in higher education is a middle class experience for which working class students are unprepared. In light of this challenge, two questions remain: How, in the 'educated, advantaged environment' of graduate school, can we talk about socio-economic class by recognizing differences and without excluding the working class voices?"
- "Now this cell phone was my ticket to feeling more comfortable in this new environment, and it served as a status symbol in my newly found culture. In fact, I remember I would walk around campus proudly holding my cell phone and act like was I either checking my messages or talking on it to give the impression that I was popular."

These "social-class ah ah moments" are just a few, representative examples of the personal narratives our students shared with us. Our students generally find eloquently simple yet powerful words to describe their emotions, start to ask the tough social class questions of our higher education community, and provide compelling examples of how the pressures of fitting in on our college campuses push some students to try to "pass" in regards to their social class status.

"We-Search": Moral Conversation

Given the social-class diversity of all the students who make their way to our classroom, our main objective is to create a space for various opinions, discoveries, and some confusion to be expressed and engaged with. Undoubtedly, there are always avid proponents and representatives for each of the topics we explore, and most times there are also opposing viewpoints at the discussion table. We want our students to learn how to talk with one another about what they believe, feel strongly about, and disagree with, without going to war with one another. To achieve this objective, we use a dialogue framework that we call *moral conversation* (Nash, Bradley, & Chickering, 2008).

We have found that with such a rich diversity of social-class backgrounds and beliefs in our seminars, we need to conduct classroom conversations in a particular way. Thus, we lay out certain ground rules at the beginning of each semester, and we expect full compliance to them. We talk about these rules, and then we revisit them, often during the course. We state, upfront and early on, that we value the *conversational process* as much as the *academic content* that we will be examining throughout the semester. Conversation and content are coequal partners during our social class unit. One without the other is incomplete.

What is *moral conversation*? Here, in a nutshell, is how we describe it: good teachers and good students are primarily interested in *affirming and enriching* each others' perspectives and viewpoints rather than finding ways to *critique and ridicule* them. We try to do this by following what we call the "Golden Rule" of moral conversation: respond to others in the class the way you would like them to respond to you. We stress that our chief responsibility to one another in our classroom is to make the other person look good. In turn, we make ourselves look good by making others look good. We make ourselves look bad when we make others look bad.

As teachers, we hold that open-minded examination of highly volatile issues such as social class and social justice can take place only if it is undertaken in a mutually cooperative, safe, educational environment. Angry, offended students are resistant students. What they usually end up learning is primarily how to defend themselves against attack. In this case, content often takes a back seat to zoning out, passive-aggression, or worse. In this regard, referring to the guilt inducing and white privilege-carping of so much conventional multicultural training, Welch (1999) says: "We have to break out of the dualistic oppressor/oppressed mindset and see the capacities for justice among 'oppressors,' the capacity for injustice among the 'oppressed'" (p. 117).

Truth to tell, many of our students first come to our classroom looking for us to be experts who can dispense the ultimate wisdom on the topics of social class and social justice—even while, developmentally, they might remain negaters, deniers, skeptics, and naysayers. We tell our students that, in a seminar such as ours, we think that we have the ability to dispense some basic information, ask the provocative questions, explore the more controversial hot buttons, genuinely empathize with their discoveries, doubts, fears, bewilderments, and misgivings, and share some of our own compelling, personal concerns about social class and social justice. But, really, this is as far as we can go. In spite of our limitations, however, we try always to convey, in a genuine way to our students, that we have no special social class or social justice agendas to push in teaching our course. We do not engage in guilt-mongering or finger-pointing. What we aim for more than anything else is for them to understand and respect the diversity of social class identities and adaptations that each of them is living in at the present time. These are the personal and collective stories that the practice of moral conversation aims to surface.

To this end we emphasize over and over again that no *conversation stoppers* will be allowed in our seminars. We prefer, instead, *conversation starters* and *conversation sustainers*. We point out (gently if possible) in our seminars whenever the following conversation stoppers rear their ugly heads: name-calling; repetitions of the same old, same old, sharp (and dull) axes to grind; self-promotion; arguing; proselytizing; settling old (or new) scores; whining about the group's/course's deficiencies; and deliberately positioning oneself on the highest moral ground while relegating others to the lowest moral ground.

Likewise, we frequently call attention to those times when genuine moral conversation is taking place. We reinforce the following good practices of moral conversation: clarifying; affirming; rephrasing; evoking (not provoking); supporting; practicing the virtues of humility, generosity and graciousness; attributing the best (not the worst) motives; looking for value in what others are saying; being prepared with relevant background information; speaking always for oneself and not for some prototypical group; and helping others to shine.

A few prompts that we use to start our conversations include: What are some questions you have around the topic of social class? Has your social class status ever placed you at an advantage, or disadvantage, of any kind? If so, how? Please complete this statement: When I think about social class, one stereotype that I think about is_____. We also ask the question, "What came up for you?" in relation to the course readings. These questions and prompts, alongside our students' enthusiastic (albeit, at times, painful) willingness to engage with the topic, often yield intense and revealing interchanges.

We end this section on the necessity of doing we-search via moral conversation with a quotation that we sometimes share with our students. This appears in the oldest and most sacred Hindu book in the world — the *Rig Veda*: *Ekam sat vipraha bahudha vadanti*: *Truth is one, but the wise call it by many names*. If this Hindu aphorism is accurate, and we believe in its basic value, then each of us in our seminars is, at best, naming our social class/social justice truths with but *one* name. Who among us, we sometimes ask our students, has the right, and the omniscience, to impose *one name* on all the rest of us?

Next Steps

In the preceding pages, we have discussed how we encourage and guide our students in their own personal exploration (scholarly personal narrative) and group/class conversations (moral conversation) regarding social class. At this time, we want to talk about exploring social class beyond the classroom setting. The exploration of this topic in the larger campus community, as well as into the community beyond the campus, is critical to social justice. We have created a brief list of text references and Internet resources to aid our readers in further learning, outreach, and educating others regarding social class. We hope that the resources and references we list below provide a variety of examples of how educators and campus leaders can be a part of the social class conversation on a local, national, and international level.

Internet and Media Resources

Class Action: Building Bridges Across the Class Divide (www.classism.org) provides resources, workshops, presentations, and organization consultations in an effort to create economic justice and inspiring action to end classism. The organization also offers workshops on the intersection of class with other identities such as race and gender. The Class Action website offers a plethora of resources for further education about social class and suggests action steps towards addressing classism.

Class Matters: The Counterculture Cross-Class Blues (www.classmatters.org) offers a wide range of information for those seeking further understanding and dissection of class and its effects on our society. Much of the website is based upon the research of Betsy Leondar-Wright, a self-defined professional middle-class activist. The website offers opportunities to engage in discussions with other on-line or via workshops in various parts of the United States. The website also offers resources regarding the intersection of class and other identities (e.g., race, sexual orientation, and gender).

Class Dismissed: How TV Frames the Working Class & Film (Alper and Leistyna, 2005) explores the intersection of race, gender, and sexuality with class. Using images from various media representation throughout the decades, Loretta Alper and Pepi Leistyna (co-producers and writers) offer a more detailed look at the portrayal of the working-class. This video challenges viewers to look past the "entertainment value" of much of the media we ingest and dissect how it may influence our thoughts, attitudes and assumptions about working class- people.

Bibliography

Adams, M., Bell, L.A., & Griffin, P. (Eds.). (1997). *Teaching for diversity and social justice*. New York: Routledge.

Alper, L. & Leistyna, P. (2005). *Class dismissed: How TV frames the working class* [film]. Northampton, MA: Media Education Foundation.

Behar, R. (1996). *The vulnerable observer: Anthropology that breaks your heart*. Boston: Beacon Press.

Correspondents of *The New York Times*. (2005). *Class matters*. New York: Times Books, Henry Holt and Company.

Duffy, J. O. (2007, May-June). Invisibly at risk: Low-income students in a middle-and-upper-class world. *About Campus*, 12 (2), 18-25.

Ehrenreich, B. (2002). *Nickel and dimed: On (not) getting by in America*. New York: Henry Holt and Company, Inc.

Freedman, D. P. & Frey, O. (Eds.)/ (2003).. *Autobiographical writing across the disciplines: A reader*. Durham, NC: Duke University Press.

Holdstein, D. H. & Bleich, D. (Eds.).. (2001). *Personal effects: The social character of scholarly writing*. Logan, UT: Utah State University Press.

hooks, b. (2000). *Where we stand: Class matters*. New York: Routledge.

Lubrano, A. (2004). *Limbo*. Hoboken, NJ: John Wiley & Sons, Inc.

MacLeod, J. (1995). *Ain't no makin' it: Aspirations and attainment in a low-income neighborhood*. Boulder, CO: Westview Press, Inc.

Nash, R. J. (2004). *Liberating scholarly writing: The power of personal narrative*. New York: Teachers College Press, Columbia University.

Nash, R.J. & Bradley, D.L. 2007. Moral conversation: A theoretical framework for talking about spirituality on college campuses. In B.W. Speck & S.L. Hoppe (Eds.), *Search for spirituality in higher education* (pp. 137-154). New York, NY: Peter Lang.

Nash, R. J., Bradley, D. L., & Chickering, A.W. (2008). *How to talk about hot topics on campus: From polarization to moral conversation.* San Francisco: Jossey-Bass/Wiley.

Reason, R. D. & Davis, T. L. (2005). Antecedents, precursors, and concurrent concepts in the development of social justice attitudes and actions. *New Directions for Student Services,* no.110., 5-15.

Rodriguez, R. (1982). *Hunger of memory: The education of Richard Rodriguez.* New York: Bantam.

Rorty, R. (1999). *Philosophy and social hope.* New York: Penguin Books.

Sennett, R. & Cobb, J. (1993). *The hidden injuries of class.* New York: Norton & Company, Inc.

Welch, S. D. (1999). *Sweet dreams in America: Making ethics and spirituality work.* New York: Routledge.

CHAPTER 11

SURVIVAL CONNECTIONS AND
SOCIAL CHANGE

Joan S. Rabin

How did I find myself so near the front, with about a million lesbians, gay men, bisexuals, transgender folk and allies strung out behind me? It was the 1993 March on Washington where the day before my love and I were symbolically "married" in front of the IRS building. What a journey! And I don't just mean the long hike through the streets of Washington to the Mall. After all, I had only just come out to myself a few years before, in my mid-forties, married for over half my life and with two children!

I have always been a lesbian; it has just taken me a very long time to figure out how to fit it all together in a pattern that worked. As the child of immigrant (and in my mother's case—refugee) parents, I spent so much time just dealing with how different I was from the mainstream of American culture. I couldn't quite grasp that it was possible to go beyond crushes on girls and greatly enjoying the company of girlfriends, to love, sex, and partnering with women.

I grew up in Queens, New York. Both my parents worked full time. There was no cultural concept of "working mothers" in our neighborhood. Everyone who was able worked to get enough money to survive. My father repaired X-ray machines and my mother was a bookkeeper.

My mother knew a person needed a lot of skills to survive in this dangerous world. She knew first-hand, having fought against the Nazis in Germany when she was in the underground resistance. She had gotten out of Germany just in time, in 1938, after everyone else in her group had been captured by the SS. My mother was going to raise her only child to be a survivor. No sissy girl nonsense: I had trucks, a cowboy outfit complete with six-gun, and lots of freedom to roam the neighborhood. My father taught me to row a boat, build a campfire, and love hiking. We spent our vacations at State campgrounds. We didn't have money for a tent so we all slept in the car. In the winter we used to drive out to Jones Beach state Park and walk along the shore. It was cold and I would have liked to have something warm to eat from the cafeteria there but we always ate sandwiches we brought from home. It wasn't until I was an adult that I realized my parents had not had the money to eat out. New York City is an international place and my mother would take me to many of the free attractions that make the city so special. The United Nations was a favorite place and so was the American Museum of Natural History. I especially loved the Bronx Zoo that we could reach by a very long subway ride. So in some ways I had an enriched upbringing.

Another aspect of that enrichment was how my parents allowed me great freedom to hike and explore on my own from an early age. They made it possible for me to feel comfortable relying on my own skills. Mom and Dad allowed me to take chances so I might fulfill my dreams. They supported my decision to stay in Israel by myself in a kibbutz (collective farm) on the Gaza border with Egypt. I was 18 and my cousin from San Francisco offered to take me along with his family on a trip to Europe and Israel in 1962. My dream had been to work on a kibbutz. When we got to Israel at the end of our vacation, I asked to stay behind so I could live on a kibbutz for a few weeks. My cousin was horrified at my staying alone and telegraphed my parents for their permission, which they promptly granted.

I have been shot at. It was strange hearing the whizzing noises going by my head. I was riding the sheepherder's horse bareback and holding on to a piece of rough twine attached to the lower jaw of the horse. Two Algerian refugee boys from the kibbutz were yelling at me in French, "Come back. You are in Egypt." Thanks to my high school French teacher I understood them and reaching forward I managed to grab the horse's jaw and pull it around so we were pointing toward home. The horse really wanted to keep going farther into Egypt but I kept struggling to get back even as he tried to brush me off under low- hanging branches in the orchard. By this time I looked like something out of a Western movie, hanging on to the horse sideways with my hand clinging to his mane and my legs wrapped around his body. When I got back I told the sheepherder and he laughed and said, "Oh yes, that horse was born in Egypt and he likes to go back and visit."

Those few weeks in Israel changed my life forever. I could build on everything I learned growing up in tough neighborhoods in New York. I took a public bus from the city of Haifa in the north to Erez, a kibbutz in the Gaza strip near Checkpoint Charlie, the border crossing to Egypt. I didn't speak much Hebrew and could read only a few words but I managed to successfully change buses in Ashkelon, and arrived at my destination in the Negev desert. I worked in the fields from 4 A.M. to 8 A.M. when we had breakfast and then until 1 P.M. when all work had to stop because of the intense heat. I made friends and got used to being awakened in the morning by the banging of the night guard's Uzi machine gun on the door and the cheerful call of "boker tov," good morning in Hebrew.

When it was time to leave Israel, I took the 6 A.M. bus north to Tel Aviv for the plane trip home. When I got to Tel Aviv I didn't have any money left (I had used my last coins to buy lunch, a roll from a bakery). I didn't have ten cents for bus fare to the airport. The driver put his own money in for me so I could get home.

As I look back as an adult and a parent I wonder how my parents could have allowed me such freedom and how I could have forged ahead with such a sense of adventure and so little fear. I think we all understood that you need to grab life while you can or succumb to the grinding survival motivation that destroys all dreams. It's hard enough to make it day to day with little money and not much hope of things getting better. An opportunity to fulfill a dream is worth taking great chances for. It tells us that we are alive and free. I think that is my greatest legacy from my parents.

Later in life I found myself with similar choices. I desperately wanted to learn how to scuba dive so I could accompany my colleague Dr. Eugenie Clark on her diving expeditions. I just barely managed to scrape through a scuba course despite almost drowning during the first lesson. I am somewhat claustrophobic and was terrified on every dive for the first two years of field research (about 100 dives). Even now after almost 300 dives I still have to be careful not to exceed my limited abilities but I love scuba diving passionately.

Dealing with the claustrophobia imposed by a facemask and regulator mouthpiece with limited airflow was one thing. Diving in a small research submarine brought on a whole new level of anxiety. But the experience was not to be missed, so down I went (twice) to study sharks. The magic of those submarine dives will be with me always and I thank my working-class heritage for giving me the toughness to do what had to be done.

One thing my background did not help with was a formal luncheon at the palace of the British Governor General of the Cayman Islands. I was busy studying the sand tilefish, *Malacanthus plumieri*, underwater when I was signaled to surface. "Hurry up," I was told "You have to be at the Governor's palace in less than an hour." With borrowed clothes and flip-flop sandals off I went hoping to get lost in the crowd of a dozen dignitaries. As part of the formal luncheon ritual the Governor invites one guest to join him for a cocktail before luncheon. Guess whom he picked? Apparently I did a poor job of hiding. So now among my memories is having a gin and tonic with the Governor General of the Cayman Islands and eating off gold-rimmed plates adorned with the crest of Queen Elizabeth II. The outrageous humor of the situation pulled me through.

School: Role models and mentors

During my 12 years in the New York City public school system I was si-multaneously surrounded by old, decaying physical structures and some highly competent, caring teachers and administrators. I started school in 1949, four years after the end of World War II. My early elementary school years coincided with the Korean War (1950-1953). I learned some-thing important on my first day of elementary school. Don't ever go in the bathrooms. They smell awful, the floors are wet, and it is dangerous. So I never drank any liquids until after I got home. P.S. 19 in Corona, Queens, NY, was well over 100 years old and didn't have many ameni-ties. The teachers were great though. It was tough in the schoolyard at recess. I never could figure out what that business with jump rope was all about and playing jacks wasn't very exciting either. Girls seemed to do a lot of boring stuff. I was called a "tomboy" and that was fine with me. It all worked quite well while I was young but the older I got the more I knew how different I was from others.

Interestingly, in the ten-year study on *Patterns of Lesbian Development* my partner and I conducted (Rabin and Slater, 2004), one of our major findings was that of the 2,067 lesbians sampled, 76% reported having felt different from other girls as a child. This compared to 54% in a sample of 136 heterosexual women who reported having felt different from other girls. It appears that feeling different from other girls is not an experience unique to lesbians. Nevertheless, feeling different from other girls characterized the vast majority of lesbians. We also asked survey respondents about having been identified as a "tomboy" as a child. Almost identical findings emerged, with 75% of lesbians having been tomboys compared to 54% of heterosexual women. (I can't help wondering, if being a tomboy is now such a common experience, why it isn't recognized as simply part of girlhood. Why give normal girl behavior a double male name, "tom" and "boy"?).

Junior High School 126 in Astoria, Queens was five stories high and almost a hundred years old. It was also the center for a drug distribution ring extending to the docks by the river. Instead of student hall monitors we had NYC police officers with guns! We did our best to ignore at it all and just clung to each other for security. Strong friendships are forged when survival itself might be at stake. I learned a lot about friendship in that junior high school. Our friendships cut across ethnic and religious divisions. Italian Catholics, Irish Catholics, Jews from various parts of Europe, all kinds of Protestants, most of us were first- generation Americans. I learned not to be too judgmental of others, that we all needed each other. I lived with an odd mixture of fear, optimism, and pride.

I read somewhere that you can always tell when someone has grown up poor because they rarely reject free food. I don't know whether there is any merit to that statement but it caused me to reflect. When someone offers me food, it feels like a connection is being offered and my refusal would sever that connection. I recall vividly how in junior high school a friend had no lunch every day because her mother was struggling to care for the five children in the family. Another friend and I would alternate bringing an extra lunch so all of us could eat together in peace.

I moved on to William Cullen Bryant High School in Woodside, Queens. It was such a tough school they filmed a documentary there called "Bad Boys." What they should have done was make a film about the many incredibly dedicated and knowledgeable teachers who gave so many of us a chance for a good life. It was in academia that I found a sense of connection, of belonging. In junior high school we had role models like Mr. Vincent DeVivo who told us of his childhood growing up during the Great Depression, making us feel we had life pretty good. Mr. John Coty role modeled breaking the rules in the name of educational excellence. Every year he assigned a book that wound up being banned by the principal for the next year. Our book was Pearl Buck's *The Good Earth*. The principal objected to the word "whore." It is Mr. Coty's courage and pursuit of excellence in the face bureaucratic interference that sustains me in my attempts to circumvent rigid administrative rules that harm rather than help my students at the university. But the most extraordinary influence was Miss Mossner, my Biology teacher in 10th grade at Bryant H. S. She actually expected us to remember what we read in our textbook and answer detailed questions on our exams. At first I found the notion outrageous, but over the course of a year I came around and wound up getting the highest grade in the school on the New York State Regents exam in biology. The chairperson of the biology department and Miss Mossner took me out for an ice- cream soda to celebrate. It meant the world to me! When you grow up in a working- class environment, role models are essential. They make it possible to envision different ways of being than what comes from family or local surroundings.

When, in 1965, I applied for admission to the doctorate program at the State University of New York at Buffalo I was asked to write an essay explaining what I intended to do with my Psychology degree. I said I wanted to make a difference in my students' lives, I wanted to be a resource for them to enhance their scholarly abilities, and I wanted to be part of a support system for students entering college. I still do; it's the only way I can repay those teachers who mean so much to me. It is all part of that sense of community and loyalty fostered by the need to hang together in an environment that is largely hostile to education and the academic enterprise overall. Those of us with aspirations toward college constituted a tiny minority both in junior and senior high school.

The funny thing is I wouldn't even have made it to college if it hadn't been for the vice-principal of J.H.S. 126, Mr. Bernard McManus. I am the first one in my family to graduate from junior high. My parents grew up in Germany. My father left school after sixth grade and got a job; my mother made it to the eighth grade before she was apprenticed to work in a pharmaceutical company. My parents could not imagine how college fit in with our lives. They assumed that I would be a secretary or something along those lines. When I shared my parents' vision for my future with Mr. McManus, he immediately demanded they meet with him the next morning. They were there even though they both had to call in late for work. My parents had great respect for educators and a directive from the vice-principal could not be ignored. He simply indicated they had to adjust to the fact I needed to go to college to fulfill my potential. He also said college was free in the public colleges of New York City. My parents left that meeting completely changed in their outlook: I was going to college!

My parents really enjoyed my junior high graduation in that big Loew's movie theater in Astoria. For many students this would be their only graduation at the age of sixteen they could legally get working papers, allowing them to leave high school if they had a job.

Queens College was quite an adventure. I commuted daily, taking two buses and a subway train each way. Everybody was a commuter since there were no dormitories. My first week at school I met someone who would change my life. Her name was Barbara and she was a sophomore pre-medical student. She came from more middle- class roots and shared that experience with me. Over four decades later we are still dear friends.

I attended all my classes and studied a great deal. At the end of the first semester I was quite satisfied with my grades (mostly B's, plus a C and a D) as were my parents. Then something happened that changed everything. My friend Barbara said, "Oh no, that won't work. Next semester those grades need to be all A's and B's." That was the crucial juncture in my career. Barbara was functioning as a mentor and was teaching me the culture of college and the appropriate goals to strive for. I had thought that just surviving and getting through college was triumph enough given my background. Barbara taught me to have confidence in my abilities and to reach high.

My poor parents! First they had to adjust to the idea of my going to college. They helped support me for my four undergraduate years and were eagerly looking forward to my graduating and getting a job. Then I go and tell them I am applying to graduate school to go for a Doctorate. in bio-psychology. Their initial response was, "We thought you were going to get a job and earn some money." I allayed their fears by explaining it was ok because if I got into graduate school, the university would pay me! I would be awarded an assistantship to cover my tuition and pay me enough to live on. "Oh, that's all right then," they said. "But what is a doctorate." they asked. I don't think they ever really understood just what getting my doctorate meant until pretty much everyone in our extended family all over the country called my parents to congratulate them when I got my degree.

The Survival Connection

One day in college I was in the locker room changing after a gym class when the young woman next to me keeled over. It turned out she hadn't eaten in a long time and was homeless because her family had kicked her out for converting to a different religion. I didn't know her but it never occurred to me not to feed her and bring her home with me. Home was a small two-bedroom apartment; so I had to share my room with her. My parents simply welcomed this stranger in need and for months she lived in our home until she reconciled with her family. The interesting part of this story is that I never particularly liked, her but in the culture of shared survival to which I belonged, bringing her home was the only response I could imagine.

Alfred Lubrano (2003) talks of his working class heritage as producing, among other things, loyalty and also a sense of connection with the people around you where you live and where you work. There is a sense of people looking out for each other and returning good deeds. The middle class, on the other hand, is socialized toward individual achievement and ambition in isolation or competition with others. This proved a problem for me as a young professional beginning to negotiate the academic world. I expected loyalty and support from colleagues reflecting the loyalty and support I offered them. Instead I slammed against the middle class world of agency over communion (Bakan, 1966), individuals looking out for themselves and disconnecting from any group ties or exploiting social connections to meet individual ambitions. I was very naïve about this middle- class world and the result was I almost lost my job.

During high school and much of college I lived in a New York City housing project in Woodside, Queens. The "projects," as we called them, were six stories high with no air conditioning and windows that only opened slightly so no one could jump out. Unlike the five-story walk-up apartment in Astoria we had lived in while I was in junior high, the projects had elevators. Ironically, while most residents were trying to escape the projects and move elsewhere, for us living in the projects was a step up. The buildings were a lot newer than the dilapidated Astoria apartment and there were some small grassy spaces and scrawny sycamore trees. My family lived there for six years and when we left the place had deteriorated to the frequent odor of urine in the elevators and halls and sometimes broken beer bottles on the outside steps. There was always an aura of danger, and I was very careful to have my body balanced when I began to enter an elevator, so that I could hurl myself backwards away from the closing door if a dangerous looking person was lurking in the corner of the elevator. Many times I just took the stairs even though we lived on the top floor. The potential danger and oppressive odors of the elevator just weren't worth it.

Aside from the physical dangers there was also a sense of emotional isolation and even abuse from many residents. The hostility toward college kids in the projects was conveyed by snide, undercutting personal remarks that made me feel isolated. I felt very different from most of the people there. The sense of powerlessness against "the system" is pervasive in working-class people. Even today I know for me there is a simmering anger and even rage dwelling just below a fairly mellow surface. Add to that the outsider status of the academic achiever in the projects and the result is a psychological legacy I would rather not have. However, when I encounter adversity in either my personal or professional life, I often remember where I come from. I take pride in having survived the slums, the fear, the danger, even the psychological isolation and the awkwardness of not having much money in a consumer-driven culture. I am not at all surprised by unreasonable rules that make it harder to do my work, care for my students or live life fully. I just keep going anyway, ignoring what I can and working around the rest. Creative perseverance is part of my heritage too.

Legacy

When my father died at age 73, he left very little money for my mother. When my mother died at 71 there was no monetary inheritance for me. After a lifetime of struggle they died without having achieved any measure of financial success. They lived very full and rich lives of deep existential meaning and I was blessed to inherit this legacy. They were hikers and campers and loved the natural world deeply. I inherited this from them as well. They were very brave people who dealt with many setbacks in life without a whimper. They never measured human importance by wealth. They treated everyone with respect. Issues of race, ethnicity, sexual orientation, and gender did not undermine this equal treatment. This also is my legacy. I am very proud to be their child and it's ok that they never really understood what a Doctorate. was. My biggest regret is that my parents died before I came out in mid-life as a lesbian. I would have loved to share the excitement and joy of that realization with them. I would have enjoyed their support as I have enjoyed the support of my children, my extended family and my partner's family.

Experiencing Discrimination

Society offers numerous barriers to success for those who are not part of the power structure of white, Christian, middle or upper class, heterosexual males. On the first day of graduate school at the State University of New York at Buffalo, I was told, "They don't like women in the lab here." It happened as I was about to start up the stairs to the building housing the animal laboratory. A third-year graduate student came out the door saw me and said, "You must be one of the new graduate students". I happily acknowledged this and that's when he dropped the bomb about women not being welcome. I had been on campus less than an hour when that fateful encounter occurred. My reaction was true to my working-class roots: I just accepted what was said and kept going. For the next year I never asked for help from anyone, not even when moving around heavy and awkward equipment. By the end of my first year in graduate school, I was the top student in my class. I had an edge because I was rooming with my dearest friend and mentor, Barbara, who was now a medical student at SUNY Buffalo. She and our other roommate, Kathy, studied all the time and I followed their pattern.

Ironically given my current status as a proud feminist, it never occurred to me that I was being discriminated against based on a biological trait, being female. I knew I consistently failed to meet society's preferred gender stereotypes so I wasn't even outraged by the unfairness of it all.

The concept of *sex* discrimination hadn't yet developed in American culture. The United States was still deeply absorbed in dealing with the recently passed 1964 Civil Rights Act barring *racial* discrimination. Even though that same Civil Rights Act (accidentally) also made sexual discrimination illegal, it would take many court cases and decades of consciousness raising for Americans to understand how the culture discriminated against girls and women.

The System and Social Change

One legacy of growing up working class is it has been easy for me to "take on the system." One thing I learned early was that rarely was the system designed to help me. If I wanted things to be better, I had to either work around the system or change it. This prepared me for working toward social change. I hated living in a country that sanctioned legal discrimination against people just because of race. In college I joined the Congress of Racial Equality (CORE) and the Student Non-Violent Coordinating Committee (SNCC) and fought for passage of the 1964 Civil Rights Act. I was appalled at America's lack of concern with the plight of Soviet Jews. I demonstrated in front of the Soviet Embassy in NYC on behalf of Soviet Jews who were being persecuted. Then there was that trip to Atlantic City in a crowded old bus to demonstrate in front of the Democratic Party National Convention, urging them to speak out against Soviet persecution of Jews. My first week of graduate school found me participating in a protest "sit-in" in the hallway in front of the University President's office. The pattern has continued to the present. I know Washington, D. C. pretty well; I've marched there so many times, most recently in April 2004 joining over a million people in the *March for Women's Lives* and reproductive freedom of choice, especially for poor women! Another act of social change came when my partner and I were among the first wave of lesbians and gay men to have a Civil Union in Vermont on August 9, 2000. Our Justice of the Peace was a lesbian. She and her partner had been the first couple to celebrate a Civil Union in Vermont.

Survival Training

Growing up in a tough neighborhood provides many lessons on how to survive in challenging situations. Just trying to enter that five-story walk-up apartment building meant squeezing past the Astoria Gents gang (the toughest in NY) lounging on the stoop. Looking for danger was a part of walking down the street or going to the store. It was automatic. Always being on alert was normal. Opportunities for creative problem solving abounded in just riding the public bus to school or finding the cheapest ways to do things.

Survival-based creative problem solving is a daily experience growing up in poor neighborhoods. It was to prove very helpful in a variety of personal and professional situations later in life. One example that comes powerfully to mind occurred during a research trip to the Red Sea. From 1986 to 1991, while I was an Associate Professor of Psychology at Towson University I was also the Project Director for my research colleague, Dr. Eugenie Clark of the University of Maryland. We studied fish behavior. As Project Director I coordinated travel arrangements for our research team. When we arrived in Israel the group had to transfer from Lod International airport to the local airport in Tel Aviv for a flight south to Eilat where we would board our research vessel in the Red Sea. We were on a tight schedule but a sandstorm had wreaked havoc with airline schedules and we faced a chaotic situation at the local airport. It was jammed to overflowing with people struggling to get on the next flight south. I had five passengers and 15 pieces of luggage, much of it research equipment, to get through that crowd. I assessed the situation and quickly realized that if we passively waited our turn we would definitely miss this last flight out of Tel Aviv to Eilat. So I had one person stay with the luggage and then, one by one, we formed ourselves into a line with me leading the way. I told everyone to pass the luggage overhead to me at the loading area. I then handed our luggage, piece by piece, over to the airline employee loading the plane. After that I gathered everyone's tickets and squirmed through the rambunctious crowd to the ticket counter. When I presented our tickets I was told that there was no room for us on the plane. That's when I told them our luggage was already onboard. With great reluctance we were allowed on the plane and everyone made it to the port city of Eilat at the southernmost tip of Israel in time for the boat's departure.

A New Mentor

In 1982 I had a midlife crisis. I was in a rut and it was hard to feel excited about life despite a good job at the University, two very special children, and what seemed like a happy marriage. In February 1982 the National Aquarium in Baltimore opened with a lecture by Dr. Eugenie Clark, a world-famous ichthyologist. I attended the lecture because my daughter had read a children's book about Dr. Clark (*Shark Lady*) and I wanted to get it autographed for her. I was so enchanted by the underwater world Dr. Clark revealed, I decided to take scuba diving lessons. I wanted a chance to enter a different world. I succeeded beyond my wildest dreams!

By 1986 I was working with Eugenie Clark as Project Director for research on fish behavior. We had clicked immediately upon first meeting. Our shared heritage of growing up in working-class households in NYC provided a strong foundation for a working relationship. Ironically, we even attended the same high school in Queens, 22 years apart, and were greatly influenced by the same biology teacher, Miss Mossner.

Coming Out

It was the scuba diving that changed my life forever. That's where I found the lesbians underwater! It was the last thing I expected. We were diving in the Bahamas, observing sand tilefish behavior. Many of the volunteer diver-researchers were women. Even the fish we were there to study (*Malacanthus plumieri*, the sand tilefish) were mostly females. Sand tilefish are sex changers; all of these fish begin as females and a few change to males as needed (Clark, Rabin, & Holderman, 1988). It never occurred to me that some of those research volunteers were lesbians, but I sure enjoyed the laughter, camaraderie, and the friendly hugs.

I finally woke up to a profound reality when I fell for one woman. I didn't know she was a lesbian. I just fell madly in love with her. It was a heck of a surprise and I never did tell her how I felt. But, at last, I was on my way back to the person I had always been but didn't know how to be. It took about a year to re-write my life, finally acknowledging all those crushes on babysitters, girls in school, teachers, camp counselors, and most especially, one particular CIT (counselor in training) at that YMCA camp when I was 14. I recalled how in junior high school Mr. DeVivo had suggested I stop spending all my time with my close girlfriends and start dating boys. I asked him why. He just said he thought it would be a good idea. I was truly puzzled. I couldn't imagine why if my current friendships felt so good I needed to be dating.

I finally succumbed to social pressure and started dating in college. By the end of my first year of graduate school I was married to another graduate student. The next ten years brought a doctorate a job as an Assistant Professor of Psychology at what was then Towson State College, and two children.

I did my bit for trying to fit in to what Adrienne Rich (1976) calls the "institution of motherhood" embedded within the "compulsory heterosexuality" of American culture. I quite simply didn't think there was a choice about getting married and having children. It was what you did. Marriage, suburbia, and children were the American dream and I thought it would make my parents happy to know I was "safe" in the mainstream of the society to which I had been peripheral for so long.

Patterns of Lesbian Development

Coming out in 1989 at the age of 45 requires a good deal of life review and reexamining past explanations for feelings. So what does a middle aged professor whose personal life has just exploded with new meaning do? A research project on the topic, of course! Not only did I get examine my own feelings about coming out in mid-life but being in academia I got to study the experience in other women, doing a major research study on lesbian development. This happened because I fell in love with a woman in the same department at the university who was an out lesbian. Together we launched a huge research project on lesbian development. Because of our concern about the paucity of data available on lesbian development in college textbooks, we have spent the last 14 years (1990-2004) collecting developmental data based on a diverse sample of lesbians throughout the United States.

We began using a 75-item questionnaire developed through a collective process with input from many lesbians. It quickly became clear that, while many lesbians are comfortable with the questionnaire format, others are blocked by it, feel it is irrelevant, or are not able to work with it. Often those who shunned questionnaires were working class and poor women. Because we particularly did not want to ignore lesbians who would be excluded by a questionnaire, a reasonable approach seemed to be to offer lesbians the choice of completing the questionnaire on their own or being interviewed with their remarks audio-taped for later data recording.

We had to go where lesbians are, rather than expecting them to come to us. Closeted lesbians, poor lesbians, and rural lesbians cannot be expected to attend public meetings/events or costly cultural events such as concerts or festivals, so they are often excluded from research. To accomplish this field-based research, we first applied for and were awarded joint university sabbaticals. We then developed a list of approximately 50 contact lesbians by writing to many women in three organizations. These women agreed to help locate harder-to-find lesbians in 14 states. The final step was to refurbish our small recreational vehicle so it could serve as transportation to remote areas, housing, and a mobile research site. This allowed us to seek women of varying socio-economic classes, ages, races, cultures, and regional experiences. We made every attempt to ensure the voices of poor women, older women, and women of color were heard (Rabin & Slater, 2005).

We also sought out and visited five different kinds of predominantly lesbian communities across the United States (residential, communal, farm, vacation, and mixed use) for interviews (Rabin & Slater, 2005). In large measure we reached many of these women who would have been omitted if we had used traditional research methods. I know all too well what it feels like to be excluded and thus have no voice. That would not happen in our study! An exciting aspect of our research trip was we encountered some lesbians who had never told their story to anyone. I found my experience of coming out in midlife paralleled that of many women in our study who made comments such as: "I've found myself," "I want to shout this from the hilltops," "Suddenly everything makes sense," "I'm filled with joy." and "I want to celebrate."

How My Past Defines How I Act And Think As A University Professor

Being working class in America means not having much power. Growing up in the 1950s as a tomboy with a strong attraction to females means feeling and being different. I am therefore quite sensitive to those in low power situations and I try to support those who are different from the group in any way.

A few years ago I was walking down the hall in the Psychology building and noticed a man in a wheelchair off to the side. I approached him and asked how he was doing. He said he was waiting to be picked up and taken to his next class. He also said I was the first person who had ever acknowledged his existence and spoken to me as he waited in the hall.

In the early 1970s I was teaching a Psychology of Learning course for the first time. In preparation for the course I created numerous examples of different kinds of learning paradigms. On the first day of class I found that one of my students was blind. I quickly realized I needed to re-write every learning example because all of them were based on visual experiences. Putting various learning paradigms into auditory, tactile, olfactory and gustatory modes was challenging and an excellent consciousness-raising experience. I was appalled when my senior-level student informed me that I was the only professor in his entire college career who had altered the course material to include him.

In that same Psychology of Learning class I had a student with great potential but no encouragement from her family to excel. Her first essay exam contained excellent ideas but was very poorly written and organized. It took five re-writes before she achieved an acceptable standard. No one had ever told her she was capable of doing better work. She continued to take courses with me and ultimately graduated with honors in Psychology. She went on to graduate school and professional success.

One of the benefits of being an employee of a state university in Maryland is tuition remission for the employees and their families. Not having to pay tuition enables many lower socio-economic class people get a college degree. At one point the State Legislature of Maryland decided to save money by denying tuition remission to staff, only allowing it for faculty families. I immediately protested this plan and advocated on behalf of tuition remission for our secretaries and other staff. We won but I was very surprised to learn how few of the faculty had supported the staff.

I have always viewed the secretaries in our department as colleagues and respected them and their contributions. In class I tell students how important the support of the secretaries is to their education and encourage them to indicate their appreciation to the secretaries. I always thank the secretaries and the student workers in our department for the work they do for me because I know that the jobs they occupy are undervalued and underpaid within the university structure. I have a tradition of bringing gifts to the office staff at the start of each academic year, when things are at their most frantic.

Recently the "living wage movement" has arisen on American campuses. Faculty and students try to force the administration to advocate for higher wages for cafeteria workers and janitors who are not state employees and are paid very poorly by outside contractors. We were successful in forcing a wage increase for the workers on the Towson campus, although it wasn't as much as we hoped to get for them.

Many at Towson University are first-generation college students and many more work long hours at outside jobs to pay their tuition and living costs. I am sensitive to the socio-economic realities of our students' lives. It is not unusual for students to get dropped from registration because they can not pay their tuition on time. If at all possible I over-enroll these students in my classes knowing how hard it is for them to get each semester's tuition together early enough. Whenever a parent asks if she or he can bring a child to class for that day I am welcoming and supportive. I keep toys in my office. If feasible I give the child a gift so being on campus with Mom or Dad is a good experience. In my Ethology and Comparative Psychology (Animal Behavior) class I require a field trip to the zoo and give extra credit for a trip to the aquarium. Admission prices are high so I emphasize that Friday night at the aquarium costs only $5 and there are reduced price coupons available for the zoo.

In my Motivation class I lecture about time pressure and stress in modern society. An example many students can identify with is being late for class because of difficulty finding a parking space, or waiting for a bus for half an hour and having three buses show up at the same time. The vigorous nods I get from some of my students to the bus example indicate that I have connected with those who don't have the money to own a car. By speaking to their lives I help to validate their experiences as equally important.

When I discuss the definition of "femininity" in my course on Sex Differences: Psychological Perspectives, I emphasize that working- class African-American women have a proud tradition of speaking out and being independent. These traits are not considered unfeminine in the traditional African-American community, whereas in middle-class European-American culture feminine women are defined as passive, dependent, and always nice. I point out that the definition of femininity in traditional African-American culture is far healthier than the definition prevailing in middle class European-American culture. Sadly, middle class African-American culture has partly succumbed to European-American definitions of femininity.

I honor my students for their achievements. I point out that many successful people got in to prestigious schools such as Harvard and Yale because of legacies, meaning a parent graduated from that school and has donated generously to the college so the child is given preference in admission. I tell my students how proud they should be of themselves for making their own way based on their own merits and not their families' wealth and power.

I come out in my classes so diverse sexual orientation students feel more comfortable and the rest of the class knows one more lesbian. I simply use a personal experience to make a point about heterosexism (which is the cultural expectation that everybody is heterosexual). My favorite is to describe what happens when I go to a physician's office and must fill out a form. Inevitably I am instructed to check off the box that categorizes me: married, separated, divorced, widowed, single. I cross out all of them and boldly write in "DOMESTIC PARTNER"!

Towson University sponsors a Diversity Weekend Retreat where students from diverse backgrounds spend time living together and participate in diversity consciousness -raising activities. These retreats are highly successful in forging long-term bonds between students from a range of racial, cultural, socio-economic class, and sexual orientation experiences. I have served on the Diversity Weekend planning committee for a number of years and attended quite a few retreats. It is important to me to participate in activities that forge bonds across the differences that separate us. Unfortunately I also go to the Diversity Weekend because homophobia can be a problem and our GLBT students need to see faculty support for them.

Fostering Social Change in Higher Education: Bringing Diversity to the Curriculum

I came to what was then Towson State College in 1970. One of the first Women's Studies Departments in the country was forming and I got drawn in. The Women's Studies Committee sent a memo to the entire Psychology Department asking that a faculty member create a new course in the Psychology of Women. There were over 20 people in the department but nobody was interested. That seemed wrong to me. Even though I was a bio-psychologist, specializing in animal behavior, I volunteered to create a course in a discipline in which I had no training. That changed my professional life permanently as from then on I would have to monitor new research findings in two entirely different specialties. I became part of a social movement bringing the new scholarship on women to the traditional college curriculum. It has been a 30 year struggle and we are still fighting to have women's lives and issues covered equally with men's in the college curriculum. Working in the areas of women's studies and diversity can be risky for attaining success in one's academic career, as I well know. Over the years I have often felt isolated as the "department feminist." But that is ok. I am accustomed to being on the outside and I just keep on doing what I believe really matters, as opposed to what gets rewarded. Now I am the "radical lesbian feminist" but it is not so lonely anymore as our department is blessed with both more feminists and more lesbians.

Over the last 14 years I have added yet another academic specialty to my professional development: sexual orientation diversity. Towson University was the first educational institution of the 11 schools in the university system of Maryland to establish a minor in Lesbian-Gay Studies. I am delighted to have been central to that enterprise, creating and teaching courses in Introduction to Lesbian-Gay Studies, Gender Identity in Transition, and the Psychology of Diversity. I also began vigorously promoting the teaching of diversity in the university curriculum.

I brought together a group of the younger faculty in my department and invited them to join me in a symposium presentation at a psychology conference. Our symposium was called *Replacing oppression with expression: Integrating feminist, cross-cultural, multi-ethnic, and sexual orientation perspectives in the teaching of psychology courses* (Rabin, Slater, Galupo, Wheeler, Fracasso, & Ayers, 1998). Our work on diversity and teaching was later expanded to two journal publications, directed by the younger faculty (Ayers, Wheeler, Fracasso,, Galupo, Rabin, & Slater 1999): *Reinventing the university through the teaching of diversity,* and *Approaches to modeling diversity in the college classroom: Challenges and strategies* (Wheeler, E. A., Ayers, J., Fracasso, M. P., Galupo, M. P., Rabin, J. S. and Slater, B. R., 1999).

In the classroom I emphasize that socio-economic class topics are also diversity issues (Ehrenreich, 2001). Of all aspects of diversity (race, ethnicity, sexual orientation, culture, age, physical ability, physical appearance, etc.) socio-economic class is hardest to teach and hardest for students to understand and appreciate, except in the most superficial ways. Television and the movies give little media attention to working class life. When I was growing up in the 1950s, television showed us our own lives. The *I Love Lucy* show was about a working- class couple living in an apartment building, as was *The Honeymooners*, with Ralph employed as a bus driver. Today television is about endless crime programs or endless wealth, neither of which reflects most students' lives. There is little depiction of working class life on television that students can learn from. (*Third Watch*, which depicts the lives of firefighters, paramedics, and police officers at home and on the job, is the exception, and well worth watching.)

In many of my courses I alert students to socio-economic class inequities in the tax structure and other institutions in the U.S. today. I point out that currently something like 10% of the population in the U.S. has about 90% of the wealth and it is getting worse. The country that the U.S. most closely resembles in socio-economic class structure is India, with a few very wealthy people and many very poor people. I also ask my students how it feels knowing that in America today one out of every five children lives in poverty, and one out of every four children below the age of six lives in poverty. To encourage the transition from passive observer to activist seeking social justice I connect my students with books that can make a difference in how they conceptualize something like poverty (Barbara Ehrenreich's 2005 book *Nickled and dimed ...On (not) getting by in America* makes a powerful impact on the human psyche).

In all my classes I integrate sexual orientation diversity factors throughout the course material. When using the word "family" I define it as a stable economic and emotional support unit headed by various kinds of people: two moms, two dads, grandparents, a single mom, a single dad, a grandmother, etc., in addition to the mom and dad pattern. Partners without children are family too.

Classroom atmosphere is vital. I explain why things happen at the university so students can begin to understand how the world works. I foster critical thinking by inviting students to bring information up in class that they have heard in other classes or from other sources which happen to contradict what I say in class. I invite class discussion on the contradictions so that we can better understand the source of the contradiction (misinformation, difference in perspective, difference in interpretation, or to show that no actual contradiction exists and to resolve the seeming contradiction). I encourage open discussion in a friendly atmosphere that is respectful of different points of view. I encourage students to question and to challenge ideas presented in class. I try to create a learning community that will remain with the student for life.

In my Ethology class I emphasize that our nearest living relatives on this planet are bonobos. Most people only know about common chimpanzees (*Pan troglodytes*) found in many places in central Africa. Bonobos are the other chimpanzee species (*Pan paniscus*) found only in a small area of central Africa. Bonobos have sex in every possible combination: male-male, female-female, female-male. Our closest relatives the bonobos live in a female-centered society that is both egalitarian and peaceful (deWaal, 1995, 2000). Female bonobos create powerful alliances with other females that are constantly reinforced with sexual contact (specifically genital-genital rubbing). "Adolescent females also typically pair up with an older 'mentor' female when they arrive in a new group and engage in sexual activity most frequently with her" (Bagemihl, 1999, p. 60). Female alliances prevent the aggression-based male dominance structure typical of the common chimpanzee (Strier, 2007).

I emphasize diversity in nature. The point is nature has many patterns, each as normal and natural as the next. If we can come to understand the diversity of nature perhaps we can begin to understand and accept the flexibility of behavioral patterns available to humans in everything from nurturing our young to patterns of sexual orientation.

Shortly after coming out I joined the Towson University Committee on Lesbian and Gay Issues. It was exciting to be part of an officially recognized group whose purpose was to deal with sexual orientation diversity issues on campus. Later I chaired the committee for three years.

The most significant project I was involved with happened unexpectedly. I was visiting Emory University in Atlanta in 1995 and discovered the "Safe Space" program run by Dr. Saralyn Chesnut, Director of the Lesbian and Gay Center. My partner, Dr. Barbara Slater and I immediately developed a safe space workshop at Towson University. The Safe Space Program has as its goal, the provision of supportive, safe environments on campus in which lesbian, gay, bisexual, transgender, and questioning students and other members of the campus community can relax and know that they will not be discriminated against on the basis of their sexual orientation.

A few institutions of higher education had safe space initiatives at that time but they were mostly offered through campus counseling centers. Our program was the only one run by faculty (Dr. Slater and I) in the country. We have offered over 25 workshops to interested faculty, staff, and students, including special presentations for the Residence Assistants, Counseling Center staff, and Health Center staff. When participants complete the safe space training they get a rainbow flag sticker complete with the Towson University logo and the words "SAFE SPACE PROGRAM" superimposed on the rainbow. Program supporters post the sticker on their door or workspace area. I met with the president of Towson University to get his permission to use the official university logo on the stickers so everyone would know the program was formally recognized by the university. One of the rewards for me is seeing rainbows all over campus.

It was lots of work, a fact neither recognized nor rewarded by the university. However, one of the strongest legacies of my working- class roots is that doing what matters is more important than doing what is rewarded. The same holds true for my work on Diversity and Multiculturalism issues, the LGBT Committee, and the Lesbian and Gay Studies Minor. I have frequently immersed myself in things that are true to my heritage but not rewarded by the "system."

My office is covered with rainbows and various other lesbian and gay symbols. It also contains pictures of different racial groups and multi-cultural artifacts. I ask myself, "What do students see when they come into my office that is a reflection of themselves?" I want students to be surrounded by diversity when they enter my office, and to feel comfortable in that their identity is acknowledged as well.

Why Activism and Advocacy? What Personal Gain Is There?

As a teacher I try to infuse my classes with the fervor of social justice and the need to stand up for human equality in all its diversity. I tell them what it was like to spend my entire childhood and young adulthood living in a country that said it was ok to discriminate against other human beings because of their race. I explain how government sanctioned racism damages every person not just the targeted group. I also point out that in the 21ˢᵗ century the only group still suffering government sanctioned discrimination is the lesbian, gay, bisexual, transgender community.

I grew up in a country in which it was perfectly legal to discriminate against a human being just because of that person's race. This damaged me and every child. How can a child learn right from wrong in a country that advocates discrimination? Just as I, as a child, felt deeply unsettled and puzzled by legal racial discrimination and segregation, today children are learning that it is ok to legally discriminate against somebody because of their sexual orientation. Every child carries dangerous psychological baggage from growing up with the government- sanctioned notion that some human beings are less worthy than others. The key to becoming an active advocate for justice is realizing that every single person is diminished by social injustice. It is not others that we are advocating for it is ourselves. We are advocating for our very humanity in celebrating the diversity that is life. Otherwise we are limited by only being comfortable with those who most closely resemble us. Everyone else becomes "the other" and eludes our comfort zone. We have a clear choice. We can advocate for diversity in our everyday lives or we can live in the endless sameness of our own small familiar space.

Poor people cannot advocate successfully for themselves because they lack the resources to bring about change. Despite the organizations that advocate for lesbians, gay men, bisexual, and transgender people the harm done by governmental and socially sanctioned homophobia is immense. The word "gay" is used in practically every school in the country to indicate something to be avoided (as in "that's so gay"). How does that make a young lesbian or young gay adolescent feel? They are in no position to stick up for themselves. Only the heterosexual majority can do that. This is where people of conscience who believe in human equality can make all the difference to the person being oppressed. It is about speaking out against discrimination when you are not the one directly affected by the negative language or act. This is what being an advocate is and always has been all about. This is an important way that each of us can help to bring about social change. Don't be passive, speak up and defend others. It makes all the difference in the world.

Bibliography

Ayers, J. F., Wheeler, E. A., Fracasso, M. P., Galupo, M. P., Rabin, J.S. & Slater, B. R. (1999). Reinventing the university through the teaching of diversity. *Journal of Adult Development, 6* (3): 163-173.

Bagemihl, B. (1999). *Biological exuberance: Animal homosexuality and natural diversity.* New York: St. Martin's.

Bakan, D. (1966). *The duality of human existence: An essay on psychology and religion.* Boston: Beacon.

Clark, E., Rabin, J. R., & Holderman, S. (1988). Reproductive behavior and social organization in the sand tilefish, *Malacanthus plumieri. Environmental Biology of Fishes, 22,* 273-286.

deWaal, F. B. M. (1995, March). Bonobo sex and society: The behavior of a close relative challenges assumptions about male supremacy in human evolution. *Scientific American, 272* (3): 82-88.

deWaal, F. B. M. (2000). Primates: A natural heritage of conflict resolution. *Science, 289,* 586-590.

Ehrenreich, B. (2001). *Nickel and dimed: On (not) getting by in America.* New York: Metropolitan.

Ford, C. S. & Beach, F. A. (1951). *Patterns of sexual behavior.* New York: Harper.

Lubrano, A. (2003). *Limbo: Blue-collar soul, white-collar dreams.* New York: Wiley.

McGovern, A. (1978). *Shark lady.* New York: Scholastic.

Rabin, J. S. & Slater, B. R. (2005). Lesbian communities across the United States: Pockets of resistance and resilience. *Journal of Lesbian Studies 9,* (1/2): 169-182.

Rabin, J. S. & Slater, B. R. (2004, February). Feminist psychology, science, and practice: The lesbian development study. Paper presented at the 29th National Conference of the Association for Women in Psychology, Philadelphia, PA.

Rabin, J. S., Slater, B. R., Galupo, M. P., Wheeler, E. A., Fracasso, M. P., & Jean F. Ayers, J. F. (1998, March). Replacing oppression with expression: Integrating feminist, cross-cultural, multi-ethnic, and sexual orientation perspectives in the teaching of psychology courses. Symposium conducted at the Association for Women in Psychology 23rd National Conference, Baltimore, MD.

Rich, A. (1976). *Of woman born: Motherhood as experience and institution.* New York: Norton.

Strier, K. B. (2007). *Primate behavioral ecology,* 3rd ed. Boston: Allyn and Bacon.

Wheeler, E. A., Ayers, J. F., Fracasso, M. P., Galupo, M. P., Rabin, J. S., & Slater, B. R. (1999). Approaches to modeling diversity in the college classroom: Challenges and strategies. *Journal for Excellence in College Teaching, 10* (2): 79-93.

IV. GLOBAL PERSPECTIVES ON SOCIAL JUSTICE

CHAPTER 12

DEMOCRACY AND UNIVERSAL HUMAN RIGHTS

An Example of Social Justice Activism at the International Level

Edward R. McMahon

Introduction

There are many ways to practice social justice activism; on the street, in the media, and in the boardroom. And those practicing social justice can range from youth and students to buttoned down university professors and corporate executives. In addition, the themes around which social justice can be exercised vary greatly. This chapter provides an example of activism in the heart of international organizations on a social justice issue of fundamental importance; that of the promotion of democracy and human rights on a global basis.

The decline in recent years of authoritarian regimes in many parts of the world has resulted in an expansion of democratic rights. This process is not seamless or assured, however. This is reflected by the continued existence of old, and the emergence of new, forms of political intolerance in many parts of the world. This issue is often viewed as abstract and beyond the ability of individuals to influence. This chapter suggests the contrary; that it is important and possible for committed individuals to master this type of subject material and to take action to initiate change.

Democracy has existed as a governance concept for at least 2,500 years, since its first articulation by Solon, Cleisthenes and Ephialtes of Athens between 600 and 450 BC. It presents us with a challenge, however. While elements of democracy are found in many different cultures, we still do not have much knowledge about its genesis and any prerequisites for its development, and how it can be best nurtured. Since the late 20th century there has been movement towards greater political pluralism in much of the world. The fragility of the current democratic opening, however, and our overall lack of knowledge about democracy, requires a comprehensive and much more coordinated global effort; not unlike those for other challenges facing this planet, such as the HIV/AIDs pandemic or Global Warming.

This chapter presents an example of an initiative designed to address one slice of this issue. The initiative has been designed to promote cooperation between the International Conference of New and Restored Democracies (ICNRD) and the Community of Democracies (CD), two important international groupings of countries which have in recent years expressed an interest in cooperating to further democracy on the global scale, but which for a number of reasons have made only modest progress in this regard. This chapter includes a) a description and background of the issue; b) a plan of action through which the issue could be addressed; and c) general reflections flowing from this experience on its broader social justice applicability.

Description and Background of Issue

Development of Democracy Concept. The promotion of democracy is one of the key social issue issues of our age. The past 40 years have been a time of significant democratic expansion. In the early 1990s Samuel Huntington developed his famous "Third Wave" argument (Huntington, 1991), which postulated that the world had previously seen modest expansions of democracy in phases from 1815-1914, and from 1945-60. Since 1974, however, the world has undergone the most sustained and far-reaching expansion of democratic rights in history. To use a highly aggregated set of figures, according to the human rights organization Freedom House 12% of the world's population in 1900 lived in countries that could be broadly considered to be democratic; today that figure is approaching two thirds of the world's population (Puddington, 2003). Even though we realize that due to varying definitional constructs these figures must be treated carefully, a wealth of supporting raw data and experiential information has in fact accrued in recent years.

A developing literature on "democracy consolidation" has focused on the protection and promotion of democracy after a country has made an initial break with authoritarian rule (Diamond, 1999). This discussion centers on ways that the initial democratic opening can be supported and strengthened, and democratic "backsliding" can be avoided. We cannot, however, afford ourselves the luxury of viewing the spread of democracy as an inevitable and ongoing process. Some random questions that generally generate more debate than consensus might include when, and under what conditions is democracy likely to take root? What is the relationship of political to economic development? What particular sets of democratic institutions are most appropriate in what contexts, and what are the elements that determine this? To what extent do regional cultural, social, and historic and other differences need to be considered? How can the rights of majorities and minorities best be balanced? In addition, history suggests that the democratization process is not necessarily iterative, and is subject to variations and setbacks. For this reason it is imperative that positive features of the contemporary period be seized to pry open the window for maximum democratic development.

Domestic vs. International Aspects of Democratization. Considerable attention has been devoted to identifying the origins and causes of successful democratization processes on the national level. These are generally sub-divided into focus on internal, or domestic causes, and external, or international factors. McMahon and Sinclair (2002) have suggested that some key internal factors include the extent and influence of civil society and political parties, as well as the structure of the economic system. External influences include the levels of bilateral and multilateral foreign aid, the demonstration effect of democratization processes elsewhere, which can be considered "carrots," and sanctions or other tools of diplomacy or even military action, which can be viewed as sticks. Often times, of course, these factors operate concurrently, so it is difficult to disaggregate them to determine their exact level of importance. And each country situation is, of course *sui generis*. Bratton (1997), however, has examined this issue in the context of democratization in Africa, and suggests that domestic causes were somewhat more important in the cases he examined.

Development of Democratic Entitlement Doctrine. One aspect of the international community's growing support for democratic forms of governance is an emerging set of norms and standards, which are increasingly seen as prerequisites for membership in the global community of democracies. A seminal work in this regard, the Copenhagen Document, was produced by the Organization for Security and Cooperation in Europe in 1990. This document spelled out explicitly the expected standards relating to democracy in participating states, especially in the critical field of electoral processes.

In addition, in recent years the related concept of a "democratic entitlement," in which citizens have a universal right to be governed according to democratic standards, has begun to take form in international law (Franck, 1992; 2001). This emerging doctrine posits that the concept of sovereignty includes the ability of people to exercise fundamental and universal rights as expressed in such internationally recognized instruments as the 1948 United Nations Declaration of Human Rights (UNDHR), the 1966 International Covenant of Civil and Political Rights, and the 1993 U.N. Vienna Declaration and Program of Action. This concept has been further explored and developed by Peterson (1997), Fox and Roth (2000), and Rich (2001).

A central challenge is how to operationalize and promote adherence to these principles. The international community's growing support for global democratic development has taken the form of defining and promoting a set of norms and standards, which are increasingly seen as prerequisites for membership in the global community of democracies. Two examples of the burgeoning literature in this regard are Franck (1995) and Clark (2003). In addition, Halperin and Lomasney (1998) critically assessed the efficacy of these standards.

Development of International Standards/Responses to Democratic Backsliding. Over the past decade it has become clear that simply spelling out expected standards of democratic performance is not sufficient to result in their adherence. Authoritarian rulers have increasingly become sophisticated in adopting the form, but not the spirit of democratic governance. Zakaria (1997) has labeled this phenomena "illiberal democracy." This term refers to any violation of democratic principles, such as suppression of free media, oppression of opposition groups, unfair electoral practices, and/or limiting legislative or judicial powers. This may be the result of an authoritarian government permitting a veneer of political pluralism to arise. When a formerly democratic government gives way to more authoritarian practices this is known as "democratic backsliding."

Work has been conducted on ways to prevent this unfortunate phenomenon. The Council on Foreign Relations (2003) issued a report entitled *Threats to Democracy: Prevention and Response.* Piccone (2004) and

Halperin and Galic (2005) followed up with supplemental analyses suggesting additional ways that democracy could be protected. One area that they emphasized was that of collective, international action to support democracy when it is under threat. This action could either be on the global or universal level, i.e through the U.N. system, or through regionally-based organizations such as the European Union or Organization of American States (OAS). Progress on these issues calls for an emerging understanding of the importance of cooperation among democracies throughout the world. They can also be designed to help insulate the democratization process from the rollback that occurred subsequent to previous waves of democratization, when countries with formally democratic institutions proved unable to consolidate them.

Role of the Community of Democracies and the International Conference of New and Restored Democracies. We now examine two important global initiatives designed to promote these ends in a comprehensive fashion. Participating countries have come together around a common theme of working together to promote democracy around the world. These have been identified as the focus of a plan of action, designed to foster synergies and cooperation between them. One initiative is the Community of Democracies (CD); the other is the International Conference of New and Restored Democracies (ICNRD).

The CD is an intergovernmental coalition of democracies and democratizing countries with a stated commitment to strengthening and promoting democratic norms and practices worldwide. The CD consists of both a governmental grouping comprised of government representatives, and a non-governmental component comprised of civil society organizations which meet as a group at biennial ministerial conferences.

The CD was inaugurated at its first biennial ministerial conference hosted by the government of Poland in Warsaw in June 2000. The initiative was spearheaded by the United States, along with seven co-conveners, which included the governments of Poland, Chile, the Czech Republic, India, Mali, and the Republic of Korea. Subsequent meetings took place in Seoul, South Korea in 2002 and Santiago, Chile in 2005. Each meeting has issued increasingly detailed lists of recommendations regarding how the CD and its member states could more effectively promote democracy worldwide.

Like the CD, the ICNRD process is based on the fundamental premise that democratization of states can be supported through international cooperation, and that mutual support, internal and external tendencies and forces endangering the processes of democratization can be surmounted.

The idea was first promoted by the Philippines, where an inaugural conference was held in 1988. Successive conferences were held in Latin America (Nicaragua - 1994), Europe (Romania - 1997), Africa (Benin - 2000), Asia (Mongolia - 2003), and the Middle East (Qatar - 2006). These conferences have developed a tripartite character, with governments, representatives from parliaments, and civil society groups participating. In Qatar 142 countries, 69 parliaments, and 97 civil society organizations were represented. One specific aspect of the ICNRD is that it has established a formal relationship with the United Nations. In 1994 then-Secretary-General Boutros Boutros-Ghali worked with the General Assembly to identify a role for the U.N. to play in this process.

A key problem is that communication and cooperation between the CD and the ICNRD has been limited. In contrast to the long list of CD criteria, the ICNRD is open to all member states in the (U.N.) U.N. Mongolia, 2006: 1). Based on the U.N. Charter, U.N. membership is open to all "peace-loving states," and does not lay out specific criteria or guidelines for determining participation. The ICNRD, like the U.N., is therefore made up of not simply democracies; it also contains a number of member states led by governments that allow little or no political pluralism. The documents that resulted from the Ulaanbaatar and Doha meetings had many similarities to the CD meeting recommendations, though the ICNRD recommendations tended to be more specific. This is perhaps because without a democracy threshold for membership, ICNRD members needed to adopt more basic and specific democratic principles than would be unnecessary for the CD to address.

Average Freedom House scores indicate that countries belonging only to the CD have the lowest and, therefore, best democracy scores, with the inclusion of countries belonging to both organizations raising the average scores somewhat. Solely ICNRD countries average still higher, showing that the ICNRD includes countries with lower democracy ratings. However, given the large number of countries belonging to both organizations, and the fact that their aggregate scores are not extremely different compared to countries only in the CD, there is a significant common constituency. At least some of these countries could serve in a bridging leadership role to develop a more effective relationship between the two groupings. In addition, the U.N. has developed a formal relationship with the ICNRD, but also seeks to use its good offices as a broker, or catalyst, for contacts between the ICNRD and the CD.

Plan of Action

I believe that pluralism in the promotion democracy is not *ipso facto* a bad thing. Conversely, however, depending upon the circumstances, a certain level of cooperation may be possible, which could contribute to a positive-sum outcome. As is true, however, in most social justice contexts, there is no exact "how-to" book written on the subject. Such a process may, at best, take place in fits and starts and in places its threads may unwind periodically. There exists, however, considerable overlap in the roster of countries which participate in both the ICNRD and CD initiatives. Many of their recommendations are similar. The reality of limited resources plus the fact that the window of opportunity for this current democratic "wave" may not be permanent, suggests a need and certain immediacy on this issue. This plan of action thus focuses on ways to promote useful cooperation between these two initiatives.

It is important to note the existence of different perspectives between these two groups and that this provides incentives as well as challenges. For example, ICNRD members could benefit from association with the greater democratic legitimacy enjoyed by the CD. Conversely, the CD could extend its impact and reach by accessing the broader audience (NGO, parliamentary, political party base and, in some cases governmental) represented in the ICNRD membership. Both groups would score public relations points by the visuals of working together as long as, from the CD point of view, this was done in such as way as to avoid diluting its position of not working with authoritarian governments.

Having background as a diplomat, a senior staff member of a democracy promotion NGO, and a published academic on the general subject, at the request of the CD Convening Group, I was invited to participate in a seminar on democracy and development, which took place in Bamako, March 29-31, 2007 and was co-sponsored by the United Nations Development Program (UNDP). The seminar was entitled *Democracy and De-*

velopment: Poverty as a Challenge to Democratic Governance; the presentation was on Regional Organizations and the role they can play in promoting democracy. This was organized in the lead-up to the November CD Ministerial Conference.

On the margins of this seminar I had discussions with the U.N. and UNDP office directors. These talks centered on ways that, under U.N. auspices, some level of congruence and coordination could be fostered between the CD and ICNRD. I emphasized that while pluralism in the world of democracy promotion initiatives is not by itself negative, the fact is that there is only limited amount of resources for such initiatives, and energy spent in competition might be better utilized in pursuing some projects and programming in a more cooperative fashion.

To further these ends I proposed a plan of action suggesting a way forward on this issue. This agenda would be proposed for recommendation and implementation by both organizations' member states. It identified the following possible themes drawn from the proceedings of both organizations which a common agenda of action could be developed.

- Deter democratic backsliding in member states.
- Refine appropriate incentives for progress in democratization, for example through expanded or adapted initiatives such as the Millennium Challenge Corporation (MCA) or the addition of a Millennium Development Goal (MDG) focusing on democratization.
- Promote collective regionally-based security forces for democracy protection.
- Strongly encourage international financial institutions (IFIs) to further recognize the inter-related nature of economic and political development.
- Induce the U.N. and its member states to more actively promote democracy, through further strengthened and empowered the U.N. Democracy Caucus and a U.N. Human Rights Council, which unambiguously promotes human rights and democratic development.
- Promote the development of peer-conducted country-level democracy audits, such as the African Peer Review Mechanism, as long as such mechanisms maintain independent integrity and quality.
- Share best practices and work with other countries to more effectively promote democracy and aid countries in their transition to democracy.

- Encourage regional intergovernmental organization cooperation, for example through the adoption of declarations or charters to promote regional cohesion and democracy.
- Link poverty reduction and democratic development.
- Provide a supportive "enabling environment" in which political parties can develop.
- Improve election monitoring and the development of mechanisms to increase transparency and other tenets of democracy.
- Promote democracy at the sub-national levels.
- Provide democracy education amongst the youth and disadvantaged sectors of society.
- Foster civil society development.

Sources: Community of Democracies Santiago Commitment, 2005 and the Final Report, Sixth Conference of New and Restored Democracies, Doha, 2006

This agenda also could include the creation of a permanent structure or structures, one of whose tasks could be the monitoring of the implementation of previous recommendations. They could take inspiration for this process from the example of the Organization for Security and Cooperation in Europe (OSCE) which, after the fall of communism, evolved from a periodic series of meetings attended by participating states, to a formal institution with a permanent infrastructure.

Realism has had to be called for in this effort; it is important to note the existence of different perspectives between these two groups. Communication and cooperation between the CD and the ICNRD has been limited. This is due in part to substantive reasons; as noted previously the ICNRD is open to any country that wishes to participate, while the CD Convening Group has developed a set of criteria to determine which countries meet a certain threshold of adherence to democratic values and practices. At its more basic level, there has been a sense of rivalry between the two groups because they are simply that: two different "competing" initiatives perceived by many to be in a subtle form of competition, with varying track records, dynamics and perspectives. To oversimplify somewhat, there has been a sense among certain CD members that the ICNRD lacks credibility, while some ICNRD participants tend to view the CD as an elitist group that picks and chooses its members on a subjective basis.

I recommended that the appropriate office in the U.N. host a meeting, perhaps in New York on the margins of the annual U.N. General Assembly, at which U.N. representatives could lead a dialogue between leaders of these two organizations. The results of such a meeting could feed into the decision-making processes of both organizations and result in a renewed commitment on the part of both initiatives to find ways with which to work with each other.

I also prepared and sent to both groups a document analyzing recommendations that emerged from the last two CD meetings (Seoul and Santiago) and last two ICNRD conferences (Ulan Bator and Doha) and which also identified areas of common focus, upon which a substantive discussion could be constructed. It also identified the membership rosters of each organization, and points out the significant overlapping membership. This document also suggested that the CD and the ICNRD have many similarities as organizations mandated to promote global democracy. In fact, over half of ICNRD member countries participate in the CD. Participation criteria in the ICNRD and CD differ significantly, however, and affect the functioning of each group. The CD specifies a comprehensive list of criteria countries must meet in order to participate, outlined in the CD Criteria for Participation and Procedures

At this writing it is too early to definitively assess the impact and results of this initiative. It is clear, however, its message has succeeded in being heard by the ICNRD and the CD leadership. For example, Article 75 of the CD's November 2007 Bamako Miniterial Consensus document explicitly endorsed intensified contacts between both organizations. Both groupings have been challenged to further consider how they could effectively work together; they have been put on notice that outsiders recognize the somewhat dysfunctional relationship to date between these two groups, and its deleterious impact on democracy promotion globally, has been noticed. At a minimum the concept of a permanent secretariat has been adopted by the CD, and was announced at their meeting in November.

Conclusion

Overall both the ICNRD and CD have similar goals, and in their documents emphasize the centrality and importance of democracy and human rights. The stated aim of both groups is to successfully spread democracy. Both groups also stated their desire to work with each other; the CD within the Santiago Commitment and the ICNRD in the Doha

Declaration. Both groups also explicitly note the importance of ensuring that their members have a solid foundation for democracy, as outlined in their recommendations. The ICNRD is, however, a less discriminating organization than the CD, with lower democracy standards for participation. These differences in participation criteria affect some specific recommendations produced by each group.

The preceding discussion suggests that there are clearly a number of different thematic areas in which the ICNRD and the CD both place considerable emphasis, and which could be areas of coordinated, if not common, focus. But communication has been lacking; this is what lead to my intervention and role in promoting inter-group dialogue. In order to increase effectiveness and efficiency, the two organizations must work together to not only promote member state practices, but the goals and methods of the groupings themselves. A more profound challenge in this regard is to actually operationalize the somewhat generalized expressions of interest in a programmatic sense. It should be possible to identify subsequent actions which are taken as a result of this enagament. For example, there may be increased contacts and visits between representatives of the two movements. The development of secretariats, which both movements have indicated will occur, could facilitate these contacts.

The more fundamental measure of success will be longer-term. It will consist of assessing what meaningful results occur as a result of heightened communication. For example, lessened suspicion and heightened actual cooperation will be a positive result. The CD and ICNRD may implement joint programming along the lines suggested above, or they may otherwise more effectively allocate democracy promotion resources as a result of increased coordination. If successful, this cooperation could lead to further democracy and respect for human rights around the world.

The following general reflections regarding social justice action planning result from this case study:

The Action Plan Developer (APD) should have credibility in the field. This person or entity can be either an interested party to the issue, or an independent neutral actor. Obviously the dynamics will be different given the role the APD plays in the implementation of the plan. If the APD is an interested party, then the Plan will likely be designed to ensure a successful outcome to its objectives. If it is neutral, then the Plan will likely be oriented towards bringing together various actors in the pursuit of a common goal; hence our interest in Collaborative Theory.   What is important is that the APD bring credibility and expertise in the subject matter to the table.

Relatedly, **the APD should enjoy the trust and confidence of the various parties**. This may not always be the case at the initiation of the Plan, as the APD may not yet be known by or have established relationships with the various actors. But it can develop.

The most effective types of Action Plans emphasize common interests/ground upon which the different actors can find agreement and build towards a positive social justice outcome. A very interesting NGO which works in the field in the international arena is Search for Common Ground (SCG). Its website (http://www.sfcg.org/) notes that there are five core principles to the Common Ground approach: a) that conflict is neither negative nor positive, but the natural result of differences between people; b) conflict can be transformed; c) finding common ground is not the same as settling for the lowest common denominator, but rather generating a new "highest common denominator."; d) the resolution of conflicts is a process, not a one-time solution; and e) that humankind is interdependent and thus the resolution of conflicts is of utmost importance.

There need to be appropriate incentives (carrots) to encourage the parties to cooperate. Alternatively, disincentives (sticks) may exist to push the parties toward cooperation. It is the responsibility of the APD to identify the most effective choice of inducements of either variety. Key considerations in this regard include the relative balance between sticks and carrots, and the proper timing and sequencing of their introduction.

A strategy for applying these incentives/disincentives is vital. Deciding when they are to be applied is a fundamental factor in determining the success of the initiative.

Bibliography

Bratton, M. (1997). International versus Domestic Pressures for Democratization in Africa. In W. Hale, Kienle, E. (Ed.), *After the Cold War: Security and Democracy in Africa and Asia.* New York: Taurus.

Clark, E. S. (2003). International Standards and Democratization: Certain Trends. In E. McMahon, Sinclair, T. (Ed.), *Democratic Institution Performance: Research and Policy Perspectives.* Westport: Praeger.

Diamond, L. (1999). *Developing Democracy: Toward Consolidation*. Baltimore: Johns Hopkins University Press.

Fox, G., and Roth, B. (2000). *Democratic Governance and International Law*. Cambridge: Cambridge University Press.

Franck, T. (1992). The Emerging Right to Democratic Governance. *American Journal of International Law, 86*(1), 1-45.

Franck, T. (1995). *Fairness in International Law and Institutions*. New York: Oxford University Press.

Franck, T. (2001). Legitimacy and the Democratic Entitlement. In *Democratic Govern ance and International Law*. Cambridge: Cambridge University Press.

Halperin, M. and Lomasney, K. . (1998). Guaranteeing Democracy: A Review of the Record. *Journal of Democracy, 9*(2), 134-147.

Halperin, M. and Galic, M. . (2005). *Protecting Democracy: International Responses*. New York: Lexington.

Huntington, S. (1991). *The Third Wave: Democratization in the Late Twentieth Century*. Norman: University of Oklahoma Press.

McMahon, E. and Baker, S. (2006). *Piecing a Democratic Quilt: Universal Norms and Regional organizations*. Bloomfield: Kumerian.

McMahon, E., and Sinclair, T. (Eds.) (2002). *Democratic Institution Performance: Re search and Policy Perspectives*. Westport: Praeger.

Peterson, M. J. (1997). *Recognition of Governments: Legal Doctrine and State Practice*. New York: St. Martin's Press.

Piccone, T. (Ed.). (2004). *Regime Change by the Book: Constitutional Tools to Preserve Democracy*. Washington, D.C.: Democracy Coalition Project,

Puddington, A. E. A. (2003). *Freedom in the World: Annual Survey of Political Rights and Civil Liberties*. New York: Freedom House.

Rich, R. (2001). Bringing Democracy Into international Law. *Journal of Democracy, 12*(3) pp. 98-99.

Threats to Democracy: Prevention and Response. (2003).). Washington, D.C.: Council on Foreign Relations Press.

Zakaria, F. (1997). The Rise of Illiberal Democracy. *Foreign Affairs, 76* (November/December).

CHAPTER 13

SOCIAL JUSTICE, ABORIGINAL LEADERSHIP, AND MINERAL DEVELOPMENT IN AUSTRALIA

Ciaran O'Faircheallaigh

Introduction

Australia's Aboriginal people experience serous economic and social disadvantage. For instance, compared to Australia's population as a whole, Aboriginal Australians have a life expectancy at birth that is 17 years shorter; suffer an incidence of kidney disease 10 times larger; are only half as likely to have a post-high school qualification; and are three times more likely to be unemployed (Productivity Commission 2007). At the same time Australia is experiencing a period of sustained economic growth associated with one the largest 'resource booms' in its history, driven in part by ever-increasing demand from China for Australia's abundant mineral resources. Many of these resources are located on the ancestral land of Aboriginal people.

A situation in which unprecedented wealth is being extracted from Aboriginal territories at the same time as Aboriginal people live in poverty and lack access to basic human services represents a profound challenge to social justice. At the same time the resources boom creates an opportunity to address this challenge, if recent changes to Australian law recognising Aboriginal title to substantial areas of land (Strelein 2006) can be used to capture a share of mineral wealth, and that wealth can be used to create social and economic opportunities for Aboriginal people (Kimberley Land Council 2008). In this situation effective Aboriginal leadership is critical in ensuring that current opportunities are turned to maximum advantage. Absence of effective leadership will mean that the current resources boom, like earlier booms in Australia's history, will pass Aboriginal people by.

This is not to suggest that in the past Aboriginal leaders have not sought to protect their people from the negative impacts of mining and tried to obtain for them a share of the wealth it generates. The case study of the Argyle diamond mine outlined below highlights the efforts of Aboriginal leaders in earlier decades. But they have faced formidable problems, including limited resources in dealing with large, wealthy mining companies; a legal context that afforded limited recognition to Aboriginal land rights; and governments concerned mainly with facilitating mineral development rather than with promoting indigenous interests. This chapter shows how a new generation of Aboriginal leaders, who have benefited from educational opportunities denied their parents and grandparents, are working with 'traditional' leaders to address these problems, to challenge existing power structures and to create more just outcomes from resource development on Aboriginal land.

Leadership in Aboriginal Australia

In order to understand Aboriginal leadership in contemporary Australia, it is necessary to consider both the nature of pre-contact or 'classical' Aboriginal society and politics[1] and the recent history of Aboriginal engagement with mainstream Australia.

Pre-contact Aboriginal societies were generally small in scale, and based around groups defined by their kinship ties and relations to specific areas of land. Leadership was contextual and contingent. Different individuals might play a leading role in different spheres of activity, and specific roles shifted from one person to another depending on their relationship to the individual or individuals around whom, for instance, initiation or mortuary ceremonies were organised. Many aspects of social and religious life were gendered, creating another limitation on the exercise of influence or decision-making by particular individuals. Thus while there were certainly powerful individuals who played leadership roles in key areas of life, their roles essentially reflected personal characteristics such as their age and wisdom; their knowledge of the land, its resources, and of the law and ritual; and their ability as fighters and defenders of their people. Individual land-owning groups exercised a high degree of autonomy in decision-making. In general, each group made its own decisions about use of resources and conduct of its social and political affairs independently of other groups. Thus there was no supra-local (for instance regional) body with the authority to take and enforce decisions in relation, for instance, to allocation or management of resources

(Edwards 1998; Hiatt 1998; Ivory 2005a; Megitt 1966; Myers 1980; Sutton and Rigsby 1982).

In summary, classical Aboriginal leadership was contextual, contingent, and localised, with little or no precedent for supra-local or regional political or social organisation.

Everywhere in Australia, colonial settlement had massive impacts on Aboriginal social and political life, impacts all the greater because of the complete absence of treaties between colonial governments and Aboriginal peoples. The specific experience of individual Aboriginal societies varied considerably, depending on the timing of colonial expansion, the suitability of different regions to European agriculture, and the presence or absence of mineral resources. In eastern, southern and south western Australia, dispossession of Aboriginal people was almost complete by the mid-19th century and some Aboriginal societies had ceased to exist. In the arid centre and the monsoonal north Aboriginal groups were more likely to be left in possession of their ancestral land, or at least remain resident on it while providing labor to the European operators of large pastoral properties.

While the impact of colonial settlement was uneven and helps to explain the great diversity that characterized Aboriginal social and political life today, it is important to recognize that in every instance its effects were fundamental and far-reaching. For example, it is estimated that the Aboriginal population of Australia fell from between 1.0 and 1.5 million in 1788 to just 90,000 in the 1920s (Butlin 1993, 139, 229). Population decline on this scale had massive impacts on Aboriginal societies, on their social and political institutions, and on their leaders and leadership structures.

The imposition of colonial rule had other and more specific effects. In general colonial authorities were ignorant of and paid no attention to Aboriginal leadership structures. Governments and the missionaries that played a key role in administration of Aboriginal settlements in many parts of Australia imposed their own Eurocentric structures that, until the 1980s, provided few opportunities for Aboriginal participation. Aboriginal settlements were highly institutionalised and regimented, and left little space for Aboriginal people to develop or apply decision-making, organisational and leadership skills. Aboriginal cultural and social practices, and the leadership that accompanied them, were often discouraged or suppressed (see, for example, Blake 2001; Brock 1993). This does not mean that Aboriginal leadership ceased to exist. It often found expression in attempts to resist the worst excesses of colonialism while maintaining a distinctly Aboriginal way of life, and the capacity of so many Aboriginal people throughout Australia to survive the massive impacts of dispossession and colonization and retain their distinct social and cultural identities and vitality provides eloquent testimony of the power and persistence of Aboriginal leadership. Importantly, leaders generally worked by undermining the dominant formal authority structures, rather than on working in or through those structures (Blake 2001; Peters-Little 2000). The latter was generally not an option available to them.

Another major impact resulted from the practice of government and missions of bringing members of different Aboriginal societies together in centralized settlements, to facilitate their control, the dissemination of European religion and, especially after the second world war, the provision of education, health and other services. In many cases large numbers of previously autonomous land-owning and language groups were drawn from a wide area to a single settlement. The result today is that these settlements, while often referred to as 'communities', are in fact comprised of distinct groups that may have different interests and do not accept the authority of other groups in the community or of structures such as elected 'community councils' (Ivory 2005b, 2005c; Peters-Little 2000). The legitimacy and authority of 'community leaders' is frequently contested from within.

Until the 1970s, Aboriginal people in Australia were in effect excluded from participation in the political mainstream. They were denied the vote in must jurisdictions until the 1960s; suffered serious limits on their freedom of movement and their right to organize politically; were denied access to educational and employment opportunities; and suffered institutionalized racism across every facet of social, economic and political life. They were also largely denied the benefits of the huge increase in state activity and government expenditures that occurred after Word war II. The result was that by the 1970s Aboriginal people lagged far behind other Australians in terms of their health, their economic status and their access to key public services such as education and housing. While there has been some improvement during recent decades in certain indicators such as infant mortality rates, little change has occurred in the general social and economic status of Australia's Aboriginal peoples. The poverty, lack of economic opportunity and serious social problems facing many Aboriginal communities is a critical part of the context for contemporary Aboriginal leadership, and current difficulties are likely to be compounded in the future by rapid population growth rates (Ivory 2005c, 1-2; Taylor 2006, 19-20). Resources are scarce, and the demands on them many and urgent.

From the 1960s onwards Aboriginal Australians gained greater access to educational opportunities and became increasingly involved in mainstream political activity. They also became very active in creating Aboriginal cultural, social and political organizations. These included Aboriginal legal services designed to challenge racism and allow Aboriginal people to exercise their legal rights; organizations that took responsibility for delivery of health, education and housing services; and regional land councils focused on winning recognition of Aboriginal land rights and on supporting Aborigines in managing and controlling their traditional lands. As Aboriginal people have achieved access to political rights and built their organizational capacity, they have achieved a significant voice in political and policy debate at state and national levels in Australia. Their political profile has also been substantially increased as a result of the growing recognition of Aboriginal rights in land, initially through legislative initiatives by state, territory and national governments, some of which proved abortive, and more recently and very importantly by the Australian High Court's 1992 *Mabo* decision. The High Court found that inherent indigenous rights in land ('native title') survived the establishment of British colonial rule in 1788, and can still survive today where indigenous peoples have maintained their connection with their traditional lands and where their title has not been extinguished by the valid grant of titles to other parties. In 1993 the federal government enacted the *Native Title Act (NTA)*, which provides a system for recognizing native title where it has survived and for a process of negotiation between developers and native title interests regarding the grant of future interests, such as mining leases, in native title lands (Strelein 2006).

As a result of the developments described above, 'Aboriginal leadership' in Australia is now complex and multi-faceted. For most non-indigenous Australians and for mainstream politicians, 'Aboriginal leaders' refers to a small group of nationally prominent individuals with substantial media profiles who have held senior offices in state or national Aboriginal organizations or in government bodies dealing with Aboriginal affairs. In reality Aboriginal leadership is much wider than this group. It includes for instance Aboriginal office holders in regional land organizations, in rural and urban service delivery organizations and in community councils, and people who play leadership roles in grass roots community movements in areas such as health, justice, arts and culture and resource management. More broadly, in much of Australia there is an extremely important and influential Aboriginal leadership at the local and regional levels whose members may not hold any formal office. These are the men and women who exercise leadership and authority because of the knowledge and experience they hold regarding Aboriginal law, custom and spiritual life and regarding the interlocked areas of kinship and rights and interests in land. Their leadership is often exercised in ways that are unobtrusive, relies on informal communication and involves building consensus among individuals and groups with an interest in a specific issue or decision. According to Ivory, such an approach has its roots in classical times:

> ... the ceremonial leader of a clan would have an intimate knowledge of ceremonies, stages, sequences, and objects. He would also have to address gathered clansmen if a situation or problem arose. He would lead the meeting but the final decision would be made in conjunction with the others present (2005).

Because it is often not associated with any formal organizational role and because of its style, white Australians often fail to recognize the significance and even the existence of leadership at this level (see, for example, Ivory 2005a, 1). However it represents a critical dimension of leadership because it can mobilize sources of legitimacy and support that cannot be mobilized through the holding of office in formal or 'mainstream' organizations, a point illustrated later in the case study. Indeed in at least some regions of Australia 'classical' sources of authority and leadership are becoming more rather than less important, as Aboriginal people use their growing control of land, resources and organizations to reinvigorate ceremonial life and modify institutions imported from the mainstream (see, for instance Ivory 2005b, 2005c).

In summary, Aboriginal leadership is fluid, multi-faceted, complex and contested. It is not organized in a hierarchy from the local to the national. The status of leaders at every level, but particularly at the local level, is often unrelated to the occupation of elected office or of formal organizational roles. Partly for this reason, but also because of the way in which Aboriginal 'communities' have been constituted and because of the enduring emphasis on group autonomy, leadership is often contested (Foley 1998; Peters-Little 2000). From a Eurocentric perspective, with its assumptions of the superiority of Weberian hierarchy, the fluid and contingent nature of Aboriginal leadership could be regarded as a major weakness. However it has arisen from key characteristics of Aboriginal societies and their struggle to survive and maintain their distinct identities within the dominant society, and it in fact offers Aboriginal people important advantages in interacting with that society. We explore this theme in examining the role of Aboriginal leaders in relation to large-scale mineral development on Aboriginal lands.

Large-Scale Mining Projects on Aboriginal Lands

Mining has occurred on Aboriginal lands throughout Australia's history, but since the 1950s the scale and extent of mineral development has increased enormously as Australia has established itself as one of the world's leading mineral producers. Historically Aboriginal people were marginalized from mineral development. They had no say in whether mining did or did not proceed or regarding the conditions under which it would occur. As a result mining projects often resulted in destruction of sites or areas of spiritual significance; caused widespread environmental damage; and generated few economic benefits for Aboriginal people. In many cases the Aboriginal owners on land on which development occurred were simply pushed out of the way, relegated to fringe camps on the edge of affluent mining towns (Howitt 1990; O'Faircheallaigh 1991). Matters began to change in the 1970s as a result of Aboriginal political mobilization and the introduction of environmental impact assessment and cultural heritage protection legislation that created some opportunities for Aboriginal people to intervene in public decisions on resource projects. The introduction of the *Aboriginal (Northern Territory) Land Rights Act 1976* allowed Aborigines in the Northern Territory to claim unalienated crown land and, where their claims were successful, to determine whether exploration (and so eventually mining) could occur on their traditional lands. However legislative initiatives in other jurisdictions were much more limited or non-existent, and it was not until the passage of the *Native Title Act 1993* that Aboriginal people in most parts of Australia had any legal basis on which to influence development on their ancestral lands.

The failure of Australian governments to recognize Aboriginal rights in land did not, it should be noted, result in Aboriginal people passively accepting mineral development. In a number of high profile cases Aboriginal groups attempted, often in alliance with civil society groups, to use direct action and political campaigns to stop developments that threatened their ancestral lands. In some cases they were successful, as in the campaign of the Jaywon people to stop the Coronation Hill gold project near the South Alligator River in the Northern Territory. However in many they were not, as in the campaigns to stop bauxite mining at Yirrkala and uranium mining in the Kakadu region, both in the Northern Territory, and oil drilling at Noonkanbah in Western Australia, where the government provided a police escort to allow drilling rigs to enter Aboriginal owned land containing sacred sites. The general failure of such campaigns reflects the power of the mining industry and the strong support of governments in Australia for the industry, reflecting in turn a belief by most Australians that placing constraints on resource development is not in the national interest (Stokes 1987).

An alternative approach for Aboriginal people was to negotiate with developers to achieve a share of the benefits created by mining and to minimize its negative impacts. Outside the Northern Territory, formal opportunities to negotiate were rare until the passage of the *NTA* in 1994. (As we shall see, this did not mean that Aboriginal leaders could not create informal channels for negotiation.) In recent years another important opportunity to negotiate with developers has resulted from the adoption by some major mining companies of 'corporate social responsibility' policies requiring them to achieve the support of affected Aboriginal communities for their mining operations. One such company was Rio Tinto, whose CEO announced in 1995 that Rio accepted the existence of native title and would work to establish positive relations with all Aboriginal communities affected its mining operations. These included the Argyle diamond mine, the focus of our case study.

Aboriginal Leadership and the Argyle Diamond Mine, 1979–2000

In 1979 the exploration arm of the Australian mining company CRA Ltd, whose major shareholder was the London-based Rio Tinto, obtained licenses to search for diamonds in the northwest of Western Australia, close to Lake Argyle. While the arrival of the pastoral industry and of government and missionaries in the late 19th century had brought many changes and resulted in most people living on cattle stations or on missions, Aboriginal people in the area maintained strong attachments to their ancestral lands, continued to adhere to Aboriginal law and custom, and maintained a vigorous ceremonial tradition. A number of ceremonies were associated with 'dreaming tracks' that traversed the region, marking the travel routes of ancestral beings during the creative period of the Dreaming,[2] and linking Aboriginal traditional owners[3] in the area to many other Aboriginal groups in surrounding regions.

The area in which CRA focused its exploration contained sites of great spiritual significance, not just in a local but also in a regional context. A number of these sites were registered with the Western Australia (WA) Museum, and as such supposedly protected by Western Australia's *Cultural Heritage Act 1972*. In late 1979 and 1980 Aboriginal people traversing the area realized that a number of sites had been damaged by CRA's activities. They approached the WA Museum, demanding that it protect the sites. When it failed to do so one of the traditional owners (since deceased and referred to here by the acronym BJ) made a Court application in May 1980 seeking an injunction against CRA on the basis that it had breached the *Cultural Heritage Act*. BJ was supported by other traditional owners with an interest in Argyle, a recently formed regional land organizations the Kimberley Land Council (KLC), and the community council at Warmun or Turkey Creek, the largest Aboriginal community in the region. On July 7 BJ withdrew his application, in the expectation that the WA Museum would act to protect the sites. In fact the Museum, under pressure from government Ministers, deferred its legal action (Dixon et al. 1990, 116-17). In the meantime CRA had applied, as it was permitted to under Section 18 of the *Cultural Heritage Act* to 'make alternative use' of a number of key sites. In the context of a mining project, this in effect would allow the company to destroy the sites. In September 1980 the Minister for Aboriginal Affairs, on the recommendation of the WA Museum, approved CRA application. CRA proceed with its exploration and, ultimately, with establishing the Argyle mine, one of the world's largest diamond producers, which became operational in 1983. One of the sites was completely destroyed in the process, and another severely damaged (Dixon and Dillon 1990).

In July 1980 BJ, two of his siblings and two other traditional owners were flown to Perth by CRA and, without the benefit of independent legal advice, signed what became known as the Glen Hill Agreement. This provided for capital expenditure of $200,000 in the first year and $100,000 per annum thereafter on a small community or 'outstation' called Glen Hill that BJ and his family had just started to establish some 30 km from the Argyle mine site. In return the signatories accepted that CRA's activities would disturb sites, and agreed to support establishment of the Argyle diamond project (CRA Exploration Pty Ltd *et a.l* 1980).

The signing the Glen Hill Agreement has been explained by some as the action of largely illiterate Aboriginal people who were duped by a wealthy and sophisticated mining company and as a result 'utterly betrayed' Aboriginal interests (Dixon 1990, 67). Another interpretation is that BJ had concluded by mid-July that there was no prospect of stopping the mine, that the traditional owners would be overwhelmed by the power of the mining company supported by the state government, as had occurred recently at Noonkanbah, and that the only choices that remained was to try and capture some benefit from the project. This was certainly how BJ himself interpreted his actions (Dixon 1990, 73-74), and other traditional owners shared his understanding of their situation:

> They gave it [the mine site] away because blackfella has no cut [power] to fight back, poor buggers. Blackfella thought, 'We have no power to stop this. We'll just have to let them go ahead'. But they thought they should get something back out of the country to help keep building up the place for the young people coming behind (cited in Dixon 1990, 75).

While there may have been widespread sympathy for the position in which BJ and his family group found themselves, the specific arrangements they negotiated caused considerable resentment among other traditional owners of the Argyle mine site and drew criticism from Aboriginal people in the region and from organisations such as the KLC. There exists in the Kimberley a strong and vibrant system of governance, sharing and exchange called *wunan*. Under this system there is pressure to reciprocate when a person is given something of value, and to share benefits that accrue to any participant within the system. However the very limited benefits offered by the Glen Hill Agreement, combined with the fact that the company insisted they be directed at capital spending, meant that BJ had almost no capacity to spread benefits more widely to include other Aboriginal people with an interest in Argyle and more broadly to comply with *wunan* obligations (Dixon 1990, 68). As a result he was subject to sustained attack by other traditional owners (Bruce and Toby 1980, Dixon 1980) and according to one observer experienced 'a rupturing of relationships and an end of the leadership role he had previously played. In time, as he marshalled greater resources ... he has regained part of his formal influence but not his formal authority' (Christensen 1990, 33).

The outcomes just described reflect the serious imbalance of power between Aboriginal traditional owners and the dominant political, economic and social system. As one traditional owner expressed it, 'The white man pushed us off our land. They give blackfella a little bit of land. Then they find minerals and they take it away from us. When are they going to give us a fair go, the bastards ...' (cited in Dixon 1980, 72). Having first tried to prevent damage to sacred sites one Aboriginal leader, coming to the conclusion that the attempt was futile, sought to gain some economic advantage from the creation of the Argyle mine. However the massive imbalance of knowledge and resources between his family group and CRA, combined with a state government steadfast in its support of the company and indifferent to Aboriginal interests, meant that the outcome could not possibly satisfy the demands of the wider Aboriginal interests in Argyle. The repercussions of this situation were, as we shall see, long lived.

Pressure immediately grew on the developer of the Argyle mine, Argyle Diamonds Ltd (ADM), to expand to scope of benefits beyond the Glen Hill Agreement. This pressure emanated from BJ himself, motivated by criticism from the wider traditional owner group; from other senior traditional owners; and from leaders of communities affected by the mine, including Warmun and another small adjacent community, Doon Doon (Dixon 1990, 86). In July 1981 ADM agreed to establish what it called a Good Neighbour Programme (GNP) to include annual payments to Warmun ($100,000) and Doon Doon ($40,000). By 1985 total GNP payments had risen to $330,000. A change of government in Western

Australia led to the establishment, in that year, of a joint ADM WA government Aboriginal Social Impact Group to address social impacts aris-
ing from the Argyle mine, and an increase in ADM's annual expenditure
to some $500,000 per annum for the next five years. However control of
expenditure and priorities still remained with ADM and the state government (Dillon 1990, 144-45).

More generally over the two decades after 1980 senior traditional
owners and leaders of affected communities engaged in an ongoing
process of (often informal) engagement and negotiation with ADM,
aimed at both extending the scope of benefits generated by the company
and gaining greater Aboriginal control over their use. Their proximity to
the mine site, their involvement as employees at the mine, and ADM's
creation of a 'community affairs' section to manage its relations with the
local Aboriginal communities all provided opportunities to engage with
company officials. This led, over time, to an incremental increase in the
benefits flowing from the project and a gradual increase in the ability of
the Aboriginal groups to determine their own priorities in allocating
funds. For instance individual communities succeeded at times in negotiating an annual allocation greater than their entitlement under the GNP,
while senior traditional owners negotiated support for outstations at
which they resided or personal benefits such as the payment of fines or
loans to help purchase vehicles or equipment. Traditional owners also
negotiated to gain access to employment at Argyle, and to provide cultural heritage training and other paid services to ADM. In 1997 the company agreed, on the basis of representations to one of its community
relations managers by certain traditional owners, to make an annual cash
payment of $100,000 to be used at the discretion of the signatories to the
Glen Hill Agreement. However as this group excluded a sibling of BJ's of
who had not travelled to Perth and also excluded many other people
with an interest in Argyle, the arrangement failed to address (and indeed
served to increase) tensions engendered by the original Glen Hill agreement. Senior traditional owners also pressed ADM to protect other sites
affected by its operations, and to do so through a systematic site identif-
cation and protection regime rather than on an ad hoc basis.

By 2002 the total flow of financial benefits to communities and signatories had reached $850,000. However this still represented only a tiny
fraction (less than 0.15 percent) of the revenues now being generated by

sales of diamonds from Argyle. In addition apart from the original Glen Hill Agreement, ADM had declined to enter into legally binding agreements, so that maintenance of its various 'community relations' expenditures was at its discretion. Further, the necessity for the traditional owners and communities to engage in an ongoing and ad hoc process of negotiation to obtain benefits allowed ADM's community relations staff to adopt a highly interventionist and often paternalistic approach in their relations with Aboriginal people.

The Argyle Diamonds Agreement, 2004

By this time a number of circumstances surrounding the Argyle diamond mine had changed. CRA Ltd had merged with Rio Tinto in 1995, making Rio Tinto the major shareholder in Argyle, and in 2001 Argyle became a wholly owned subsidiary of Rio. As mentioned earlier, Rio had determined in 1995 that it would seek to establish positive relationships with Aboriginal communities affected by its mines. Argyle was due to exhaust the ore that was accessible by open pit mining by about 2007 and it had been assumed that mining would then cease, but in 1999 Rio decided that ADM should investigate the possibility of moving its operations underground and continue mining, possibly until 2020. In either case, Rio would want an agreement with the Aboriginal traditional owners of Argyle, as a foundation on which to build a continuing relationship with them or, in the event of closure, as the basis for an 'exit strategy' that would resolve outstanding issues and so protect Rio's reputation.

In 2001 Argyle approached the KLC and asked for its participation in establishing a negotiation process with traditional owners that would lead to a comprehensive agreement between them and the company. The KLC was established by Kimberley traditional owners in 1979 as a regional, grassroots regional political organization to assist them oppose developments threatening their cultural heritage sites and traditional lands and win recognition of their Aboriginal rights. The KLC had also, in 1995, been recognized by the federal government as the Native Title Representative Body (NTRB) for the region, and as such performed a number of statutory roles under the as *NTA*, including assisting traditional owners to lodge and pursue native title claims and certifying agreements between Aboriginal landowners and developers. The KLC's day-to-day operations were managed by an executive director, and in

2001 a young Aboriginal man was appointed to this position who had been born and brought up in the Kimberley, worked for Aboriginal organizations there, and had then completed a law degree and worked with a major commercial law firm in Perth.

In September 2001 the KLC and ADM signed a Memorandum of Understanding that set out ADM's intention to negotiate a comprehensive agreement with traditional owners and the basis on which the KLC would assist traditional owners in the negotiations; and dealt with a range of practical matters including funding for the negotiation, which would be provided by ADM. At this stage it was envisaged that the negotiation process would be concluded by June 2003. In April 2002 the KLC started preparing for negotiations, retaining specialist anthropological, legal and financial consultants and seeking, in conjunction with ADM, to establish a committee that could oversee the negotiation process and ensure it generated a favourable outcome for traditional owners. Initially a negotiation committee was proposed composed primarily of office holders from local Aboriginal organisations such as community councils. However the KLC and ADM quickly concluded that this body would not be properly representative of, or be regarded as legitimate by, the traditional owners. They also concluded that substantial ethnographic work was required to establish the composition of the traditional owner group and to and appropriate decision making processes based on Aboriginal law and custom. In addition, the history of Argyle over the previous two decades, and especially the exclusion of key Aboriginal people from decision making and from benefits created by the project, had caused considerable distrust and conflict among traditional owners and between the KLC and traditional owners. The KLC therefore spent a considerable amount of time documenting decision-making processes; fully identifying traditional owner groups; bringing traditional owners together, helping them to work through their differences and building trust between them and the KLC; and establishing a structure that could oversee the negotiations.

A second Negotiation Committee was established that included all of the traditional owner groups with an interest in the Argyle lease area, with more substantial representation afforded the groups with immediate and primary interests (Argyle Diamond Mines and Kimberley Land Council 2003). This Committee consisted of a mix of senior traditional owners, who were knowledgeable about affected lands and Aboriginal law and custom but who had little formal education and whose knowledge of English and experience of formal negotiations was limited; and younger traditional owners who were less authoritative in matters of land, law and custom but had more formal education and experience of working in non-Aboriginal contexts. The Committee also included senior Aboriginal people who, while not traditional owners for Argyle, were connected to the area through dreaming tracks and stories. These individuals would monitor the agreement making process and their presence would add to its legitimacy and the legitimacy of any outcomes from it. In contrast, a feature of the earlier engagement between BJ's family group and CRA Exploration had been a failure to involve senior law people in key decisions regarding the Argyle site (Christensen 1990, 38). A further 'Framework Agreement' was signed in June 2003 between the KLC and ADM extending the time frame for the negotiations and providing additional funding to support it.

The senior traditional owner who had originally led the opposition to Argyle and his immediate family refused to participate in the negotiation process, and refused to be represented by the KLC. BJ was reportedly still bitter regarding what he saw as his abandonment by the other traditional owners and the KLC after the signing of the Glen Hill Agreement, and concerned that the benefits he had managed to negotiate would be diluted under a new agreement. He insisted that ADM should maintain the existing arrangements in relation to community and individual payments and that any new agreement would have to include a settlement negotiated between ADM and him.[4] During 2003-2004 both ADM and senior traditional owners and law people, supported by KLC staff, made repeated attempts to persuade him to join the Negotiating Committee, but without success.

Critical to the negotiation process was the development of what were called 'Traditional Owner (TO) Rules', referring to key negotiating positions to be put to the company by the traditional owners. The 'TO Rules' emerged from an extensive dialogue, particularly in two three day meetings conducted on traditional owners' country, between the Negotiating Committee, the KLC's Executive Director, and KLC staff and specialist consultants. Negotiating Committee members would articulate their aspirations, concerns and priorities. Consultants would provide information in relation to Rio Tinto policies and to other agreements that it had negotiated; to ADM's existing and planned operations; and regarding negotiation options in relation to specific issues such as financial compensation, protection of Aboriginal cultural heritage and promotion of Aboriginal employment and business development. All involved would engage in analysis of ADM's motivations and strategies and regarding effective negotiation strategies. From this dialogue emerged what were generally very short documents (usually less than one page), written in plain English, setting out the Negotiating Committee's position on each issue.

To take one very significant example, the first 'TO Rule' in relation to protection of Aboriginal cultural heritage was 'No means No'. As mentioned above, under Western Australia's cultural heritage legislation, if Aboriginal traditional owners opposed mining of a particular site (in other words if they said 'No'), a mining company could, as Argyle did in 1979, request the relevant Government minister to give it permission to damage or destroy the site. The traditional owners were saying to Argyle that it should make a legally binding commitment to them not to exercise its right to request that the Minister allow it to damage or destroy a site unless the traditional owners first approved such a course of action. In other words, if they took the position that exploration or mining should not take place in a specific place because of the damage it would cause to cultural heritage sites, Argyle would accept their decision thus, 'No means No'.

The development of the TO Rules were critical because they expressed, in simple English words that were understood by all the traditional owners and by the company, core negotiating principles and positions. When negotiations were under way, the traditional owners could use the TO Rules in evaluating and responding to company positions and to ensure that the discussion remained focused on issues that were of primary importance to the traditional owners.

The negotiations were at times protracted and difficult, continuing throughout 2003 and into 2004. At times the Negotiating Committee felt under considerable pressure to accept the company's offers, in part because there was no guarantee that the underground mine would proceed. If it did not, only limited time would remain in which to secure benefits for the traditional owners from ADM's operations, and the longer the negotiations took, the less time would be available. Senior traditional owners and law people played a critical role in maintaining the cohesion of the Negotiating Committee and in insisting that ADM accept the core 'TO Rules'. The senior law people played a particularly important role in ensuring that individuals who had only minor or indirect interests in the Argyle lease did not attempt to highjack the discussions or claim for themselves greater influence than they were entitled to under Aboriginal law and custom.

Older Negotiation Committee members, lacking confidence in their ability to express themselves in English and in some cases reluctant to criticise white people, were sometimes hesitant to express positions forcefully to company representatives or to criticise negotiating positions put by ADM. As a result younger traditional owners with more formal education played an important role at the interface with the company, as they were much less hesitant about putting positions assertively and criticising the company. However final decisions were taken by the senior traditional owners, as required by Aboriginal law and custom.

By mid 2004 agreement had been achieved on a majority of issues, but a few key matters were still outstanding and the Negotiating Committee was, with the support of the KLC's Executive Director, holding a strong position on these. At this critical juncture BJ intervened, writing to ADM and stating that he would not accept the legitimacy of any agreement negotiated in his absence. This weakened the ability of the Negotiating Committee and the KLC to hold firm, as did the fact that funding for the negotiations would soon expire and there was no guarantee that ADM would renew it. An agreement was finalised in mid 2004 and signed in September 2004.

The traditional owners achieved a number of their key objectives. In particular, they secured the 'No means No' rule in relation to cultural heritage, meaning that ADM will not seek government approval to damage or destroy a cultural heritage site without the consent of traditional owners. Given the history of the Argyle project, this outcome was of profound significance to the traditional owners. In addition, the Negotiating Committee secured, for the first time, substantial financial compensation for the traditional owner groups, and extension of individual payments to previously-excluded senior traditional owners. A significant proportion of compensation payments is allocated to long-term investment, with the result that when Argyle closes (now expected to be in 2018) the traditional owners will have a significant capital base that can continue to generate an income for them into the future. Funds are also allocated to support mens' and womens' cultural activities; education, business and community development initiatives by individual traditional owner groups; and health, housing and other initiatives in conjunction with government or private sector partners (Galganyem Trust and Kilkaya Trust 2006). All payments to traditional owners groups and to communities now result from a legally-binding contract, rather than from ad hoc discretionary arrangements. In addition, measures were agreed:

- to avoid inadvertent damage to cultural heritage sites and to manage sites already affected by ADM's operations;
- that require ADM to consult traditional owners in relation to environmental management of, and closure planning for, the Argyle project;
- to promote Aboriginal business development and maximise Aboriginal employment at Argyle;
- ensure that resources are available to support effective implementation of the agreement (Argyle Diamonds Ltd et al. 2004).[5]

Traditional owners and the KLC were disappointed in some aspects of the agreement, including the fact that financial benefits for traditional owners are based on gross profits, and so are more unstable and less certain than benefits based on ADM's revenues, the preferred alternative for traditional owners; and that ADM's commitment in relation to environmental management is only to consult the traditional owners and not to afford them a role in decision making.[6]

Conclusion and Analysis

Aboriginal leadership has been in evidence throughout the history of the Argyle project. Senior traditional owners and community leaders sought to use the very limited means available to them to prevent damage to their sacred sites from exploration at Argyle. When this failed and they were faced with the inevitability of a major mine on their traditional lands they sought, over two decades and in the face of a company possessed of overwhelming power and resources, to minimise damage to their sites and to use any available means to secure for themselves a share of the benefits generated by mining. In this they achieved some success. However the benefits they secured constituted only a tiny proportion of the wealth taken from their country, and this fact combined with the manner in which the original Glen Hill Agreement was signed and the exclusion of many traditional owners from a share in the benefits led to bitterness and disunity. This situation partly reflected the decisions of BJ to focus on securing benefits for his immediate family group. This decision is understandable given the poor living conditions and limited economic opportunities facing Aboriginal people in Australia. However it left him unable to draw on the leadership potential represented by other traditional owners for Argyle and by influential law people from the wider region.

After 2001 the involvement of another level of Aboriginal leadership in the form of the Kimberley Land Council and its executive director allowed the traditional owners to take advantage of changes in company policy and the status of the Argyle project to greatly expand the benefits flowing to traditional owners. With financial support from ADM, the KLC and traditional owners worked hard to build a strong negotiating platform, and in the process to overcome the fissures that had developed among traditional owners and between them and the KLC over the previous two decades. Both older and younger traditional owners on the Committee played key roles in pursuing negotiation goals and securing a favourable outcome, and they were supported in doing so by specialist consultants recruited by the KLC. Twenty years earlier the absence of such specialised technical advice had left the senior traditional owners isolated and vulnerable in dealing with a powerful multinational mining company. Thus the interaction of Aboriginal leadership at different levels was crucial, at the local level in the form of traditional owners deriving their authority from Aboriginal law and custom, and at a much broader regional level in the form of an Aboriginal organization deriving part of its authority and resources from the mainstream legal and political system.

The decision of one senior traditional owner to stand outside the negotiation process militated against an even more favourable outcome. As discussed earlier, traditional Aboriginal society was characterised by a high degree of group autonomy, but also by a substantial capacity to enforce discipline and cohesion within groups through the control by senior individuals of mundane and sacred knowledge, both essential to survival. Contact with European society and the arrival of a cash economy, has served to weaken the ability of the wider group to control the behaviour of individuals and families within the group. The result in the case of the Argyle negotiations was an inability of the wider group, which had agreed to jointly pursue a common goal, either to forcefully incorporate, or to marginalise, an individual whose actions had the potential to undermine the collective effort. Such limits on coercion represent an important constraint on contemporary Aboriginal leadership.

Much of the leadership displayed by Aboriginal people was neither charismatic in nature, associated with holding of formal offices, or particularly evident to a casual observer. The incremental winning of increased benefits over the period 1981-2002 was achieved through a series of low-key, direct engagements between traditional owners and company officials. The most vocal participants on behalf of traditional owners in meetings between the Negotiating Committee and ADM were younger Aboriginal people and KLC consultants, yet without the leadership of older traditional owners the Committee could not have been effective or indeed even functioned. An uninformed observer would probably not even notice the senior law people sitting quietly at the back of negotiation meetings. Yet their interventions were crucial in ensuring that the power of senior traditional owners was not usurped, thus allowing unity to develop and the Negotiating Committee to perform effectively, and helping to confer legitimacy on the outcome of negotiations.

The role of younger Aboriginal people who have benefited from greater access to educational opportunities, including the KLC's Executive Director, was equally important, highlighting the key place of education in pursuing social justice. Looking to the future, social justice can only be achieved for Australia's Aborigines if many more Aboriginal people across Australia's resource-rich regions complete high school and university, and obtain the skills necessary to negotiate with mining companies and governments and to take up positions of influence within these institutions. An important initiative in this regard is under way in Cape York in northern Queensland. The Cape York Institute for Policy and Leadership was established in 2004 through a partnership involving Cape York Aboriginal leaders, Griffith University and the Queensland and Australian governments. One of its key aims is to develop the leadership capacity of young Cape York Aboriginal people, and it has established a number of programs designed to support them in gaining entry to university, completing their courses, and developing their careers. For example the Institute's Higher Expectations Program (Tertiary) targets talented Cape York young people aged 17-30 with high achievement and leadership potential, and provides them with long-term support to undertake a successful tertiary career and maximize their opportunities for educational achievement, career development and effective leadership within their communities. To overcome the multiple disadvantages faced by students from Cape York, the Program provides a specialized and comprehensive support program. The Institute not only offer practical material assistance through scholarships, it also strengthens students' academic, social and emotional capacities, and for the duration of their studies participants receive a combination of holistic case management, leadership training and professional mentoring. The Program places strong family support and community identity at its core, and upholds as a core value that each participant should in time contribute to their homeland of Cape York (Cape York Institute for Policy and Leadership 2008).

The establishment of similar initiatives across Australia would greatly assist in ensuring that Aboriginal peoples achieve an equitable share of Australia's wealth and the opportunities associated with it, and in ending the social injustice currently experienced by so many Aboriginal Australians.

Notes

1. There is considerable debate regarding the nature of politics and of political leadership in classical Aboriginal society, reflecting the absence of any written record created by Aboriginal people themselves, a general lack of interest and understanding among early non-Aboriginal observers, and in many cases the self-interest of settlers in suggesting that the people they displaced lacked any coherent system of property rights or governance. In addition the diversity that characterized Aboriginal requires caution in offering generalizations. However a number of broad points can be made about pre-contact society and politics that continue to have considerable relevance to contemporary Aboriginal Australia and so to Aboriginal leadership. This is the context for the discussion here.

2. The Dreaming refers to the time long ago when creation figures moved across the landscape and created not only the forms the land now takes, but also the law that governs peoples' interactions with the land and each other and the lan-

guages and ceremonies that constitute key elements of their culture. See Rose 1996: 22-33. for a fuller discussion of Aboriginal concepts of the Dreaming.
3. The term 'traditional owner' is used in Australia to refer to those people who, under Aboriginal law and custom, hold rights in particular areas of land.
4. Authors' notes, Argyle Diamonds negotiations, March 2003–September 2004.
5. Unlike many comparable agreements the Argyle diamonds agreement is not confidential, except for its financial clauses. The text is available at http://www.atns.net.au/agreement.asp?EntityID=2591
6. Authors' notes, Argyle Diamonds negotiations, March 2003–September 2004.

Bibliography

Argyle Diamonds Ltd and Kimberley Land Council (2003) 'Framework Agreement'. Unpublished.

Argyle Diamonds Ltd, Traditional Owners and Kimberley Land Council Aboriginal Corporation (2004) 'Argyle Diamond Mine Participation Agreement – Indigenous Land Use Agreement', Unpublished, http://www.atns.net.au/ agreement.asp?EntityID=2591

Blake, T. (2001) *A Dumping Ground: A History of the Cherburg Settlement*. Brisbane: University of Queensland Press.

Brock, P. (1993) *Outback Ghettos: A history of Aboriginal institutionalisation and survival*. Melbourne: Cambridge University Press.

Butlin, N.G. (1993) *Economics and the Dreamtime: A Hypothetical History*. Cambridge: Cambridge University Press.

Cape York Institute for Policy and Leadership (2008) Higher Expectations (tertiary) program. www.cyi.org/au/heptertiary.aspx accessed 24 April 2008

Christensen, W. (1990) 'Aborigines and the Argyle Diamond Project', in R. Dixon and M. Dillon (Eds). *Aborigines and Diamond Mining: the politics of resource development in the East Kimberley*, pp. 29-39. Nedlands: University of Western Australia (UWA) Press.

CRA Exploration Pty Ltd ... and members of the Gidja and Mirriwung tribes of the Kimberley (1980). 'An Agreement made the 20th Day of July 1980'. Unpublished.

Dillon, M. (1990) '"A Terrible Hiding": Western Australia's Aboriginal Heritage Policy', in R. Dixon and M. Dillon (Eds) *Aborigines and Diamond Mining: the politics of resource development in the East Kimberley*, pp. 40-54. Nedlands: University of Western Australia (UWA) Press.

Dixon, R. (1990) 'Aborigines as Purposive Actors or Passive Victims?, in R. Dixon and M. Dillon (Eds) *Aborigines and Diamond Mining: the politics of resource development in the east Kimberley*, pp. 66-94. Nedlands: University of Western Australia University of Western Australia Press.

Dixon, R. and M. Dillon (Eds) (1990) *Aborigines and Diamond Mining: the politics of resource development in the East Kimberley*. Nedlands: UWA Press.

Dixon, R., C. Elderton, S. Irvine and I.Kirkby, 'A Preliminary Indication of Some Effects of the Argyle Diamond Mine on Aboriginal Communities in the Region', in R. Dixon and M. Dillon (Eds) *Aborigines and Diamond Mining: the politics of resource development in the east Kimberley*, pp. 108-129. Nedlands: University of Western Australia (UWA) Press.

Edwards, W.H. (1998) 'Leadership in Aboriginal Society', in W.H. Edwards (Ed). *Traditional Aboriginal Society* 2nd ed., pp. 161-181. South Yarra: Macmillan Education Australia.

Foley, G. (1998) 'Land Rights Battle Should Include Freehold: Foley', *Land Rights Queensland*, February.

Gelganyem Trust and Kilkkayi Trust (2006) *Future, Country. Gelganyem, Kilkayi.* Kununurra: Gelganyem Trust and Kilkkayi Trust.

Hiatt, L.R. (1998) 'Aboriginal Political Life', in W.H. Edwards (Ed). *Traditional Aboriginal Society* 2nd ed., pp. 182-196. South Yarra: Macmillan Education Australia.

Howitt, R. (1990). *All they get is dust: Aborigines, Mining and Regional Restructuring in WA's Eastern Goldfields.* Sydney: Economic and Regional Restructuring Research Unit, University of Sydney.

Ivory, B., (2005a) 'Finding Tek: Indigenous governance and leadership in the Thamarrur region (Port Keats). Paper presented to the North Australia Seminar Series, Australian National University, Darwin, 8 June 2005.

Ivory, B. (2005b) 'Kunmanggur, legend and leadership: A study of Indigenous governance succession in the northwest region of the Northern Territory'. Canberra: Centre for Aboriginal Economic Policy Research (CAEPR), Australian National University.

Ivory, B. (2005c) 'Leadership: Issues and principles from the Thamarrurr (Port Keats) region of the Northern Territory, Paper delivered to the CAEPR-Reconciliation Australia Workshop, Darwin, 5 December 2005.

Meggitt, M.J. (1966) 'Indigenous Forms of Government Among the Australian Aborigines' in I. Hogbin and L.R. Hiatt (Eds) *Readings in Australian and Pacific Anthropology,* pp. 57-74. Melbourne: Melbourne University Press.

Myers, F. (1980). 'The Cultural Basis of Politics in Pintupi Life', *Mankind,* 12, 3, 197-214.

O'Faircheallaigh, C., (1991). 'Resource Exploitation and Indigenous People: Towards a General Analytical Framework', in P. Jull and S. Roberts (eds), *The Challenge of Northern Regions,* pp. 228-71. Darwin: North Australia Research Unit.

Peters-Little, F. (2000) *The Community Game: Aboriginal Self Definition at the Local Level.* Canberra: Australian Institute of Aboriginal and Torres Strait Islander Studies (AIATSIS).

Productivity Commission (2007) *Overcoming Indigenous Disadvantage: Key Indicators 2007 Report.* Canberra: Commonwealth of Australia.

Rose, D.B. (1996) *Nourishing Terrains: Australian Aboriginal Views of landscape and Wilderness.* Canberra: Australian Heritage Commission.

Shaw, B. and Toby, J. (1990) '"We Still Got the Idea": Opportunity, Not identity, in the East Kimberley', in R. Dixon and M. Dillon (Eds). *Aborigines and Diamond Mining: the politics of resource development in the East Kimberley,* pp. 40-54. Nedlands: University of Western Australia (UWA) Press.

Stokes, J., (1987). 'Special Interests or Equality? The Mining Industry's Campaign Against Aboriginal Land Rights in Australia', *Australian – Canadian Studies,* 5, 1, 61-78.

Strelein, L. (2006). *Compromised Jurisprudence: Native Title Cases since Mabo.* Canberra: Aboriginal Studies Press.

Sutton, P. and Rigsby, B. (1982). People with "Politiks": Management of Land and Personnel on Australia's Cape York Peninsula', in N. Williams and E. Hunn (eds), *Resource Managers: North American and Australian Hunter-Gatherers*, pp. 155-171. Canberra: AIATSIS.

Taylor, J. (2006) *Indigenous People in the West Kimberley Labor Market*. Canberra: CAEPR.

 # LIST OF CONTRIBUTORS

DeMethra LaSha Bradley is the Doctoral Assistant to the President and Provost at the University of Vermont (UVM). She is also an Ed.D. candidate in the Educational Leadership and Policy Studies program at the University of Vermont.

Audrey Cooper is a Ph.D. candidate in Anthropology at American University. Her research centers on users of Vietnamese Signed Languages in deaf education and deaf social movements, along with broader questions about language ideology and relationships of body, language, citizenship, and representation.

Elijah Edelman is a Ph.D. student in the Department of Anthropology's Race, Gender and Social Justice program at American University. His work focuses on situated modes of resistance among U.S. based Female-to-Male trans people.

G.L.A. Harris is an Assistant Professor in the Mark O. Hatfield School of Government at Portland State University. She received her doctorate in Public Administration with a concentration in Public Management from Rutgers University. Her research interests include examining issues of social justice and civil rights.

Susan Brody Hasazi is the Stafford Distinguished Professor of Leadership and Special Education and Director of the Doctoral Program in Educational Leadership and Policy Studies at the University of Vermont. She holds an Ed.D. from Boston University.

Noor Johnson is a doctoral student in anthropology at McGill University. Her research focuses on the impact of environmental change on the Inuit in the Canadian Arctic and on transnational social justice activism on climate change.

Richard Greggory Johnson III is the editor of *A 21st Century Approach to Teaching Social Justice: Educating for Both Advocacy & Action* and he is an Assistant Professor of Educational Leadership and Policy Studies at the University of Vermont. His first book (with Dr. Kenneth Oldfield) is *Resilience: Queer Professors from the Working Class* (SUNY Press, 2008). Dr. Johnson holds graduate degrees from Golden Gate University, DePaul University and Georgetown University.

Khari LaMarca returned to do a doctorate in Anthropology (RJSJ) after a thirty-year professional career in international and public health.

William Leap is Professor of anthropology at American University (Washington DC) His publications include key works in American Indian English, language and AIDS, gay men's English and, more recently, language, sexuality and late modernity.

George Stuart Leibowitz is Assistant Professor at the University of Vermont's Department of Social Work and teaches courses in assessment, substance abuse, mental health, and social welfare policy. He holds a doctorate in Social Work from the University of Denver.

Edward R. McMahon holds a joint appointment as Research Associate Professor of Community Development and Applied Economics, and Political Science at the University of Vermont program. He is an alumnus of Georgetown University's School of Foreign Service.

Michelle Marzullo is a Ph.D. Candidate in Anthropology concentrating in Race, Gender, and Social Justice at American University in Washington, DC. She holds a Master's degree in Human Sexuality Studies from San Francisco State University.

Robert James Nash has been a professor of Interdisciplinary Studies at the University of Vermont for 40 years. He has published extensively on his interests in educating for pluralism of all types, including political, social class, and religious difference. Dr. Nash is an alumnus of the Georgetown University Graduate College.

Ciaran O'Faircheallaigh is Professor of Politics and Public Policy at Griffith University, Brisbane, Australia. Dr. O'Faircheallaigh has published numerous articles and books in the fields of public policy, resource economics and resources policy, negotiation, social impact assessment and Indigenous studies.

Irvin Peckham has taught English at the high school and college levels. He has been the writing program director and director of graduate studies at the University of Nebraska at Omaha and is currently the writing program director of the University Writing Program at Louisiana State University.

Andrew Quinn is an assistant professor of social work at the University of North Dakota. His interests lie in human behavior and qualitative and quantitative research methodologies. In addition, he holds an interest in the application of technology to social work education and how technology can promote social justice.

Joan S. Rabin is an Associate Professor of Psychology at Towson University. During her 38 years at TU she was part of the birth of the Women's Studies Program in the early 1970s, creating courses such as Sex Differences: Psychological Perspectives and Gender Identity in Transition. Dr. Rabin and her partner, Dr. Barbara Slater, founded the Safe Space Program at TU in 1995; her most recent work has focused on issues of sexual orientation diversity.

Bruce Reeves is an Assistant Professor and Field Coordinator with the Department of Social Work at the University of North Dakota. He received his Master of Social Work degree from the University of Utah, Salt Lake City, and has worked as a social worker for the past 25 years in a variety of settings.

Katharine Shepherd is an Associate Professor in the Department of Education, Special Education Program, at the University of Vermont. Currently, Dr. Shepherd teaches courses in collaborative consultation, special education assessment, leadership and social justice, and systems of services for individuals with disabilities and their families.

Efleda Tolentino is Assistant Professor in the Early Childhood Program of Long Island University. Her teaching is inspired by her work with young children and her students, and teachers in the field. She holds her doctorate from NYU.

Jeffrey A. Trumbower is Professor of Religious Studies and Dean of the College at Saint Michael's College. Dr. Trumbower obtained his doctorate from the University of Chicago in 1989.

Jillian T. Weiss, currently Associate Professor of Law and Society at Ramapo College, has a J.D. and a Ph.D. in Law, Policy & Society. Her research is directed towards social issues involving "gender identity" and transgender persons.

INDEX

Studies in the Postmodern Theory of Education

General Editors
Joe L. Kincheloe & Shirley R. Steinberg

Counterpoints publishes the most compelling and imaginative books being written in education today. Grounded on the theoretical advances in criticalism, feminism, and postmodernism in the last two decades of the twentieth century, Counterpoints engages the meaning of these innovations in various forms of educational expression. Committed to the proposition that theoretical literature should be accessible to a variety of audiences, the series insists that its authors avoid esoteric and jargonistic languages that transform educational scholarship into an elite discourse for the initiated. Scholarly work matters only to the degree it affects consciousness and practice at multiple sites. Counterpoints' editorial policy is based on these principles and the ability of scholars to break new ground, to open new conversations, to go where educators have never gone before.

For additional information about this series or for the submission of manuscripts, please contact:

> Joe L. Kincheloe & Shirley R. Steinberg
> c/o Peter Lang Publishing, Inc.
> 29 Broadway, 18th floor
> New York, New York 10006

To order other books in this series, please contact our Customer Service Department:

> (800) 770-LANG (within the U.S.)
> (212) 647-7706 (outside the U.S.)
> (212) 647-7707 FAX

Or browse online by series:
> www.peterlang.com